the MAPLE LEAF FOREVER

the MAPLE LEAF FOREVER

BRIAN McFARLANE

AT BAY press

WINNIPEG

The Maple Leaf Forever

Design and layout by Lucas c Pauls and M. C. Joudrey.

Published by At Bay Press November 2024.

Library and Archives Canada cataloguing in publication is available upon request.

ISBN 978-1-998779-42-0

Printed and bound in Canada.

This book is printed on acid free paper that is
100% recycled ancient forest friendly (100% post-consumer recycled).

MIX
Paper | Supporting responsible forestry
FSC www.fsc.org FSC® C016245

First Edition

10 9 8 7 6 5 4 3 2

atbaypress.com

Canada Council for the Arts | Conseil des arts du Canada

MANITOBA ARTS COUNCIL | CONSEIL DES ARTS DU MANITOBA

We acknowledge the support of the Canada Council for the Arts.

With the generous support of the Manitoba Arts Council.

TABLE OF CONTENTS

The Maple Leaf to us was the badge of courage, the badge that meant home. It was the badge that reminded us all of our exploits and the different difficulties we got into and the different accomplishments we made. It was a badge that meant more to us than hockey...hoping that the possession of this badge would mean something to the team that wore it, and when they skated out on the ice with this badge on their chest they would wear it with honour and pride and courage, the way it had been worn by the soldiers of the first Great War in the Canadian Army.

— Conn Smythe

As an organization, we wanted to get back to our roots, when Conn Smythe first changed the team logo to the Maple Leaf in 1927. Inspired by the badge that he and his fellow Canadian soldiers wore during World War I, Smythe wanted his team to wear the badge with 'honour, pride and courage.' This is our goal for the next chapter in Leafs history. We are committed to restoring the Toronto Maple Leafs to a proud and prominent place, and this classic logo will connect the team's championship legacy with an exciting and proud future for our players, our city and for our fans.

— Brendan Shanahan,
President and Alternate Governor, Toronto Maple Leafs

This book is dedicated to a beloved Maple Leaf, Börje Salming

INTRODUCTION

WELCOME TO what is quite possibly the longest introduction in the history of hockey book publishing.

Let me begin *The Maple Leaf Forever,* not with the early days of the fascinating Toronto Maple Leafs hockey franchise, but with recent seasons, campaigns that stirred hopes that a Stanley Cup championship, the first since 1967, would be a long-awaited reward for excellence.

In the past decade, the Leafs have become one of the most productive and successful teams in the NHL. But a championship hasn't happened. Not even close. And that makes everyone connected with this famous franchise frustrated and very, very sad. Regular-season excellence is commendable but fades in comparison to the exhilaration and giddy thrills of a Stanley Cup landing in the grasp of Leaf Nation.

If only we knew the answers to the questions *Why has it not happened?* and *When will it happen?*

In 2019–20, their rise to the top under new captain John Tavares and young scoring stars Auston Matthews and Mitch Marner was not as rapid as predicted, and the season was suspended on March 12, 2020, as a result of the COVID-19 pandemic.

One game during this first part of the season was notable. On February 22, the Leafs lost to David Ayres and the Carolina Hurricanes. Ayres was an emergency backup goalie, or "EBUG," and he happened to be the Maple Leafs' practice goalie and a former part-time Zamboni driver for their farm team.

NHL play resumed in August. The Leafs played the Columbus Blue Jackets in a qualifying playoff round (a series unique to the 2020 playoffs), and lost the best-of-five series, three games to two.

Early in 2020–21, a coaching change was made. On November 20, with only two wins in their past sixteen games, the Maple Leafs fired head coach Mike Babcock and replaced him with Sheldon Keefe, head coach of their AHL farm team, the Toronto Marlies. The team improved, winning thirty-five of their fifty-six games and topping their division.

Auston Matthews netted a league-high forty-one goals, becoming the first player in team history to win the Maurice "Rocket" Richard Trophy, and was also named a finalist for the Ted Lindsay Award, given to the league's MVP as voted on by players. Marner and Matthews both finished in the top five in league scoring. But in the first round of the playoffs, the Leafs flopped after going up three games to one against the Montreal Canadiens. Toronto's defeat to the less-than-mighty Habs in seven games closed out the fifth consecutive year in which the Leafs had lost in the opening round.

In 2021–22, the Maple Leafs set franchise records in wins (fifty-four) and points (115) and qualified for the playoffs for the sixth consecutive season. Matthews and Marner again led the way, with the former collecting a career-high sixty goals and the latter putting up ninety-seven points. Then came a first-round playoff clash with the Tampa Bay Lightning, the defending Cup champs—a huge opportunity to erase memories of nightmarish first-round expulsions. The Leafs might have won, but did not. They dropped Game 7, by a score of 2–1. Another playoff heartbreak for the Leafs and their fans.

The Leafs might say, "But we were good. Really good. Check the numbers." And the regular-season stats would back them up:

Record	54–21–7	(4th in NHL)
Power Play	27.27%	(1st)
Penalty Kill	82.05%	(8th)
Goals For	312	(2nd)
Goals Against	252	(14th)

Despite the glossy numbers, the Leafs weren't good enough at crunch time—in the postseason. Lightning goalie Andrei Vasilevskiy saw to that, but so did Toronto's vaunted power play, which went a dismal 4-for-28 (14.3 percent), including 0-for-3 in Game 7.

Perhaps what the team needed was one player—I think of former Leafs like Doug Gilmour or Darryl Sittler—to generate a brilliant goal or two through sheer determination, guts and willpower beyond belief. If not Gilmour or Sittler, think Börje Salming, Lanny McDonald or Wendel Clark.

In 2022–23, another fifty-win season was enough to trigger a fresh wave of Stanley Cup optimism in Leaf Nation. Toronto, with 111 well-earned points, gained home-ice advantage against Tampa Bay in another first-round matchup. The Lightning had skidded downhill in the last month of the season, losers eight times in eleven games. So, there was a chance. And lots of hope.

During the regular season, Ilya Samsonov had provided solid goaltending, and while Marner fell one point short of one hundred, he set a franchise record by scoring at least one point in twenty-three consecutive games, the longest such streak in the NHL in seven years. Then there was Auston Matthews with forty goals—which at this point in his career could be considered an off year—matched by William Nylander's career-high forty. Always reliable John Tavares scored a respectable thirty-seven.

A slide in Morgan Rielly's defensive play caused some alarm, but surprisingly, he became a playoff hotshot, more reliable and likeable than Santa Claus. He was heroic, if not *super*-heroic, like Sittler in '77 or Gilmour in '93.

Despite their late-season stumble, the Lightning proved once again to be a formidable foe. But this time—finally—the Leafs prevailed. Tavares, who left the New York Islanders at the peak of his brilliant career because he had always wanted to be a Leaf (he remembered wearing Leaf pyjamas as a kid), scored the overtime winner in Game 6 at Amalie Arena. The Leafs found themselves in a hockey realm most of them had never visited before: the second round. After all, the last time a Toronto team had advanced was in 2004.

Tavares and the Leafs moved on against another slick team from the Sunshine State—the Florida Panthers, who'd just upset the mighty Boston Bruins. And as Vasilevskiy had done the year before, another stellar Russian goalie stood in their way: Sergei Bobrovsky, a $10 million-a-year man with skill and determination. He was a fitness fanatic who spent more time in the Panthers weight room than anyone.

"He goes nonstop," a teammate said. "Always stretching, always learning something new. He is extremely dedicated to being the best he can be."

The Leafs dropped the first three games, as the acrobatic Bobrovsky played a starring role, before eking out a 2–1 victory. With a loss in Game 5, they were toast—second-round losers who played like they didn't deserve anything more. Again and alas, no one among their big gunners mustered a lick of leadership—no clone of Gilmour, Sittler or McDonald—to show them how playoff charges can be important game changers.

Sid Seixeiro, a popular, opinionated Toronto broadcaster, roasted them on TV. Following their 3–2 loss to Florida in Game 2, a game Toronto had led 2–0, Sid growled loudly, "What's this? The road is clear for the Maple Leafs to do damage...and they're blowing it." Seixeiro called out Tavares for a mistake on the Panthers' game-tying goal, and ripped William Nylander for "giving up" on the Leafs, despite being one of their best players against Tampa Bay.

Seixeiro castigated regular-season stars Auston Matthews, Mitch Marner and Michael Bunting, accusing them of being playoff "screw-ups."

"The biggest mistakes on the ice were from their most important people," he fumed.

He described coach Sheldon Keefe, who had guided the team to three of its four winningest seasons, as "clueless."

"Keefe's not putting the right lineups on the ice."

He closed out his rant by saying, "You need to play sixty minutes to win."

Perhaps Sid ran out of spit and time to lecture the higher-ups—team president Brendan Shanahan and general manager Kyle Dubas—let alone the anthem singer and Zamboni driver.

Seixeiro's admonishment of a team *co-owned by his employers* was the strongest ever heard publicly from a Rogers or Bell employee.

Slightly more than sixty percent of his viewers thought Sid was "dead on" with his critique.

The Big Thinkers at Maple Leaf Sports and Entertainment decided to fire Dubas and replace him with Brad Treliving, the former GM of the Calgary Flames. But Coach Keefe and the "Core Four" of Matthews, Marner, Nylander and Tavares remained intact. While the club managed to scare the hell out of Boston in the first playoff round, some sloppy defensive play in OT in Game 7 allowed the Bruins to win. Once more, the Leafs found themselves on the wrong side of the handshake line at the TD Garden.

As in 2022, the most obvious Toronto weakness was its woeful power play: 1-for-21 (4.8 percent) in the series, a success rate you might expect from a Junior B team facing the Bruins.

To be fair, this edition of the team showed some gumption in coming back from a 3–1 series deficit—and until Pastrňák's overtime winner, Boston did not hold the lead at any point in the final three games of the series. But can anyone remember when Toronto playoff performances have been fun to watch? Six straight Game 7 losses dating back to 2013 amounts to a decade of frustration, not fun. For such big stars to play like nervous Nellies over and over again is baffling.

In the off-season, coach Sheldon Keefe was told to pack up and leave, but on April 11, 2024, Brendan Shanahan marked his ten-year anniversary as team president—with little to show for it. While the Toronto brass pondered next steps, I reflected on a time when Stanley Cups often wound up in Toronto. Few will remember because it happened so very long ago.

FOUR CUPS IN THE '60S

THE 1960s was an era like no other, the beginning of a long-running love affair that blossomed between the Toronto Maple Leafs and their millions of loyal fans. I was there. I lived it and I loved it—until Harold Ballard took control.

When I was a young hockey announcer in the 1960s, I was fortunate enough to witness Toronto teams win three Stanley Cups early in the decade and a fourth—with me in the famous Gardens gondola (the broadcast booth)—in 1967, Canada's Centennial Year. It was the era of just six NHL clubs, Pierre Trudeau, the Beatles, the Cuban Missile Crisis, long hair, drugs, the miniskirt, *Playboy* magazine, etc.

Those Leafs teams were all worthy champions. Successful and proud. I liked the '67 Leafs in particular because they were old and wise and winners, but about to be dismantled, a team forced to sacrifice a lot to six new expansion teams with odd names like Penguins and Seals and North Stars. And their final mammoth feat—a Cup win on home ice in 1967—came as a stunning surprise.

It was the Centennial Year, and the Stanley Cup finals matched up Canada's two teams. Toronto against Montreal. The Habs were overwhelming favourites to send the huff-and-puff Leafs reeling off to some seniors' home. Yet the mighty Canadiens were humbled by Terry Sawchuk in Game 6 at Maple Leaf Gardens. Toronto GM/coach Punch Imlach boldly put all his "oldtimers" on the ice for the final seconds of that game, some so aged they risked pulling a groin just lifting the coveted old mug for a photo op.

It was my first Cup as a broadcaster. It would turn out to be the last to be embraced by the city of Toronto. My wife and I, after crashing the victory party (we were not invited), would get to sip from the famous trophy in the foyer of Staff Smythe's house. I recall Eddie Shack cackling nonstop as he danced as fast and erratically as he ever skated, perspiration flying in all directions off his prominent nose, and Gary Smith, the team's third-string goalie—a tall, blond, handsome man—making a late arrival with a Dolly Parton lookalike on his arm, complete with the famous Parton cleavage—a riveting attribute.

"You're gawking," my wife reminded me.

"So? Everyone's gawking."

Now, in 2023, as I hobble into my nineties, I dare to think I might witness another Stanley Cup parade in Toronto. Few people still standing can say, "I saw the Leafs win *four* Stanley Cups." Or even five or ten, harking back to Bill Barilko's winning goal in 1951 and beyond. I heard Barilko's marker on the radio. His came against Montreal more than a year before there was hockey on CBC-TV. Oddly, all five final games in '51 required overtime.

Scanning back to the '40s, you'll find four more Cups won by the Leafs in that war-torn decade. Any other old dudes leafing through these pages who remembers those? And surely there are one or two old codgers approaching one hundred who vaguely recall their fathers taking them to the brand-new Maple Leafs Gardens to witness the 1932 Cup win. No, I don't recall that series. I was less than a year old. Toronto won that Stanley Cup behind the "Kid Line," which featured three future Hockey Hall of Fame members—Charlie Conacher, Busher Jackson and Joe Primeau—all under the age of twenty-six.

HOW LONG WILL THIS GO ON?

I OFTEN wonder if the team I idolized as a child, whose games I broadcast as a pro, might still be seeking to break their Cup-less string a hundred years from now. Is it really possible that this agonizing drought could go on endlessly?

My friend Joe Bowen, the Leafs' current radio play-by-play voice, shares my concerns. Hockey blogger Howard Berger imagined Bowen saying, in frustration, "I'm seventy-one and I've been doing this job [calling Leaf games loudly] for the past four decades. I'm thinking retirement and I can't help but wonder if I'll ever—and I mean EVER—get to call a Leafs' Stanley Cup game?"

To which Berger added, "It's a question that Bowen has frequently pondered during this longest famine in Leafs history."

Ponder this: There's a chance that no person alive today will ever see the Leafs get their mitts on the Stanley Cup. Now, that's a scary, scary thought, but it's just that—a thought, not a prediction. Think of the Vegas Golden Knights. They've been around since yesterday (seven years, actually) and they've already won a Cup.

In order for us to hear Joe's mighty voice call his first Cup final match, the Leafs must not only match their first-round victory in '23, but capture *three more* best-of-seven series in the same playoff year. Joe knows such a feat is possible but highly unlikely, considering the team's past playoff efforts.

We all know that hockey is a rise and fall game, with teams rising to the top, then falling back. The Leafs are at or near the top, but must find the formula that earns them a long-awaited Stanley Cup. And it must happen soon, before competitors catch up, before the inevitable slide begins.

In no time, Joe Bowen's voice, like mine, will be more a bleat than a bellow. But there will always be shouters and chanters hollering, "Go, Leafs, Go!"

Yes, always.

Perhaps the Buds will snap their Cup drought on the hundredth anniversary of the '67 victory and some PR person for the team will call to ask my opinion. I may not hear the phone ring. In 2067, at age 136, I may be deaf.

If I do answer and hear someone shout, "Brian, the Leafs finally won the Cup!" I may reply, "The Cup? What Cup? Who are the Leafs? Is this a joke?"

If they insist that I come and join in the celebration, I may tell them, "Sorry, this is my night to go dancing at Club Temptation."

Surely, I'll be hockeyed out by then.

Silliness aside, in the past three seasons, the Leafs have iced their best regular-season clubs in franchise annals. A treat to watch. But in the postseason, they've been wretched at times.

The most loyal and resilient fans in professional sport will talk about coaching decisions and management choices and a lack of "killer instinct" until the cows come wandering home and the puck is dropped on a new season—the current one. They (the fans, not the cows) are acutely aware that the most skilled team in franchise history needs a "fix," and they are demanding a remedy from the Big Thinkers.

This frustrating era is so unlike the first seasons of the beloved Leaf franchise, when the coveted Cup often appeared to be within easy reach. It was about as heavy as a jug of beer back then, and it kept falling into canals and being left at roadsides when tires needed fixing. King Clancy recalled it being in his Ottawa home one summer and players dropping cigar butts in it.

EARLY-DAY DRAMA

HOCKEY HISTORIANS reviewing the state of hockey prior to the formation of the NHL and the birth of the Toronto Maple Leaf franchise will quickly discover that one fact stands out: Toronto teams showed a thirst for Stanley Cup action—at home and away—shortly after the beginning of the last century, when there was tremendous interest in the game in places large and small. Hall of Famer Cyclone Taylor told me that when he played in the early 1900s, fans would stand outside train stations in blizzard conditions just to get the scores of far-off Cup games via telegraph.

In 1902, when a Toronto team, the Wellingtons, played for the Stanley Cup in Winnipeg, it was difficult to get game results promptly. So, an official in Winnipeg would notify *The Globe* newspaper office in Toronto of the score. *The Globe* in turn would call a man working late at the Toronto Street Railway, who would blast a whistle three times if Toronto had won the game and twice if they had lost. Apparently, people could hear the late-night shriek of the whistle everywhere in Toronto and were disappointed on the night of the deciding game when there was no third blast—Winnipeg had won the series. The next day's newspapers would provide all the details.

In Winnipeg, there was such a rush for tickets to that best-of-three series that four men at the front of the ticket line were almost crushed to death against the arena doors. All four were trampled and unconscious when pulled to safety. Their bodies were passed over the heads of the onrushing mob until fresh air revived them and they were able to rise and muscle their way into the line again, this time at the end of it.

The series was highlighted by some unusual scenes.

For the warmups, the Winnipeg players wore long gold dressing gowns over their uniforms.

In the middle of one game, a Newfoundland dog jumped on the ice, precipitating a merry chase.

At one point, a high shot lodged in the rafters and players below tossed their sticks toward the arena roof, hoping to dislodge the puck. The one whose stick knocked it loose received an ovation and probably took a little bow.

Chummy Hill of the Wellingtons scored a goal—with half a puck. When the puck split in two, Hill whacked the half he controlled into the net and the referee said, "I'm calling it a goal."

Another puck was shot into the crowd at one point and the spectator who caught it did not throw it back—as was customary—but put it in his pocket as a souvenir. His to keep.

How many pucks have been carried off by fans since then? Easily a million, I'd guess.

During play, snow sifted down through cracks in the arena roof and formed little lines on the ice.

You don't see such things at a hockey game today.

A number of fans travelled all the way from central Saskatchewan to see the 1902 games, at a cost of roughly $200 each—almost a year's wages for some.

TORONTO ALMOST UPSET THE MIGHTY WANDERERS

SIX YEARS later, in the spring of 1908, the Montreal Wanderers were the hottest team in hockey. In the 1907 season they'd established a record that has never been matched, going undefeated and averaging over ten goals per game. In one game, they routed the Montreal Victorias 16–3, and in two outings against the Montreal Shamrocks they won by 18–5 and 16–5. Ernie Russell, their top scorer, compiled the staggering record of forty-two goals in the nine games he played. The Wanderers were so popular that crowds of seven thousand filled the arena for their games. Before one game with Ottawa, hundreds of fans outside the building became frustrated when they were turned away at the gate—there were no more tickets to be sold. Fans stormed the arena, breaking down doors and windows and scrambling to get inside. Freeloaders. Young boys scrambled up the rafters and clung there, away from the ushers and privy to a view that Foster Hewitt would have appreciated.

The formidable Wanderers were always in the annual chase for the Stanley Cup in those years, winning the trophy in three straight seasons. In 1908, they walloped Ottawa 9–3 and 13–1 in one Stanley Cup series. They immediately accepted a challenge from the Winnipeg Maple Leafs and crushed the westerners by scores of 11–5 and 9–3. And yes, there was a Maple Leafs team in Canada long before Conn Smythe.

That triumph seemed like a fitting end to a hugely successful season. But just as the mighty Wanderers were preparing to put their skates away, they were handed a third Stanley Cup challenge, this time from a Toronto club, the Pros, champions of the Trolley League, the first outright professional league in Canada. The Trolley League was so named because teams travelled by electric trolley between games in hockey hotspots like Toronto, Brantford, Guelph and Berlin (later named Kitchener).

But the arrogant Wanderers treated the Toronto challenge with disdain, as a joke. "Toronto doesn't have a chance against us," a Wanderers spokesman told reporters. "If the Cup trustees order us to play a two-game series against Toronto, it will be a travesty. We'll more than double the score against them. So let's make it a one-game affair and get the season over with."

The Cup trustees agreed and the Toronto boys were given only one chance—sixty minutes and time's up—against the wonderful Wanderers.

The referee appointed for the game in Montreal was twenty-three-year-old Frank Patrick, who, with his brother Lester, would one day form an entire league in Western Canada, introducing rules that changed the face of the game. The Patricks, who were enterprising players, managers and owners, were brilliant pioneers of the game. And pretty good referees as well, it appears.

On March 14, 1908, fans of the Wanderers bet huge sums that their heroes would double the score on the visitors, even though Toronto had young Newsy Lalonde in their lineup. Lalonde had been the leading scorer in the Trolley League, with twenty-nine goals in nine games.

In the early minutes of the game, the Toronto club stunned the Montrealers with their speed and poise. The score seesawed back and forth and was tied four times. Montreal's legion of supporters exhorted the champions to pick up the pace, for they were in grave danger of losing huge wads of wagers. During a stop in play, fans motioned three or four of the Wanderers, including goaltender Riley Hern, over to the side boards. "You promised to double the score on these chaps," they shouted. "If you pull up your socks and do it, there'll be some bonus money for you to divide up after the game."

While the players were listening to these enticements, one of the strangest goals in Stanley Cup history was scored. Referee Patrick, ignoring the distraction at rinkside, dropped the puck at centre ice and Lalonde fired it quickly toward the Wanderers net. His aim was true and the disk sailed past the opposing players, who scrambled back too late to prevent the goal.

However, Lalonde's empty net goal so fired up the champions that they stormed back with two goals of their own and won the game by a 6–4 score. The Wanderers retained the Stanley Cup, but their supporters lost a bundle when the score wasn't doubled. The Toronto boys, on the other hand, had been in on the wagering and returned home with a pot of $2,500 to divide amongst themselves. It was a small fortune in that era.

Unfortunately, Lalonde moved on to star with other teams, notably the Montreal Canadiens, but his scoring skills in two stints with Toronto teams were unbeatable. In a total of twenty games, he scored sixty-one goals. That's three goals per game, folks. Simple math.

In a six year NHL career (five with the Habs), he played in ninety-nine games and tallied 125 goals. Two of his career goals were gifts. He played for Montreal in Ottawa one night and the hometown fans went ballistic when a goal for their team was disallowed. When referee Cooper Smeaton dropped the puck at centre ice, the Ottawa men stood still and watched as Lalonde skated in alone and scored on the Ottawa goalie, who said, "Be my guest."

Another faceoff, another solo skate by Lalonde, who slipped a second puck past his goalie friend, who wished him well but refrained from patting him on the back.

Joe Malone was another prolific scorer who, while playing for Quebec City, scored seven goals against Toronto in an NHL game played on January 31, 1920. No NHL player has scored more. Fellow historian Stephen Smith reminds me that Malone was twenty-nine years old at the time and the final score was Quebec 10, Toronto 6.

Smith says, "It was a frigid night, so cold that Corb Denneny, the Toronto centre, had his right hand badly frozen during the game."

Those were the days.

Wait. Did I just hear someone mutter, "You were right. That was the longest introduction to any hockey book—ever! Are you finished?"

Yes, I am. But stay with me. I promise you some good stuff just ahead.

THE TURBULENT TEENS

TORONTO'S FORGOTTEN CUP SUCCESS

THE FIRST time the Stanley Cup was won by a Toronto hockey team was in 1914, when the Blueshirts were members of the National Hockey Association, the forerunner to the NHL. Playing on the vast ice surface of the new Mutual Street Arena—whose dimensions were reported as 230 feet by ninety-five—the Blueshirts swept a best-of-five series against a team from Victoria, British Columbia, the champions of the Pacific Coast Hockey Association. Two names on the Victoria roster catch the eye. Goaltender Bert Lindsay is one—he was the father of Hall of Famer Ted Lindsay. The other is Jack Ulrich, the first deaf hockey player to play for the Stanley Cup. He was hailed in the *Victoria Daily Times* at the beginning of the 1912–13 PCHA season as one of the better backcheckers in the game. In 1914–15 and 1915–16, Ulrich played in the NHA with the Montreal Wanderers and Toronto Blueshirts, scoring a total of five goals in twenty-six regular-season games.

Ulrich once wrote an angry letter to *The Toronto World* newspaper, objecting to its use of the nickname "Dummy."

"At the coast they never called me 'Dummy' in the paper. It is vulgar to call [me] that. Why not call me Jack or Silent? Suppose you are deaf, how would you like to be called 'Dummy'? I am not [a] dummy; I am deaf, that is all."

He also wrote, "What do you mean by writing in the paper that I have to depend on Mr. Patrick for directions while in the game. I never depend on him, except his signals for me to go to the bench or come on the ice. And you wrote I was not a goal-getter. How could I score a goal when I was on the ice for only a few minutes?"

Immediately below Ulrich's letter, *The World* ran an apology.

Jack Ulrich retired from hockey after the 1916 season, never having heard the roar of the crowd. In 1927, he died of acute appendicitis in Detroit, aged thirty-seven.

A NEW LEAGUE IS BORN DURING A WORLD WAR

THE INAUGURAL season of the NHL, 1917–18, was a turbulent one. Not as tempestuous as the world war that had been raging overseas, but still an agonizing one for a small group of league organizers who, at season's end, felt relieved to have kept pro hockey alive in Eastern Canada.

Somehow, the newly formed league had weathered a series of bewildering events, beginning on the eve of the season opener when the owner of the Montreal Arena—often called the Westmount Arena—said he was fed up with the poor calibre of hockey displayed by the two NHL clubs based there, the Canadiens and Wanderers.

"I'm going to toss both clubs from my rink if they don't sharpen up," he threatened. "And I'll let the pleasure skaters have all the ice time."

That's how one man—a sourpuss with clout—felt about pro hockey back then.

Fortunately, the Wanderers won their first-ever game over Toronto by a slim margin of 10–9. A mere seven hundred fans attended, many of them soldiers and veterans just back from battle. They saw the Wanderers' Dave Ritchie score the NHL's first goal one minute after the first puck was dropped, and in the same period, they witnessed Montreal's Harry Hyland notch the NHL's first hat trick. Hyland went on to score five goals in the first sixty minutes of NHL play. Meanwhile, on the same night, the Canadiens' Joe Malone was scoring five goals in *his* first NHL encounter against Ottawa, but that game started later than the one in Montreal, so Malone missed out on being the fastest man at anything on opening night. The delay was caused when the Ottawa men demanded more money before performing—and waited until they got it.

(Modern-day fans should be made aware that Auston Matthews's four-goal NHL debut wasn't the unprecedented feat many thought it was and were told it was.)

The Wanderers' first victory would also be their last. After a couple more sparsely attended home losses, they rang out 1917 with a defeat in Ottawa. A few days later, their season went up in smoke—literally. On January 2, 1918, the Westmount Arena burned to the ground, forcing the Wanderers to withdraw from the circuit. The record book shows that they went 1–5; they were 1–3 in games they actually played, but two scheduled opponents claimed victories by default after the fire.

Prior to the season, the owners of the Quebec franchise had decided not to ice a team, so the folding of the Wanderers left only three teams competing in the NHL: the Montreal Canadiens (who were sharing the Westmount ice with the Wanderers and hastily made arrangements to play across town at the rinky-dink Jubilee Rink), the Ottawa Senators, and Toronto—a team with no nickname, although "Blueshirts" or "Torontos" would serve. Toronto skated off with the NHL championship, and then the Stanley Cup, at the season's end. Within months, this team would be sold and be officially named the Arenas.

A little over a year later, there was another homeless hockey team in Montreal. On April 23, 1919, the Jubilee Rink burned down, forcing the Habs to move to the Mount Royal Arena, which opened in January 1920. Surely, one of the management's first moves was to purchase plenty of fire insurance.

THE HABS' FIRST ENCOUNTER WITH TORONTO

AN ACCOUNT of the first meeting of the Canadiens and the Toronto "No-Names," played at the Mutual Street Arena just seven days into the NHL's inaugural season, appeared in *The Mail and Empire* on December 27, 1917:

"It was a rousing performance by the home team, which scored four unanswered third-period goals for the 7–5 victory. The Canadiens are no longer the Flying Frenchmen!"

The Arenas might have been slow to start that night, trailing 5–3 at the end of the second period, but they skated the Canadiens into the ice in the third. Only Vézina's "impossible saves," said to be "a marvel of efficiency," kept the score close.

Of course, *The Mail and Empire* might have been a little hasty in proclaiming that the Canadiens were doomed to forever skate in slush. An NHL-record twenty-three championships, following their 1916 title won while they were in the old National Hockey Association, might suggest otherwise.

The Habs set another record on January 10, 1920. Montreal and the Toronto St. Patricks splurged to the tune of twenty-one goals in a 14–7 Canadiens win. Several previous games had seen teams combine for nineteen goals. The 14–7 shootout now shares the record with a December 11, 1985, meeting in which the Edmonton Oilers overwhelmed the Chicago Blackhawks 12–9. Can you believe Wayne Gretzky did not score a goal in the romp? He was too busy collecting assists, tying the league record of seven, set in 1947 by Detroit's Billy Taylor—who, as a youngster, served as the Leaf mascot.

TORONTO'S FIRST CUP IN THE NHL

DURING THE NHL's inaugural season, when the Ottawa Senators skated out for a game in Toronto, their bench was empty—they had no substitutes on hand. How did the Toronto club react? Their manager reciprocated by emptying his own bench. It was the only NHL game ever played with the minimum of twelve players involved. One can imagine the howls of outrage from those who did not get to play—and did not get paid.

ALF SKINNER

Later, "Bad Joe" Hall of Montreal and Alf Skinner of Toronto tried to decapitate each other in a vicious stick-swinging duel. Both were arrested and hauled into court, where a lenient judge said, "What do you expect? They're hockey players," and released them with suspended sentences.

Canadiens scoring ace Joe Malone, on loan from the dormant Quebec club, scored forty-four goals in twenty games that season, an amazing goals-per-game pace.

Toronto and Montreal wound up tied in the standings and met in a two-game, total-goals playoff. Toronto won the league championship, 10–7.

Decades later, hockey historian and NHL.com writer Dave Stubbs raised questions about the upset.

How, he wondered, could the Canadiens, winners of a Stanley Cup in 1916, be knocked off by a still-diapered temporary franchise that had been cobbled together pending the resolution of a Toronto ownership dispute?

By a team that, in fact, had no official name at all, known loosely as the Blueshirts or simply Torontos?

How indeed could this newcomer, outscored 55–39 in ten games by Montreal that season, knock off the Canadiens 10–7 in a two-game, total-goals semifinal playoff, on their way to a five-game Stanley Cup victory over the Pacific Coast Hockey Association's Vancouver Millionaires?

However they managed it, in 1918, the Toronto Hockey Club captured the Stanley Cup over Vancouver, the Pacific Coast Hockey Association champion, edging the visitors three games to two on home ice. The westerners wore very little padding and took a pounding. The fifth game was tied 1–1 in the third period when Toronto's Corb Denneny slammed home the winning goal and became Toronto's first NHL playoff hero. Alf Skinner led all playoff scorers with eight goals in seven games. The Blueshirts became the first NHL club to win the Stanley Cup, snatching it back from Seattle, the previous season's champs and the first US-based team to win it.

JACK ADAMS

RUSTY CRAWFORD

OLD-TIME PLAYERS WERE MEAN AND VIOLENT

JACK ADAMS was one of the first star players in the NHL and a Stanley Cup winner in Toronto long before he made a bigger name for himself as the long-time coach and manager of the Detroit Red Wings.

Adams spent four seasons with the St. Patricks, playing on a line with hotshot scorer Babe Dye, and was the team's leading scorer in 1925–26.

As a youth in 1914–15, he played with his hometown Fort William Maple Leafs. He came east to play for Peterborough and Sarnia teams before turning pro with Toronto in 1917. He once talked about the violence he encountered in many of those old-time games.

> *Hockey is a tough game nowadays, it's true, but I don't mind telling you that the game today is a picnic compared to what it used to be. The Rusty Crawfords, the Joe Halls, the Sprague Cleghorns and the Billy Coutus of decades ago have no counterparts in the game now. If you were lucky enough to skate by them in one piece, they'd turn and hook their sticks at your face or crack you over the head.*
>
> *I've been involved in professional hockey as a player or coach or manager for forty-three years and I say the modern players just don't know how hard and mean their game once was.*
>
> *That Rusty Crawford was a lean, hawk-faced, wicked little guy with a big hooked nose. He was the most cold-blooded of men, absolutely fearless, who'd cut his own players in practices if the action got a little out of hand. The first morning I met him he said, "Son, don't take anything from anybody. Not even in practice."*
>
> *One game stands out in my mind as the most brutal I ever took part in. The Arenas played the*

Canadiens [for the NHL championship] in the spring of 1918, and we won the first game 7 to 3 in Toronto. It was a two-game total goals series, with the second game in the old Jubilee rink in Montreal, and the winner qualified to meet Vancouver in the Stanley Cup final. There was never a game like that second one. I got deep cuts over the eye, down one cheek, and under my chin. When it was over, I was taken to the Montreal General Hospital for hemstitching. I needed twenty-two stitches, as it turned out, and all the cuts were dripping blood when I was led into the emergency ward. My sister Alma was nursing there then, and by coincidence she was on duty when I arrived. She didn't even recognize me.

We lost the game, 4 to 3 but won the round 10 to 7. I have an old newspaper clipping about that game:

"The Blues," it says, using a nickname for the Arenas, "refused to quit. Canadiens hammered and battered these game youngsters. They put Ken Randall out of the game for keeps, cut Jack Adams' head to ribbons, battered Rusty Crawford from head to foot, sent Harry Mummery hobbling off halfway through the period with one leg limp from a sweeping slash, broke the teeth of goalkeeper Harry Holmes, knocked out Harry Meeking and Alf Skinner, and bumped every other opposing player on the ice—but the Blues didn't quit. It was the most punishing game ever played in an NHL final. An unforgettable picture was chunky Jack Adams dashing up and down the boards with blood streaming from cuts over his eyes and ears."

I was there, too, on the night nine years later when a violent-tempered veteran named Billy Coutu attacked a referee and was barred from

> *hockey for life for the assault. This was right after the Ottawa Senators, with whom I closed out my playing career, had won the Stanley Cup by whipping Boston in a game that concluded with a wild brawl on the ice. Coutu, a Bruin defenceman that season, led a surge of Boston players toward referee Jerry Laflamme when the game ended. They engulfed the referee, knocking him to the floor near the referee's room in the Ottawa Auditorium, and cutting and bruising his face. The league president, Frank Calder, fined or suspended five players for the brawl and for the attack on Laflamme. Coutu was the main culprit. In addition to his life suspension, he was fined a hundred dollars.*

Adams added, "With a few exceptions, the old-timers weren't vicious men. Rough-hewn but rarely ruthless. With most of them, hockey was a part-time exercise that brought in a few extra dollars.

"Salaries were so low that few men could make the game a career.... When I signed with Charlie Querrie, who ran the Arenas, for $800, his payroll for nine players totaled $5,350."

Future Hall of Famer Jack Adams played centre for the Arenas before joining Vancouver in the PCHA, where he scored one of the most unusual goals in history. By accident, he knocked the puck into his own team's net and somehow got credit for the goal. It vaulted him into fifth place in the PCHA scoring race.

RASCAL RANDALL PAYS A FINE

DURING THE 1918–19 NHL season, a husky, short-tempered pepper pot named Ken Randall became one of the most talked-about performers on the Blueshirts. Vulgar obscenities flowed from his mouth in games—even as team captain—as he hurled verbal bile at

KEN RANDALL

referees and opposing players alike. His conduct earned him many trips to the penalty box, as well as a number of fines.

In a February game, the Arenas suffered a 9–0 humiliation by Montreal. Late in the game, Randall clobbered shutout-bound goalie Georges Vézina and was tossed from the game by referee Lou Marsh. Randall cursed the arbiter loudly, and some fans covered their ears. After tongue-lashing Marsh in a return match, Randall was again thrown out—and suspended by league president Frank Calder. Randall was ordered to apologize to Calder and Marsh and to pay a hefty fine of $35 before he could be reinstated.

Randall's biographer (and grandson), J. Shayne Randall, states that a friend convinced Ken to place three dollars in pennies—along with thirty dollars in bills—in a brown paper bag and present it to referee Marsh before the next home game. And that's what happened. But somehow, the bag contained excrement along with the cash. After opening the bag and sniffing, Marsh dropped it to the ice. The bag burst open and coins rolled in all directions. Randall and his mates were ordered to collect them all, then find fresh coins. Another version of the story holds that young fans leaped onto the ice and collared the change.

Randall's prank enraged team manager Charlie Querrie, who ordered his captain to change into his street clothes. But only after he helped with the ice cleaning.

Randall played in the city's very first professional game, in 1912, when the Blueshirts hosted the Montreal Canadiens, losing 9–5 in front of four thousand fans at the Arena Gardens on Mutual Street.

When the NHL was born, Randall was named captain of the team that wound up winning the Stanley Cup in the spring of 1918. He won a second Cup with the team, renamed the St. Patricks, in 1922, though he'd relinquished the captaincy by then.

Shayne Randall of Peterborough, Ontario, wrote about his grandfather's life on ice in a 2017 biography, *The Pepper Kid: The Life and Times of Ken Randall, Hockey's Bad Hombre.* Shayne, now in his seventies, is the son of Fen Randall, the eldest of Ken's nine children, and is a great-uncle to Doug Gilmour, the twenty-fourth player to wear the franchise's *C*.

Shayne Randall says, "I think my grandfather suffered from what we'd call CTE [chronic traumatic encephalopathy] today. He was really beaten up. At the end of the season, it would take him a month to recover. He really took a lot of punishment." Calculating how many concussions Ken Randall sustained in his twenty-six-year hockey career is impossible, but the many blows from fists and sticks he took to his head "left him in a traumatic state near the end of his life."

Ken Randall died in 1947. He was fifty-eight.

I would like to write more about the colourful characters from Toronto's hockey past. Owners and managers Eddie Livingstone and Charlie Querrie, Hall of Fame players Reg Noble, goaltender Hap Holmes, Harry Cameron, fearless Rusty Crawford and so many others. But I must move on or I'll never get to Turk Broda, Johnny Bower, Darryl Sittler and the two M's, Matthews and Marner.

THE TWENTIES

FOSTER WASN'T THE FIRST

IN THE early 1920s, a slim young radio announcer would gain fame as the play-by-play caller of hockey games played at Toronto's Arena Gardens. Foster Hewitt, born on November 21, 1902, was a *Toronto Star* columnist who every week broadcast on the newest wonder of the age, radio.

Foster's dad was the sports editor at the *Star* and served for sixty-three years as secretary of the Ontario Hockey Association. One afternoon in 1923, Foster was dispatched to the arena on Mutual Street, where he helped install broadcast equipment for the newspaper's radio station, CFCA. He was also told to be ready to broadcast a game that evening, a playoff game between senior teams from Kitchener and Toronto—that is, if no one else could be found. Nobody was located, so that evening Foster Hewitt broadcast his first hockey game. He would remain Canada's "voice of hockey" for the next half century and beyond—an incredible fifty-six years.

Foster thought that the date of his debut was March 23, 1923. But records indicate that no game was played that night. Researchers say the first game he worked was probably on February 16, 1923. Foster performed the play-by-play of the third period (and three overtime periods) using a telephone mouthpiece from within a tiny, enclosed glass booth at ice level that continually fogged up, especially during the three extra periods, obstructing Hewitt's view of the contest.

Several games were broadcast on radio that season with Foster at the microphone. But Hewitt was not the first play-by-play hockey broadcaster. My journalist friend Eric Zweig has done diligent research into hockey broadcasting—as I have with less diligence—and we can assure you that on February 8, 1923, the first radio broadcast of a hockey game was transmitted from the Mutual Street arena with Norman Albert handling the play-by-play of the third period of an OHA playoff match. North Toronto beat Midland 16–4 that night. Six nights later, on February 14, Albert was on the air again for the first broadcast of an NHL game—the Toronto St. Pats defeated the visiting Ottawa Senators 6–4. Norman Albert is known to have broadcast one more game that year. Those third-period-only broadcasts were the first of their kind.

On February 16, Foster Hewitt first hooted, "He shoots, he scores!" during a game between two senior clubs—the Toronto Argonauts and Kitchener Greenshirts. Hewitt quickly became famous, while Norman Albert quickly became forgotten.

Zweig says, "Foster Hewitt must have known that Norman Albert preceded him, but over the years he did very little to dissuade people from believing that he had been the first."

Hewitt would often declare the date of his first broadcast as March 22, 1923. If that was indeed his first game, then an announcer in Regina, Saskatchewan, named Pete Parker preceded him by a few days by calling a game between the Regina Capitals and the Edmonton Eskimos, making Parker the second man to broadcast a game.

For forty years, Hewitt was Canada's leading hockey play-by-play broadcaster for the General Motors (later Imperial Oil) hockey broadcast on Saturday nights. Hewitt became famous for his opening words:

"Hello, Canada, and hockey fans in the United States and Newfoundland."

And even more famous for five words he shouted in the final few seconds of his career.

"Henderson has scored for Canada!"

Three generations of Hewitts—William, Foster and Foster's son Bill—are Hall of Fame inductees. How's this for an alliterative fun fact—the Hewitts: a family full of famers.

JEAN BELIVEAU, FOSTER HEWITT AND DAVE KEON

THE ARENAS BECOME THE ST. PATS

IN 1919, Charlie Querrie, the general manager of the Toronto Arenas, found out the club was up for sale, and on December 7, he and four partners—Fred and Percy Hambly, Paul Ciceri and Richard Greer—purchased the team. With new owners came a new name—the St. Patricks, a moniker borrowed from a local senior amateur squad—and new green and white uniforms.

There would also be a number of unfamiliar faces in the lineup. Jack Adams, Rusty Crawford, Hap Holmes, Harry Meeking and Alf Skinner had departed for points west, while the reactivation of the NHL's team in Quebec City cost Toronto Harry Mummery and Dave Ritchie. Among the new acquisitions was a future Hall of Famer, and the St. Pats didn't have to look far to find him: Babe Dye had scored thirteen goals in just nine games for the amateur St. Pats in 1918–19.

In 1921, the St. Pats won the second half of the NHL's split season, putting them in the league final against Ottawa. On the night of the first leg of the two-game, total-goals series, the Toronto players dropped a bombshell on the hockey world: they refused to take the ice until they'd been given a hefty cash bonus. Officials were stung and called the players "greedy mercenaries." The *Toronto Daily Star* wrote, "This high-handed action has given the players a black eye with the public." Nonetheless, the players got their bonus, only to be blanked, 5–0 and 2–0. Ottawa went west to Vancouver and defended their Stanley Cup title.

The St. Pats were able to knock off the Senators, 5–4 in the 1922 NHL final, and they hosted the Vancouver Millionaires in a best-of-five Stanley Cup series. In keeping with NHL rules, the ice was marked off with a forty-foot, no-offside area at centre ice, and there was a twenty-foot no-offside area for defencemen in front of each goal. But Pacific Coast rules required more lines to be added, dividing the rink into three equal sections. "Why, the bloomin' surface looks more like a football gridiron," moaned St. Pats manager Charlie Querrie.

When Toronto clinched the Stanley Cup with a 5–1 romp in Game 5, Lou Marsh wrote in the *Star*: "Vancouver has no excuses.

When they were whaled Saturday night at their own game of seven man hockey, they practically quit cold. That stood out like a carbuncle on a fat man's neck. Dye, the St. Pats' lazy one, scored four times and acted like someone had sifted red pepper into his flannels."

It would be another ten years before Toronto fans witnessed a third Stanley Cup. By then, the city's hockey champions would be known as the Maple Leafs, performing in an enormous world-class arena before sellout crowds.

Toronto's first two Cup-winning teams should have been a bit embarrassed when their goals-against averages were revealed. In 1918 it was 4.91, and in 1922 it dropped to 4.04.

OLYMPIC STAR REFUSED TO TURN PRO

DURING THE mid-1920s, the St. Pats (and every other pro club) sought the services of star forward Harry Watson, top goal getter on Canada's 1924 Olympic hockey team. Watson averaged seven goals per game in Chamonix, France, as Canada won gold, outscoring opponents by a 110–3 margin. But Watson turned down all offers—it was said Toronto put up $10,000—and entered the business world. Insurance became his new passion.

How could anyone with a solid chance for hockey stardom make such a choice? It's a good question.

Conn Smythe tried again to sign this sought-after star. As longtime Leaf employee Frank Selke later told it, Smythe sent him to the bank to withdraw $5,000 in small bills, then invited Watson over to his office. Watson arrived to find the cash spread out across Smythe's desk. There'd be more where that came from, he was told. This was merely a signing bonus. Even so, Smythe's powers of persuasion fell short of the mark.

Still, on February 19, 1927, newspapers proclaimed that Watson had indeed agreed to become a Maple Leaf, and might even appear in uniform against the Montreal Maroons in their very next game. Just as quickly, the papers backtracked. Nearly a century later, a document

HARRY WATSON

surfaced that put the spotlight on just how close the Leafs actually came to signing the man known as Moose.

In 2021, the Hockey Hall of Fame received a treasure trove of St. Patricks- and Leafs-related papers covering the years 1925 to 1931. Among them was a letter, signed by Watson, stating that he would agree to play for the Leafs in 1927–28, *if* they also managed to acquire a couple of his Olympic teammates—any two of Hooley Smith, Dunc Munro and Beattie Ramsay. The Leafs managed to sign Ramsay, but couldn't swing a deal for Smith or Munro, both of whom lined up for the Montreal Maroons that season.

Watson had survived the Great War as a teenage flying ace. In 1918, he shot down six planes, including four in five days, two weeks before his twentieth birthday. He left hockey as the game's greatest amateur.

When Canada plastered Sweden 22–0, the Swedes lined up every player in front of their goalie but still failed to blunt the attack. In a 33–0 shutout of Switzerland, Watson scored an astonishing thirteen goals. He was later elevated to the Hockey Hall of Fame and the IIHF Hall of Fame for his efforts, and his 1924 feat of filling the nets was recognized in 2008 as the IIHF's fifty-third most significant story in hockey history. One would think it would rank higher on the list, much higher.

DYE FIGURES IN SMYTHE'S DISMISSAL

HARD-SHOOTING HOCKEY player Cecil Dye, a Toronto boy coached by his mother, became a fixture with the Toronto St. Pats in the early years of the NHL.

Better known in hockey circles by the nickname "Babe," Dye was a high-scoring forward throughout the '20s. Long before there was Rocket Richard's fifty goals in fifty games, there was Dye's thirty-eight goals in twenty-nine games. In Dye's first 172 NHL games he scored 177 goals—a pace that was not equalled until Gretzky came along. And just forty-five assists.

Assists were hard to come by in those days. Irvine "Ace" Bailey, one of the few Toronto players to win the NHL scoring title, a feat he

BABE DYE

accomplished in 1928–29, posted twenty-two goals and ten assists in forty-four games for a league leading thirty-two points. Puny numbers by today's standards. But look at Ottawa's Cy Denneny. In 1923–24, he led all NHL scorers with a mere twenty-four points—twenty-two goals and two assists. How about Joe Malone? In the NHL's first season, 1917–18, he won the scoring crown with forty-four goals and only four assists. In Malone's first three NHL seasons, he played fifty-two games, scoring ninety goals with only sixteen helpers. I met him once in a Montreal hotel lobby and we chatted. He was a good-looking man, long retired. I should have sought an interview or an autograph.

When Dye, a stocky little guy who also excelled in pro baseball and football was in his prime, Conn Smythe, coach of the University of Toronto hockey team, was gaining fame as a college coach. Smythe guided his Varsity team into Boston each season for clashes with U.S. collegians at the old Boston Arena.

His coaching methods and outspoken opinions caught the attention of Charles Adams, owner of the NHL's Boston Bruins. In 1926, when Adams learned that the New York Rangers were about to be awarded a franchise in the NHL, he advised the Rangers' president, Colonel John Hammond, "You should grab this guy Smythe before some other team does."

Hammond grabbed him.

Smythe plunged into his job and arranged for the Rangers' training camp to be held in Toronto. He displayed an amazing ability to sign top-notch talent, landing stars like goalie Lorne Chabot, Bill and Bun Cook, Frank Boucher and Ching Johnson. Many would go on to Hall of Fame careers.

But young Smythe apparently missed the boat on one player—Babe Dye. And the mistake would cost him his job. One night, Smythe took a break from hockey. He and his wife attended a movie. When they returned to the hotel where the Rangers were quartered, he encountered the anger of Colonel Hammond.

"Your night at the movies just cost us the services of a great player," he berated Smythe. "The Black Hawks have purchased Babe Dye from St. Pats. We could have had him for $14,000."

"So what?" snapped Smythe, "Dye's not my kind of player. Sure he's a scorer but he's not a checker. Never will be. I wouldn't take him for a dollar."

Hammond was astounded. Barney Stanley, the Chicago Black Hawks' coach, had assured Hammond that Dye was one of the greatest players in hockey. Dye had broken empty seats in the stands with his blasts. He'd scored a number of goals from outside the blue line. Nobody did that.

King Clancy told me when we wrote a book together, "The guy had a shot like a cannon. And yes, he'd score goals from centre ice."

Stanley told Hammond in a follow-up conversation, "Obviously, Smythe knows nothing about the pro game. How come you hired the guy? Especially when Lester Patrick, an experienced hockey man, was available."

Hammond acted on Stanley's advice and fired Smythe. He then contacted Patrick and offered him the astonishing sum of $18,000 to take over as Rangers manager.

Patrick drooled over the talent Smythe had left him. In Patrick's second NHL season—without Babe Dye, and without Smythe—the Rangers won the Stanley Cup.

SMYTHE AND HIS BACKERS BUY THE ST. PATRICKS

IMMEDIATELY AFTER being cut loose by the Rangers, Smythe met with his friend John P. Bickell, a part owner of the Toronto St. Patricks. He told Bickell his club needed changes and that he, Smythe, was the man to make those changes. But Bickell had already decided to hire Mike Rodden, a sportswriter and part-time referee.

"Good luck," Smythe said. "But I'm telling you, Rodden will be a disaster." Later, when the Pats stumbled through a few games, Bickell called Smythe to tell him he'd been right about Rodden and to ask if he'd still be interested in managing. Smythe said yes, but only if the offer included a share of the club. When Bickell mentioned that a promoter with designs on moving the team to Philadelphia was offering $200,000 for the St. Pats, Smythe convinced Bickell he must keep the team in Toronto. "You'll never regret selling the team to me, even though I can't match the Philadelphia offer."

Bickell liked Smythe's enthusiasm and energy and vision. He liked Smythe's idea for a name change for the club. And his burning desire to build an arena like no other. He provided the money and the enthusiasm that enabled Smythe to achieve the franchise that would make Smythe—not Bickell—famous. Thanks to Bickell, Smythe found some backers and bought the club for $75,000 down, with another $75,000 to be paid within thirty days.

SMILING JACK WAS AS IMPORTANT AS SMYTHE

DID YOU know that an incredible sportsman nicknamed "Smiling Jack" was the owner and president of the Maple Leaf hockey club for a number of years?

As a hockey historian, I must confess I knew little about Bickell's role in hockey for a good part of the last century. Yet his list of his accomplishments is astonishing. It appears that Bickell was more responsible than any other person for the construction of the NHL arena I worked in for decades—Maple Leaf Gardens in Toronto.

I hear you saying, "That can't be possible. I know hockey. And Conn Smythe deserves all the credit for the building of the Gardens."

My response: There's no way Smythe deserves all the credit. As much acclaim, if not more, should go to a fascinating figure who befriended Smythe back in the 1920s.

John Paris Bickell was born in 1884 in the tiny community of Molesworth, Ontario, a hamlet halfway between Wingham and Listowel that is not nearly as ugly as the name would imply. Jack's life began with the traumatic loss of loved ones. He was six years old when his father, David Bickell Sr., died at age thirty-five. Two years later, his younger brother, David Jr., also passed away. He was just four years old. An older brother would die at age thirteen of appendicitis.

The strange sequence of deaths left Jack the only male in the family, with a mother and baby sister to care for. To his family's amazement,

Jack Bickell grew up to graduate from college, chase after gold in the Klondike and own a brokerage firm by the time he was twenty-three. He was a millionaire by age thirty.

I've been in touch with a Bickell relative, Graham MacLachlan of Calgary, who coauthored a book published in 2017, *J.P. Bickell: The Life, the Leafs and the Legacy*.

MacLachlan has spent years researching his distant relative, who never married nor had children of his own. He was struck by the number of different industries J.P. so prominently influenced in the early twentieth century.

"If anybody in Canada has owned gold or silver, flown in a plane, been to a sporting event, been in a mine or a hospital or benefited from medical research, been in a movie theatre, that person has been touched by J.P. Bickell," says MacLachlan.

So widespread were his interests that MacLachlan said, "I just kept saying, 'This can't be the same guy.' It's simply too remarkable. The whole story just goes on and on."

Bickell sold his company in 1919, but by 1926 he was a senior partner in the New York brokerage firm Thomson McKinnon, where he focused on his mining interests, having invested in McIntyre Porcupine Mines in Schumacher, Ontario, in 1911.

Bickell's role as president of McIntyre Porcupine earned him a place in the Canadian Mining Hall of Fame. By the time of Bickell's death in 1951, shareholders had been paid more than $62 million in dividends.

"Everything the man touched literally turned to gold," MacLachlan says.

Along the way, he added pro hockey to his portfolio.

At the age of forty, he partnered with Nathan Nathanson, with whom he helped establish the Famous Players movie theatre chain, to purchase the Toronto St. Patricks hockey team. Bickell would be associated with NHL hockey in Toronto—as a shareholder, executive, and board member—for the rest of his life, playing a prominent role in seven Stanley Cup triumphs along the way.

The role of Conn Smythe, whom Bickell brought aboard in 1927, has been somewhat overrated. Smythe himself, to his credit, often raved about Bickell's leadership and fundraising efforts at the time.

With Bickell at the helm, and Smythe playing a secondary role, the team was rebranded as the Maple Leafs.

"He was all about civic duty," MacLachlan says. "He was said to be the largest taxpayer in Canada for a number of years. He was such a Canadian patriot, especially if it involved the Maple Leaf."

In 1931, the team would move into a superb new arena, Maple Leaf Gardens. Bickell, not Smythe, was the first president of the company formed to manage the hockey team and the rink. He helped lay the cornerstone of the arena with Lieutenant-Governor W.D. Ross on September 22, 1931.

(I was ten years old on that occasion and can recall reading all about it—after I was done with the comics page—in the *New Liskeard Speaker*—before I went for a skate.)

"You could say, without exaggerating, that Bickell was the cornerstone of the whole project," Smythe would tell *Toronto Star* sportswriter Milt Dunnell following Bickell's death.

In 1978, J.P. Bickell was inducted posthumously into the Hockey Hall of Fame as a builder.

Smiling Jack was a board member of the Wellesley Hospital, the Canadian Bank of Commerce, the Art Gallery of Toronto (now the Art Gallery of Ontario), the National Trust Company (now part of Scotiabank) and the International Nickel Company of Canada.

In 1922, he helped finance the Mississauga Golf and Country Club in Port Credit, where he once made a 215-yard hole-in-one. In 1931, Bickell was a director of the Toronto Maple Leafs baseball team.

In the 1930s, Bickell took flying lessons and flew with a friend to China, just in time to witness the Japanese dropping bombs on China prior to the Second World War. In 1938, he purchased an eight-passenger Grumman Goose, an amphibious plane, for his personal use. As a fervent patriot, Bickell donated two aircraft he owned to the Royal Canadian Air Force at the outbreak of war in 1939.

During the Second World War, as president and chairman of Victory Aircraft in Malton, Ontario, Bickell focused his attention on moving planes from factories to airfields, a job that helped stop Hitler's forces from invading Great Britain. Victory built Lancaster bombers at a rate of one a day. After the war, he was instrumental in the company's transition to A.V. Roe Canada, and remained that company's chairman until his death in 1951.

Bickell's greatest legacy lives on—in what he has done for others. After his death, the J.P. Bickell Foundation was established, endowed with $13 million from Smiling Jack's fortune. As of 2017, the foundation had made grants totalling more than $160 million. The main beneficiary has been Toronto's Hospital for Sick Children.

"If you think of Sick Kids Hospital, you have to think J.P. Bickell," MacLachlan says. "It was really to honour his family."

Jason Wilson, coauthor of Bickell's biography, writes that Bickell was "not flawless." He often drank to excess, and gambled and caroused with his cronies (Harold Ballard may have been one) at the King Edward Hotel. Bickell never married, but was known to support three mistresses. Despite these "imperfections," he was a kind and generous man. Not exactly a household name today, but he should be.

In 1953, the Maple Leaf Gardens board of directors commissioned a trophy, the J.P. Bickell Memorial Award, to recognize members of the Maple Leaf organization for their outstanding service. But since 1972, it has been presented only six times. It's a shame that it has been all but forgotten, locked away somewhere in Scotiabank Arena. There are good men and women working for the Leafs who deserve the recognition such a trophy would bring.

I'm so pleased you read to the end of this story. I speak for Smiling Jack Bickell when I say on his behalf: GO, LEAFS, GO!

"GOOD-BYE ST. PATS! HOWDY MAPLE LEAFS"

IN 1927, when Conn Smythe, with Bickell's consent, officially changed the team's name from St. Patricks to Maple Leafs, it was no big deal. It merited a one-column item on page ten of the *Toronto Star*, while a report in *The Globe* said, "Good-bye St. Pats! Howdy Maple Leafs."

What *was* remarkable was that the change occurred in midseason.

Initially, the team's new colours were to be red and white, but the

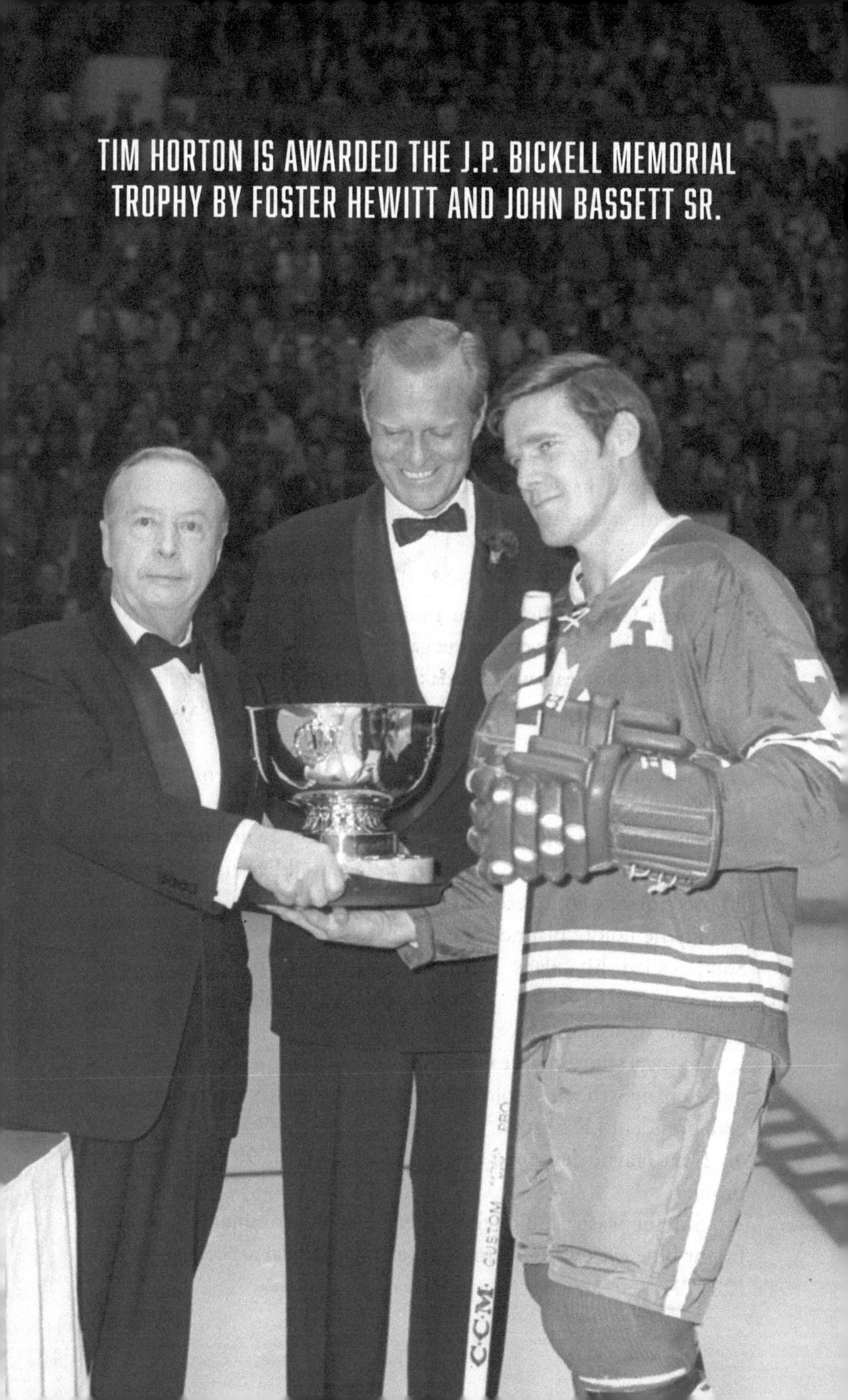

TIM HORTON IS AWARDED THE J.P. BICKELL MEMORIAL TROPHY BY FOSTER HEWITT AND JOHN BASSETT SR.

Leafs were wearing white sweaters with a green maple leaf on the front for their first game on February 17, 1927. Months later, on September 27, Smythe announced a change to the blue and white colours the team wears proudly to this day.

Smythe named himself as team governor and general manager, and even decided to coach the team. Handling multiple duties made him the face of the Maple Leafs—the chief decision maker.

He was quick to develop feuds with referees and NHL general managers. Boston's Art Ross was a favourite target. Smythe sent Ross a bouquet of roses one day after learning the Bruins boss was suffering from hemorrhoids. A note inside directed Ross to place the prickly stems where they'd be most effective. "Shove them there" was the message in Latin.

Smythe knew from the beginning that his team needed a new arena. The Arena Gardens held eight thousand people, including standees, and was packed for every home game. Though they were selling out consistently, the Leafs weren't making much money compared to their rivals in New York, Boston, and Chicago, all of whom played in new, and larger, arenas.

It would take over a million dollars to construct a new building, and Smythe got backing from the Sun Life insurance company for half a million. He found a site on Carlton Street owned by the Eaton's department store chain, a location he favoured because it was at the intersection of two streetcar lines.

Smythe boldly planned the construction of Maple Leaf Gardens. Some called his plans "Smythe's Folly." As the grand opening approached, fans were wagering on how long it would take for Smythe to fill the thousands of seats being installed.

I'm suggesting Smythe would have made none of these moves—the name change, the new colours, the Gardens—without the blessing of club president J.P. Bickell.

Trent Frayne described a young Smythe in a 1999 *Globe and Mail* profile:

"Smythe wasn't a big fellow, but he could dominate a room. His bright blue eyes were his most revealing physical aspect—warm and welcoming sometimes, colder than ice cubes other times. He was often intimidating, as often charming. He believed in playing hunches and he believed in luck; mix his superstitions with his practical ability and you had him, a belligerent Irishman. He was stocky and big-chested. He wore pearl grey spats and an off-white Borsalino fedora. He could be somewhat acerbic."

I remember him wearing those spats as he strolled through the Gardens. But I dared not ask why he wore them.

DAY WAS THE FIRST OF MANY LEAF GREATS

IT'S ODD that two of Toronto's greatest early day pros would have the shortest surnames in hockey: Cecil "Babe" Dye and Clarence "Hap" Day.

Other than King Clancy, Day is the player who dominated the first quarter century of Maple Leafs hockey.

Day started his pro career with the St. Patricks as a winger, before dropping back to defence. He was among the first to don a Maple Leaf sweater in 1927, and by the time he had retired, he had served as the team's captain and coach. And although he was never officially named the general manager, from 1955 through 1957 he was responsible for the day-to-day operations of the team.

Day was born in Owen Sound, Ontario, on June 1, 1901, and grew up in the Midland area. He missed one year of minor hockey because he was required to buy his own sweater (for $3.75) and could not scrape up the money. He played junior in Midland, then moved up to senior hockey with the Hamilton Tigers, where he became a star.

He was also a top student and found time to study pharmacy at the University of Toronto. When Maple Leaf Gardens was under construction in 1931, Day would persuade Smythe to let him open a pharmacy in one corner of the new arena.

In 1924 Hap signed with the St. Pats for $5,000, more money than any previous Toronto hockey player had received. Three years later he was the first captain of the Leafs and wore the Maple Leaf on his chest with pride until 1937, when he was traded to the New York Americans. He played one last season, then worked as an NHL referee before taking over the Leaf coaching reins in 1940.

Former teammate Ace Bailey said, "Hap Day was the best defenseman ever to play for the Leafs."

In 1932, Day captained the Leafs to their first Stanley Cup (over the New York Rangers), won on home ice at Maple Leaf Gardens. As a coach between 1940 and 1950, he would be in the winner's circle much more often—the team captured five Stanley Cups in his decade behind the bench.

Writer Al Nickleson wrote of Clarence "Hap" Day in the 1950–51 Maple Leafs program: "He's a living example of a truly great athlete, who never smoked or drank and who, as a kid, trudged a total of ten miles in bitter cold so that he might practice hockey at a rink in Owen Sound."

Ten miles, Al? Really?

THE GARDENS GOES UP, DYE GOES DOWN

THE GARDENS went up in record time—six months—and at a nominal cost, with some workers accepting Gardens stock in lieu of wages. They were true believers.

In the Leafs' first season at the Gardens, 1931–32, they were the best on the ice—Stanley Cup champions.

By then, Babe Dye's star had fallen.

His first season with Chicago was a good one—he scored twenty-five goals. But he broke a leg, and his scoring touch all but vanished after that.

He tallied but one more goal in his NHL career—with the New York Americans. In 1930, Smythe showed empathy and gave Dye a six-game trial with the Leafs but he scored no points and was done.

Early in his NHL career, Dye was also a star outfielder with the minor-league Buffalo Bisons. He was so skilled that in 1923, Connie

Mack, the famous owner and manager of the Philadelphia Athletics, offered $25,000 for his contract. But for whatever reason, he remained a Bison.

One winter, he lost some teeth in a hockey game, and in baseball season he was chasing a fly ball when his false teeth popped out and fell in the grass. He stopped to look for his dentures while the base runner celebrated an inside-the-park home run.

Dye lost his father as a child and said his mother had taught him how to play hockey. His booming shot twice earned him the NHL scoring title. In 1922, he led the St. Pats into the Stanley Cup final against Vancouver. He scored nine of his team's sixteen goals in that series.

Trivia buffs will have fun with this question: Can you name the forward who was voted number thirty-one on the list of the top one hundred Maple Leafs of all time—without scoring a single point as a Leaf? Sounds impossible, right? Well, Babe Dye played in his final six games as a Leaf without earning a point. All of his other points (203 goals, forty-nine assists) were tallied with the Toronto St. Patricks, Hamilton Tigers, Chicago Black Hawks and New York Americans.

And though his name has been all but forgotten, his goals-to-games ratio remains the fourth-best in NHL history, behind only Mike Bossy, Mario Lemieux and Cy Denneny.

I lift my glass to you, Babe. Molson's of course, the hockey brew.

A footnote: four other players on the Leafs' top one hundred list—Reg Noble (number fifty-five), Harry Cameron (seventy-seven), Jack Adams (ninety) and Corb Denneny (ninety-five) are Hall of Famers who never played a game for the Leafs. They all played for the St. Patricks.

THE MOANER WRITES ABOUT THE MAJOR

AT ONE time, Ted "The Moaner" Reeve was synonymous with sports in Toronto. He played for two Grey Cup–winning teams as a football player, and twice won the Mann Cup, awarded to the top senior men's lacrosse team in Canada. From 1923 to 1971, he covered sports for *The*

Toronto Telegram, and when that paper went out of business he joined the brand new *Toronto Sun*. During his days with the *Tely*, he wrote these words about Conn Smythe:

> *Smythe himself is worth the price of admission. He holds all records for circling a rink. In the early days he would pop up in so many parts of the Arena, shouting hoarsely at players or referees that he often gave the impression a large crowd was present.*
>
> *He has jumped out on to the ice in New York, and been escorted by the police out of the Boston rink. He gives pep talks in the dressing rooms that make the liniment boil over.*
>
> *Blunt, quick-tempered and overbearing, he has enough enemies to fill the Gardens—which would be all right with him if they paid to get in. He has also a wide streak of sentiment and kindness. A few of his players dislike him. All of them respect him, and some of the older or smarter ones would play for him until they dropped. The team itself has a college spirit that is seldom equaled on a campus.*

THIRTIES THRILLS

A SPECTACULAR ARENA OPENS

MAPLE LEAF Gardens was my second home for half a century.

It opened in 1931—the year I was born, and thirty-five years before I broadcast my first game there. By the mid-1960s it possessed a heritage that today's swanky North American ice palaces may never acquire.

Construction began on June 1, 1931, and proceeded at warp speed—the Gardens was open and ready for play in under five months and two weeks.

Embedded in the cornerstone, laid at the southeast corner of the building, was a manuscript stating the artificial ice would be manufactured by three sixty-ton machines with enough capacity to cover the cement floor with a sheet of ice about three-quarters of an inch thick.

Roughly nine miles of piping was embedded in the cement floor to carry the fluids from the ice-making machines, although I've often questioned that statistic. Nine miles? Perhaps if the pipes were the size of drinking straws.

In addition to the arena, the building housed a gymnasium, a billiard room and a bowling alley.

The Gardens was an instant success. It was filled to capacity on opening night, November 12, 1931, when the Leafs lost 2–1 to Chicago. The wife of Leaf defenceman Alex Levinsky said, "My gosh, they just finished the roof before the game. And everybody showed up wearing fancy clothes. We worried about being covered in sawdust."

One month later, the arena was home to a unique church service that not only filled the seats, but forced organizers to turn away an estimated twenty thousand people standing in a drizzle outside.

The Gardens soon became home to a number of first-time events: professional lacrosse and basketball, indoor softball, soccer and dog racing. One night during the dog races, the mechanical rabbit broke down. The dogs skidded to a halt and then trotted off to take a nap—or perhaps sniff out some hydrant.

Prior to a rodeo in the '60s, several tons of dirt and straw were laid over the ice surface. But getting the crap—and that's what it was—off again in time for a game with Detroit presented a huge problem. Manure and urine stained the ice and created an inauspicious "first": brown ice for an NHL game. It infuriated Conn Smythe, who insisted that the Gardens be spotlessly clean at all times.

My late friend Tommy Gaston, who'd watched the Leafs play in the Mutual Street Arena as a boy, recalled the opening of the Gardens.

"My dad made sure I had a suit and tie on," he said. "It was a real event. You walked in the first time and stopped to gasp. That dome high over centre ice was so massive. Lots of tuxedos and top hats. Everything smelled new and the lights were so bright."

I saw my first game there in the mid-1930s. I remember the awesome size of the arena, the frantic speed and energy of the players, and a trip to the men's room to pee—into a long trough used by twenty or thirty patrons simultaneously, gallons of urine going through a hole at the end of the trough to who knows where. I wondered if the Leaf players used a similar trough in their dressing room. Years later, there was no trough. It had been sold to a farmer who fed his pigs from it. A collector would have paid a thousand dollars for it—maybe more.

DICK IRVIN: A GREAT PLAYER AND COACH

IN 1913, Dick Irvin, born in Hamilton, Ontario, in 1892, scored all nine goals in a senior hockey game as his Winnipeg Monarchs defeated a strong Toronto team, 9–1. The scoring outburst earned him a unique

DICK IRVIN

place in the popular syndicated newspaper feature, *Ripley's Believe It or Not!*

A few years later Irvin moved west, playing and starring with teams in Regina and Portland. In 1926, Irvin and his teammates on the Portland Rosebuds were sold en masse to a new NHL franchise, the Chicago Black Hawks (the nickname was two words back then). As team captain, Irvin played brilliantly for Chicago, finishing second in the NHL scoring race in 1926–27, a point behind Bill Cook of the Rangers and four ahead of Howie Morenz.

Early in his second season in Chicago, he suffered a fractured skull, and although he came back to play a third year, the injury hastened the end of his playing days.

After his recovery, Irvin was hired to coach the Hawks, who had finished with the worst record in the NHL two years in a row. In one of those seasons, Vic Ripley, their leading scorer, collected a mere thirteen points (his career high was twenty), some distance behind Gretzky's record of 215 season in 1985-86.

In his only full season as coach, Irvin led the Hawks to a record of twenty-four wins, seventeen losses, three ties and a trip to the Stanley Cup finals, but they lost to the Canadiens and the team's owner, Major Fred McLaughlin, released him in September 1931. This came as no surprise because McLaughlin changed coaches the way some people change their socks and shirts.

McLaughlin would make fifteen coaching changes in eighteen years. Godfrey Matheson, who got the job when he met McLaughlin on a train, was one early hire. Matheson lost the job after two games.

In 1931–32 the Toronto Maple Leafs were winless after five games and manager Conn Smythe convinced Irvin to sign on as Toronto's coach. Under the bright lights of the brand new Maple Leaf Gardens, he achieved the ultimate reward by guiding his Leafs to the Stanley Cup—a perfect way to wrap up their inaugural season in their new home.

Irvin would lead the Leafs to the finals six more times, but could not deliver another Cup to Toronto.

After nine seasons in Toronto, Irvin moved on to Montreal, where the Canadiens' fortunes were plunging. Again, Irvin moulded a winning combination, guiding the Habs to Cup wins in 1944, 1946 and 1953. His 1943–44 team lost only five games out of fifty.

Irvin finished his amazing coaching career back in Chicago in 1955–56, taking over a club that had squatters' rights to the NHL basement for seven of the previous nine years. Before he could begin one of his patented rebuilding jobs, he found himself battling cancer. He died in Montreal in May of 1957.

Irvin missed the playoffs only twice in twenty-seven seasons and passed along his love for the game to his son Dick, the Hall of Fame hockey broadcaster.

During his final season, Irvin told a *Sports Illustrated* reporter that he knew exactly how many NHL goals he'd seen: 8,705. "My players have scored 4,721 goals and been scored on 3,984 times," he claimed. "And my hockey travels have carried me over a million miles, most of it by train." At the time, he reigned as hockey's winningest coach. Today, a chap named Bowman claims the record.

One of the highlights of Irvin's annual training camp in Montreal was the final scrimmage, pitting the rookies against the veterans. Those sessions were often frantic.

Irvin would smile and say, "Some kids earned their ticket to the NHL by busting their arse in that final day of camp."

SHRIMP GETS IN THE GAME—WELL, ALMOST

ONE YEAR in the 1930s, the Toronto Maple Leafs limped into the NHL playoffs with several players sidelined by injuries. Desperate for help, they called on a local lad, Shrimp McPherson, to don the blue and white. In the event of another injury, Shrimp would get his big-league chance.

Midway through one game, Shrimp's moment came. He was instructed to replace an injured Leaf who was hobbling from the ice to the bench. In his eagerness to play, Shrimp jumped on the ice too soon. His skates had no sooner hit the Gardens' slick surface than the referee signalled a penalty. "Too many men on the ice!" he roared, pointing at Shrimp.

Red-faced, McPherson headed back to the bench while one of his teammates was sent to the penalty box. He didn't get another chance.

According to hockey historian Mike Ferriman, Shrimp has the dubious distinction of being the only player in NHL history to incur a penalty without ever playing a single second in the NHL.

NHL records show no evidence that Shrimp played in any NHL game. But he enjoyed a fine minor-league career and was living in St. Louis when the Blues gained entry to an expanded NHL in 1967. It was there that he finally made his way back to the NHL—as the team's assistant trainer.

He passed away in Oakland, California, in 1974, following a game between the Blues and California Golden Seals.

McPherson's obituary began: "Former Toronto Maple Leaf centre ..." But *was* he?

WHAT'S IN A NAME?

HERE'S AN oddity about the Leafs' first Cup, in 1932: Conn Smythe's eleven-year-old son Stafford became the youngest person to have his name engraved on the Stanley Cup.

And his name was spelled correctly. That's a claim Jacques Plante could never make. He won the Stanley Cup five years in a row and his name was spelled differently each and every time.

Conn Smythe insisted that the names of seventeen investors be engraved on the Cup. To find room for them, five players only had their surnames stamped in the silver: (Harold) Darragh, (Frank) Finnigan, (Bob) Gracie, (Earl) Miller and (Fred) Robertson. When the Cup was redesigned during the 1957–58 season, the names of the investors, as well as the five players, were removed—even though the five players took part in every playoff game and met the requirements to be on the Cup. And without those seventeen investors, there was plenty of room to include them.

KEN DORATY

DORATY ENDS LONGEST GAME

ON APRIL 3, 1933, a record crowd of 14,539 filled Maple Leaf Gardens for the fifth and deciding game of the semifinal playoff series between Boston and Toronto. When the attendance was announced, many said a larger crowd would never see a hockey game in Toronto.

At the end of the amazing marathon, decided by a 1–0 score at 4:46 of the *sixth* overtime period, players and fans agreed it was a playoff game like none ever witnessed before.

The *Toronto Star* offered a concise synopsis of the action:

> *When the first puck was dropped, there was no inkling that the teams would still be skating at 1:48 the next morning, in the sixth period of overtime. That's when the red light flashed and a mighty roar from the fans rocked the Gardens. That's when little Ken Doraty took a pass from Andy Blair and whipped the puck past Bruins netminder Tiny Thompson. It was the only goal of an incredible marathon. Thompson had been sensational and had faced 114 shots. In the Leaf net, Lorne Chabot had faced 93 shots and stopped them all.*
>
> *Doraty, at 124 pounds, was tiny and Blair had been hobbled by a recent injury. They were two unlikely heroes.*
>
> *After the fifth overtime period, some players wanted to call a stop, but NHL President Frank Calder gave the order: "Play on. Play to a finish!"*
>
> *The goat of the game was Boston's ace defenseman Eddie Shore. Blair intercepted Shore's cross-ice pass and slipped the puck over to Doraty, who raced in and scored!*
>
> *Doraty was able to dive into the net and retrieve the puck, a souvenir of the greatest goal he would ever score.*

> *Boston coach Art Ross took the devastating loss like a true sportsman. He found King Clancy in the crowd and shook him by the hand. It was the same hand he'd turned into a fist earlier in the season when a few of Clancy's verbal darts had hit home and a snarling Ross had threatened to use his knuckles on Clancy's nose. Or more likely, his mouth.*

The following day, Lou Marsh, veteran sports editor of the *Star*, wrote of Doraty's golden goal:

> *The gink who breaks up these epic hockey matches is always some meek and lowly punk.*
>
> *The gent who broke up last night's titanic struggle was the midget of the team—Ken Doraty—little undersized runt as far as big league hockey players go...lightest and smallest player on the roster... the kid who hauls down the thinnest envelope...last sub on the relief corps. Now get me right—I don't intend to insinuate that Ken Doraty, who played the hero's role last night, is literally a punk. He is a gallant and game young man, but he is just plain lucky to be on the Leaf payroll!*

Hey Lou! Sounded to me like you *did* think Doraty was a punk.

Critics of Marsh's game account objected to his use of the words *punk* and *undersized runt* to describe the twenty-seven-year-old Doraty. Many accosted Marsh outside the *Star*'s offices. "You'd better apologize. I'm about the same size as Doraty myself. And you better not call me a runt!"

Ken Doraty ended the longest game ever played at Maple Leaf Gardens. Three years later, the marathon would be eclipsed by one in Montreal between the Red Wings and Maroons that lasted a dozen or so minutes longer.

During the next season, Doraty established a record that can never be broken. When the Leafs met Ottawa on January 16, 1934, the game was tied 4–4 at the end of regulation time. The overtime rule in that era required a full ten minutes of extra play—no sudden-death endings. Doraty rattled in three goals in the extra frame and the Leafs won the contest 7–4. Doraty became the only NHL player ever to score a hat trick in overtime.

ACE BAILEY'S FINAL GAME

ACE BAILEY was in his late eighties when I visited him one day in 1990. He lived close by, in a seniors' home in North Toronto. Bailey was one of the few Toronto players to win the NHL scoring title, a feat he accomplished in 1928–29.

He told me about the night of December 12, 1933, and a game in which a savage check delivered in anger—and from behind—by Bruin tough guy Eddie Shore ended Bailey's career and left him near death with a fractured skull.

Bailey was a superb right winger who played for both the St. Pats and the Leafs during his abbreviated eight-year career. Three times he was the Leafs' scoring leader. And he became the first player in North American sports to have his number retired.

Here's what happened that night at the Boston Garden.

Bruins defenceman Eddie Shore led a Boston rush toward the Leaf zone, but he was tripped up by King Clancy at the blue line. When no penalty was called, Shore rose to his feet, glowering. By this time Clancy was deep in the Boston zone, and Ace had dropped back to the blue line to cover for him. Shore charged up from behind Bailey and struck him with such force that he was thrown into the air.

Bailey's head hit the ice and he lay on his back as though his neck were broken. His legs began twitching.

The Leafs' Red Horner rushed up to Shore and threw a punch to the jaw that knocked him out cold. Both Shore and Bailey were carried off on stretchers.

Conn Smythe was following Bailey's stretcher when he was punched by a fan. Smythe punched back. Clancy raced over, brandishing a hockey stick, and the fan fled.

Bailey lay in the small room where he'd been taken. One of the doctors on duty at the rink came in, took a look and said, "Get an ambulance here and get it fast!"

He added, "If Bailey is a Catholic, someone should call a priest."

Eddie Shore, with sixteen stitches in his skull, came into the room and apologized to the groggy Bailey.

Bailey is reported to have slurred a response, "That's all right, Eddie. It's all part of the game."

It was an eternity before the ambulance arrived. Fortunately, at the hospital there were two neurosurgeons who were particularly skilled in dealing with Bailey's type of injury. Two delicate operations were performed seven days apart. Internal damage was so severe the surgeons offered little hope for his survival, but Bailey's fighting spirit was a factor they might have overlooked. At one point, a nurse on duty rushed in to save Bailey's life when he swallowed his tongue.

She stayed for hours, urging him to "keep fighting, Ace. Everybody is praying for you."

It was true. All across Canada, fans were praying for his recovery. Thousands of get well cards arrived at the Boston hospital. There was a nationwide sigh of relief when it was announced that the crisis was over.

Ace was quick to credit Dr. Donald Munro, one of the Boston neurosurgeons, for his survival. Bailey told me in 1990, a few months before he passed away, "It was Dr. Munro who saved my life. He drilled a hole in each side of my skull. There was a blood clot in there. Took him a couple of hours to get it all out. He polished off a large glass of brandy when he finished.

"Dr. Munro let me come home to Toronto and a few weeks later I got a letter from the Bruins. Inside was a cheque for $7,800, part of the gate receipts from a game between the Bruins and the Maroons. With that money we bought some property and built a house on it. It cost us exactly $7,800. Then, when they held the big benefit game for me at

Maple Leaf Gardens, we received another cheque, this one for about $20,000. That money was placed in a trust company and they sent us a cheque every month for years."

It was during the Toronto game, a forerunner to the annual All-Star Game, that Bailey and Shore met again at centre ice. When Shore offered his hand and Bailey took it, the crowd erupted in a tremendous ovation.

"I was never the type of man to hold grudges against anybody," Ace told me. "With my dad, it wasn't quite the same story. My dad, after listening to Foster Hewitt describe my injury on the radio, became distraught. He headed for Boston packing a loaded gun. He decided he'd shoot the man who'd nearly killed me. Fortunately, Conn Smythe and Frank Selke got wind of it and notified the Boston police, who took care of the situation."

With his career over, Bailey coached teams at the University of Toronto and Conn Smythe hired him as a penalty box official for Leafs games at Maple Leaf Gardens. He must hold a world record for most time spent in a penalty box; he was a fixture there for the next forty-seven years. Harold Ballard dismissed him before he reached the half century mark, and Bailey remained bitter about it for the rest of his life. "I didn't even get a thank you note from Ballard for all those years I put in," he complained. "Others did when they were let go, but not me. I saw the letters signed by Ballard and I told him about it once. He said, 'Ace, I didn't send any letters.' I said, 'Oh, yes you did. I saw your signature on them.' He said, 'Not my signature. One of my staff must have signed it.' I said, 'Harold, I know your handwriting and it was your signature.' He snarled, 'Okay, then I lied to you.' And I said, 'Harold, thanks for admitting it. Now you can take this job and stuff it up your keister.'"

THE FIRST PENALTY SHOT WAS ON GARDENS ICE

ARMAND MONDOU played on the left wing for the Montreal Canadiens for a dozen NHL seasons from 1928 through 1940, winning a pair of Stanley Cups along the way, in 1930 and '31.

Born in 1905, Mondou was the first NHLer to take a penalty shot after the league installed a new rule in 1934. It happened on opening night that year, Saturday, November 10, after the Leafs' Bill Thoms tripped Georges Mantha of Montreal as he broke in on Leaf netminder George Hainsworth.

The puck was placed in a ten-foot circle located thirty-eight feet from the goal—just inside the blue line. Mondou was chosen as the shooter, and he had the option of standing in the circle and firing away, or skating at the puck from farther back. Hainsworth was not allowed to advance more than a foot off his line.

The twenty-nine-year-old Mondou decided on a top-speed approach for the league's inaugural penalty shot. That was after Hainsworth switched his regular goal stick for "a lighter one."

Toronto's *Globe* wrote of the history-making shot: "The fans were quite interested, but Mondou's shot was a dud. It never left the ice and Hainsworth stopped it with his usual nonchalance."

The Leafs won the game, 2–1.

CLANCY COULDN'T LICK A POPSICLE

KING CLANCY was traded from Ottawa to the Leafs in 1930 and found himself starring on Toronto's Stanley Cup-winning team in the spring of 1932. And he told me a delightful story of a playoff game he played against Boston a few years later.

> *In March of 1936, the Leafs met the Bruins in the playoffs. I remember it was one of those two-game, total goals to count series. Well, the Bruins jumped in front by shutting us out 3–0 in Boston. Left us peeking out from behind the old eight ball.*
>
> *In Game 2, back in Toronto, the Bruins opened fast and took a 1–0 lead. [Eddie] Shore was the big cheese for the Bruins, the best player on the ice in both games. So, I decided to try and throw him off*

his game. In the Leaf room before the third period, I told my teammates, "Don't worry, men. I've got Shore in my hip pocket."

Early in the period, Shore was caught for some infraction and that made him furious. I skated up to him and said, "Geez, Eddie. That was a rotten call. You didn't do a thing to deserve that penalty. The referee must be out to get you."

My words must have registered because suddenly Shore wheeled around and fired the puck at referee Odie Cleghorn. Hit him right in the ass. Bull's-eye! Now, Cleghorn was a tough as Shore—maybe tougher—and he wouldn't stand for that. He hollered, "Okay, wise guy. That'll cost you another ten minutes in the box."

What a break for us! With Shore in the penalty box, the Bruins sagged. We scored four goals to tie the round. Then we scored two more goals and went on to wallop the Bruins 8–3 in that game. Knocked them right out of the playoffs.

Yes, there was a time when a Leafs team scored eight playoff goals in a game against the Bruins.

Clancy continues:

Did you know Shore used to skate out on the ice before games in Boston wearing a long gold dressing gown over his uniform? What a showman! And the music would blare "Hail to the Chief" while he waltzed around the ice.

And I'd needle him. I'd skate up to him and say, "You look so lovely in that gown, Eddie. I hope you'll be wearing it in the game. I'd love to see you get all tangled up in it and fall into the boards and then start crying for a penalty."

He'd glare at me and say, "I'm going to kill you tonight, Clancy."

And I'd say, "You try it, Eddie, if you're not afraid of taking a good licking in front of all your adoring fans."

Of course we both knew I couldn't lick a Popsicle. I think I was in a hundred fights and never won a single one of them.

A NIGHT FOR THE KING

AS A star defenceman, King Clancy sparked the Leafs to a Stanley Cup triumph in 1932. He retired during the 1936–37 season and coached the Montreal Maroons the following season. Then he turned to refereeing, and became one of the most respected officials in the game. He coached the Leafs from 1950 to 1953 and served the club after that as assistant general manager and "vice president in charge of nothing."

Here's the King, talking about a special night held in his honor at Maple Leaf Gardens. It was March 17, 1934—St. Patrick's Day.

Can you believe they talked me into getting dressed in a green uniform with a big white shamrock stitched on the back? They had me wear a long, white beard, and somebody placed a crown on my head.

Then, wearing my royal robes, I was ushered in on a makeshift throne. When the float reached centre ice, I stepped down. Then everything went black because either Charlie Conacher or Day threw a mittful of chimney soot in my face. They showed no respect for royalty at all.

But it turned out to be a fantastic night. They gave me a grandfather's clock and a silver tea

KING CLANCY, HAP DAY AND JOE PRIMEAU

service for my wife. I think I was the first Leaf player ever to be given a night.

SELKE TAKES A HIT

WHEN FRANK Selke took the job as Conn Smythe's assistant in 1929, the job description might have read "possible death-defying consequences."

One night in the '40s, while attending a Leaf game in Boston, Selke, who'd switched seats with Smythe, was accosted by a Bruins fan. Selke had stood and cheered a Leaf goal when the man struck him in the face with a program. Another Leaf goal resulted in a second attack. Then the man's companion, a much bigger chap, hauled off and punched Selke in the nose. Police were called and the two thugs were hustled away.

Only then was Selke informed of their notoriety.

"The big, tough guy was Beano Breen," he was told. "He's a dangerous Boston gangster. And the little guy with him is his trigger man. They're probably guilty of at least a dozen murders in Boston."

Selke thought Bruins manager Art Ross, who was always angry at Smythe, might have had something to do with the seating arrangement. After all, Selke had been sitting in Smythe's regular seat.

Later, Selke learned of Beano Breen's death. At a wedding reception, of all places, two men stepped up and shot him in the face and head.

Later still, when the Bruins played in Toronto, Selke heard Art Ross telling reporters all about the demise of Beano Breen and how detectives had not yet made an arrest.

Selke stepped forward and asked, "Mr. Ross, his murder was a week ago Wednesday, right?"

"Right."

"And the Leafs played in Boston that night, right?

"Right."

"And you'll recall it was Beano Breen who punched me in the nose earlier in the season, right?"

"Right."

"Well, nobody would expect a small, mild-mannered fellow like me would be the triggerman in a gangland shooting, would he?"

"No, not likely."

"But I did have a couple of hours to kill when I was in Boston that day."

With that, Selke turned and melted into the crowd.

ALFIE MOORE'S FINEST MOMENT

ON THE afternoon of May 5, 1938, minor-league goaltender Alfie Moore sat nursing a cold beer in a Toronto tavern. That's how I'll begin this story, although others may cast doubt on its veracity.

Moore had given up all hope of getting a ticket to the first game of the Stanley Cup final between the Chicago Black Hawks and Toronto Maple Leafs. The opening faceoff at the Gardens was just hours away. Then Alfie got the surprise of his life. Two Chicago players, Johnny Gottselig and Paul Thompson, barged into the tavern and began looking around.

Alfie jumped to his feet and called out, "You guys got an extra ticket for the game tonight?"

The Chicago players rushed over and pulled Alfie to his feet. "Come along with us, Alfie. We're taking you to the game, and you won't need a ticket."

"What are you guys talking about?"

Gottselig grinned. "Alfie, you're going to be the Chicago goalie tonight. And you better play the game of your life against Toronto."

That spring in in the 1938 playoffs, thanks to the stellar goaltending of Mike Karakas, the Chicago Black Hawks had stunned the Montreal Canadiens and New York Americans in a pair of best-of-three playoff series.

But in the final, it looked as if the Hawks' Cinderella ride was about to come to an end. The Leafs had outpointed Chicago 57–37 in the regular-season standings, and in the deciding game of the semifinals,

Karakas broke a toe that remained badly swollen. He would not be able to play in Toronto.

Bill Stewart, the Hawks' rookie coach, pleaded with Leafs owner Conn Smythe to let him employ Davey Kerr, the New York Rangers' regular, as a substitute. But Smythe was no fool. "Forget about Kerr," he snarled. "He's one of the best around. But I'll let you use a minor-league goalie in our system—Alfie Moore. That is, if you can find him."

The two men argued until they almost came to blows. Then Stewart threw his arms in the air and turned to Gottselig.

"Go find Moore," he commanded.

Moore was hauled from the tavern and hustled to the Gardens. He threw on a sweater and some goaltending gear and heard a buzz from the fans when he was introduced as the Hawks' goaltender. He stopped a few pucks in the pregame warmup, then pronounced himself ready.

But was he? It didn't appear so when Gordie Drillon scored on the first Toronto shot of the game.

However, if Leaf fans expected Moore to surrender under a barrage of shots, they would be disappointed. He pulled himself together and managed to blank the Leafs the rest of the way. The Hawks won the game, 3–1. As he skated off the ice, the grinning goaltender couldn't resist thumbing his nose at Conn Smythe.

Perhaps it was the thumb that did it. Smythe was so outraged with the outcome of the game that he refused to allow the Hawks to use Moore in Game 2 of the series. Paul Goodman, a Chicago farmhand, was recalled in time for the second match, and Toronto won, 5–1. Karakas declared himself fit for Game 3 at Chicago Stadium, and he played brilliantly, backing the Hawks to 2–1 and 4–1 wins. The Cinderella Black Hawks had captured the Stanley Cup.

Asked what he thought his contribution was worth, Alfie Moore said, "How about $150?" The grateful Hawks paid him double that amount and threw in a gold watch, a memento he treasured long after his one-shot Stanley Cup heroics were history. Moore played in only twenty-one regular-season games in his entire NHL career, none of them with Chicago; and yet, his name is engraved on the Stanley Cup. Not for a second did he believe that would ever happen.

Blackhawks coach Bill Stewart had a remarkable career—or, you might say, two of them.

Born in Fitchburg, Massachusetts, he played several years in baseball's minor leagues, at one point signing a contract with the Chicago White Sox. But he was never able to crack a big-league lineup, and eventually he turned to managing and umpiring in the minors. He was already keeping busy in the winter, coaching and refereeing hockey games.

In 1928, the NHL hired Stewart as the league's first-ever American-born referee. A few years later, in September 1933, he made his debut as a big-league umpire. By the time he retired his whisk broom in 1954, he had officiated in 3,192 regular-season games, four All-Star Games and four World Series. In both sports, he was considered one of the best.

Believe it or not, in 1937, he took a break from his duties as NHL referee-in chief and signed on as coach of the Black Hawks. He joined the team for training camp almost immediately after working his first World Series, a "Subway Series" between New York's Yankees and Giants. Just six months later, he would play a key role on hockey's grandest stage, guiding Chicago to their second Stanley Cup championship. It's surprising Hollywood didn't make a movie about this versatile sportsman.

The following season, the Hawks won their first four games, but lost ten of their next seventeen, and the plug was pulled. "I sure didn't last long as a hockey manager," Stewart said. "I thought I'd be getting a new long term contract with a big raise. Instead, the team owner fired me."

And imagine an owner firing a coach after he won the Cup. That should never happen—although, come to think of it, it happened years later to the Habs' Al MacNeil.

Paul Stewart, who refereed for years in the NHL, is a proud grandson of Bill's. Paul became the first American to referee more than one thousand NHL regular-season games. He was also a solid player who skated in twenty-one games with the Quebec Nordiques in 1979–80, making him the only American to both play and referee in the NHL.

Both Stewarts are in the United States Hockey Hall of Fame.

GENTLEMAN JOE AND THE BIG BOMBER

WE'VE MET Busher Jackson. Now let's turn to the other two stars who formed the first great line in Toronto hockey history.

Joe Primeau played all nine of his NHL seasons with the Toronto Maple Leafs, and his clean play earned him the nickname "Gentleman Joe." He was born in Lindsay, Ontario, and raised in Victoria, British Columbia. His family moved to Toronto when Joe was still a youngster. He played with the St. Michael's College School juniors, and for the 1926–27 season Frank Selke arranged for him to play with the senior Marlboros. In 1929–30, Primeau's pro career finally took flight when Leafs coach Conn Smythe put the twenty-three-year-old centre on a line with a pair of eighteen-year-old rookies, Charlie Conacher and Harvey "Busher" Jackson. The Kid Line was born. The three young players—all superstars, Stanley Cup winners and Hall of Famers in the making—complemented each other's style perfectly.

In 1931, the Leafs moved into Maple Leaf Gardens and won the Stanley Cup that season, led by the incomparable Kid Line.

In his playing days, Primeau was also involved in business, and he retired early from the game in 1936, at age thirty, to build his company, Joe Primeau Block. In 1944–45, with the business well established, he returned to St. Mike's as coach and won the coveted Memorial Cup in his first season. He then coached an RCAF team stationed in Toronto, finally then hooked up with the Marlboro seniors, whom he led to the Allan Cup championship in 1949. In 1950–51, he became coach of the Maple Leafs and won a Stanley Cup in his first year. He's the only man to coach teams to the Allan, Memorial and Stanley Cups.

Charlie Conacher was the most famous of the famous Kid Line.

If Babe Dye had the hardest shot in hockey during the '20s, Charlie Conacher matched him for velocity in the '30s. Conacher's blasts soon earned him a nickname—the Big Bomber—as a member of the most prolific line in early Leaf history. Right wing Conacher, centre Primeau and left wing Jackson finished at or near the top of the scoring lists for the better part of the decade.

The Conachers, a family of ten siblings, were involved in sports from dawn to dusk. Charlie was the best hockey player in the clan, but not by much. His older brother Lionel, once named Canada's best all-round athlete, was a star on ice, and his younger brother Roy bested Charlie by one goal in career scoring. All three have been inducted into the Hockey Hall of Fame.

Charlie's son Peter was an NHLer, and Lionel's son Brian played on the Leafs' last Cup winning team, in 1967.

Have I forgotten anyone? Yes, brother Bert Conacher had big-league talent, but he lost an eye playing the game and had to give it up.

Charlie Conacher was the best right wing in the game for most of the '30s. He was an explosive scorer who used his size—six foot one, and two hundred pounds in his heyday—to his advantage. He could beat goalies with his booming shot, and he'd bowl right over anyone who dared to thwart him in his head-on dashes to the net.

Between 1930 and 1936, Conacher either led or tied for the league lead in goal-scoring five times. He was a Second Team All-Star in his second and third years in the league, and a First Team selection for three consecutive seasons beginning in 1933–34.

Bob Davidson joined the Leafs in 1935 and roomed with Charlie. But he had none of Charlie's scoring prowess. Davidson compiled a mere thirty goals over his first seven seasons. When he retired, he became the most famous scout in the Leafs organization. Every kid in Canada knew his name and hoped he'd show up to one of their games one day. He told me, "Charlie Conacher was a great fellow. As his roomie, I really felt out of place because he was so popular. Any time we were on the road, the reporters would come to his room to get a good story from Charlie. I would just lay back on the bed and listen to all this stuff. They never even said hello to me."

Conacher's bash and bang style of play may well have cost him a long career. After nine years with Toronto, he'd lost a step, so he was sold to the Detroit Red Wings, where he played for one year before moving to the New York Americans for two seasons. He retired from play in 1941 but stayed in the game as a coach, guiding the junior Oshawa Generals to a Memorial Cup championship in 1944. He moved up to coach the Chicago Black Hawks for three seasons in the late 1940s. After a game in Detroit, in which Charlie assaulted referee Bill Chadwick for not calling a penalty against the Red Wings, reporter Lew Walter approached Coach Conacher to ask about the confrontation. Charlie's response was an overhand right to the jaw. "Yeah, I punched him," Conacher confessed. "Walter called me 'the worst of all the coaches to talk to.' I don't have to take that from anyone.'"

Charlie Conacher was hugely popular in his Leaf days and beyond. I met him once on the golf course, but when we tried to converse, he had difficulty talking. Throat cancer. He died in 1968.

Over many years, the Charlie Conacher Research Fund has raised millions for cancer research. His son Pete, who made it to the NHL, is one of the finest chaps you'll ever meet.

THE BUSHER LOST EVERYTHING

HE LEARNED to skate wearing girl's skates, stumbling around the outdoor ice on Poverty Pond in Toronto's west end. His skates and sticks were hand-me-downs, discarded by older kids. It was the 1920s, and the kid hustled newspapers to raise a little spending money.

He grew up to become one of the NHL's flashiest performers, a player once described by Frank Selke as "the classiest player of all time." He was the fastest forward on the Leafs' famed "Kid Line," and his name was Harvey "Busher" Jackson.

As a teenager, following a Memorial Cup triumph in 1929, Jackson joined the Leafs, teaming up with Charlie "Big Bomber" Conacher and "Gentleman" Joe Primeau. The line would become the most famous trio in early Leaf history.

In 1932, Jackson celebrated his twenty-first birthday by winning the NHL scoring title with twenty-eight goals and twenty-five assists. He was listed as the youngest scoring champion to that date—in 1981, Wayne Gretzky won the scoring title at age twenty.

The late Red Burnett, then a young sportswriter for the Toronto Star, once said of Jackson, "He had everything: appearance, stickhandling ability, more shifts than a racing car. The Busher had size and strength, packed into an almost perfect physique."

Jackson's offensive skills netted him 241 goals during a fifteen-year career. But the on-ice skills that vaulted him to superstardom were offset by weaknesses away from the arena. An addiction to alcohol was one—a costly one. On his bio were two failed marriages, a series of business failures and unsuccessful coaching stints. He died too young—at age fifty-five, hobbled in his last few years by a liver ailment.

I would meet him occasionally in the press room at Maple Leaf Gardens. His shabby clothes and lined features gave him the appearance of a very old man. On one occasion, he appeared wearing a brace to protect a broken neck suffered in a fall down a flight of stairs. "And I wasn't drinking when I fell," he insisted.

This was the fabulous forward whom Conn Smythe tried to keep out of the Hockey Hall of Fame.

My broadcaster friend Dick Beddoes protested. "Mr. Smythe, bar him from the Temperance Hall of Fame or even the Chivalry Hall of Fame but for God's sake, not from the Hockey Hall of Fame, where performance on the ice should be the important criterion."

Beddoes was echoing sentiments expressed by Jackson's linemate, Charlie Conacher. "They inducted Joe and me into the Hall and totally ignored Busher. We should have gone in as the Kid Line. That's how we're going to be remembered."

Jackson died in the summer of 1966, and five years after his funeral, he was finally reunited with his Kid Line comrades in the Hall of Fame. Beddoes wrote a fitting final paragraph: "There is no humanity in an institution which waits five years to salute an individual just to be sure he is very dead. Flowers are worthless unless you are alive to smell them."

THE FORTIES DYNASTY

THE LEAFS DOMINATED THE DECADE

NHL hockey in the 1940s began in disarray because of wars raging in Europe and the Pacific. Conn Smythe, who'd served in the Great War, was eager to get involved on European battlefields, and he expected some of his Leafs to follow his example. Many of them did.

Foster Hewitt's *Hockey Night in Canada* broadcasts were often recorded, edited, and transmitted to the BBC in England, to be broadcast to Canadian forces training or fighting overseas—an immense morale booster.

During the 1939–40 season, before signing up again for duty overseas and prior to a game at Boston, Smythe paid for an ad in *The Boston Globe* which stated:

> *Attention Hockey Fans! If you're tired of seeing the kind of hockey the Boston Bruins are playing, come to the Garden tonight and see a real hockey club, the Toronto Maple Leafs.*

Bruins manager Art Ross was enraged with Smythe's insult, even after his Bruins won 3–2 in overtime.

Before sailing off, Smythe concluded that coach Dick Irvin lacked the ability to deal with player issues while the boss was gone, so he convinced the Montreal Canadiens to hire Irvin. Smythe then named Hap Day as his team's new coach.

The new Leaf idols were top scorer Gordie Drillon and slick centreman Syl Apps.

Moncton's Drillon was the last Leaf player to lead the NHL in scoring—in his second season—1937–38. He teamed up with the great Apps to score twenty-six goals and fifty-two points in forty-eight games. He was a First Team All-Star and captured the Lady Byng Trophy for sportsmanship. In goal for Toronto was the previous year's Vézina Trophy winner, Turk Broda.

Drillon's legendary scoring punch was offset by a defensive disinterest. On opening night at Maple Leaf Gardens one season, Drillon skated past goalie Broda before the opening faceoff and tapped him on the pads. "See ya in the spring," Broda called after him.

The Toronto club, much like the current edition, had gained a reputation for being "non-finishers" after several playoff clashes, but Smythe was convinced that Coach Day would soon turn his team's fortunes around. He would be proven right: the decade saw the Leafs win the championship five times, helping ease the gloom and doom of the wartime years.

Eventually, the deadly battles in Europe ended and hockey players returned home and shed their battle dress for hockey uniforms as they engaged in the more familiar battles—ones they actually enjoyed. Leaf teams would shine throughout the decade.

LEAFS FALL SHORT AGAINST THE RANGERS AND BRUINS

THE 1939–40 Toronto Maple Leafs finished third in the NHL standings and swept their best-of-three quarter-final series with Chicago.

In the semifinals, things turned ugly when their opponents, the Detroit Red Wings, faced elimination in Game 2. No fewer than twenty-eight players were involved in a game-ending brawl at the

Olympia. The Leafs' Red Horner was willing to take on all of the Red Wings—and even a lady who attacked him, yanking on his hair and smacking him with her purse. The Leafs won most of the fights and, more important, won the game and the series.

The New York Rangers captured the first two games of the final at home, and then, because the circus took over Madison Square Garden every spring, they were forced to play all remaining games in Toronto. The Leafs won Games 3 and 4 with Turk Broda starring in goal. In the fifth game, Muzz Patrick scored the overtime winner for New York, and Bryan Hextall was the hero in extra time in Game 6. The Rangers lugged the Stanley Cup back to New York for the first time since 1933.

When the 1940–41 NHL regular season ended, two young Leafs—Syl Apps and Gordon Drillon—were tied for the team scoring lead with forty-four points. Drillon had one minor penalty all season, while Apps had three. Both fell short of Boston's Bill Cowley, who topped all scorers with forty-seven.

That year's edition of the team finished second among the NHL's seven teams, and met the first-place Bruins in the semifinals. Toronto took two of the first three games in the series, but dropped three of the next four—all of which were decided by a score of 2–1.

The following season, the Leafs finished in a manner that was even harder to believe.

AN INCREDIBLE COMEBACK

THERE MAY be only a handful of doddering Leaf fans who actually witnessed the Stanley Cup final series in 1942. It pitted the Leafs, coached by Hap Day, against Jack Adams's Detroit Red Wings. There has never been a playoff series quite like it, although the Oilers–Panthers final in 2024 came close.

For starters, the Leafs were fortunate to be in the final. In the first round of the playoffs against New York, the NHL's top team, it took a goal by Nick Metz with five seconds left in the third period of the deciding game to propel the Leafs into the final round.

Playing for the Cup against the Red Wings, the Leafs were odds-on favourites. Hadn't they finished the regular season with eight more wins and fifteen more points than Detroit? But they stumbled through the first two games on home ice and lost them both. Then they dropped the third game, played in Detroit. Leaf fans were frustrated and furious and blamed Coach Day for the impending disaster. Sportswriter Andy Lytle of the Toronto Star wrote, "Except for the gate receipts and the records, there is little apparent use in prolonging this series."

Hap Day confessed that Detroit's style had his team buffaloed. In those days there was no centre-ice red line. The Wings simply worked the puck over their blue line and then fired it into the Toronto zone. Day conceded that defenceman Bucko McDonald was "worn out" and that Gordon Drillon's playing style "isn't suited to the Wings' shoot-and-chase approach. I plan to bench them both."

"And who'll replace them?" he was asked.

"There's Ernie Dickens and Don Metz," he replied. "They're green, but I can use them."

Metz, with only two goals all season, was an unlikely replacement for Drillon, who had tied for eighth in the NHL scoring race. Dickens was another two-goal man, a lad who'd played in only ten NHL games.

In Game 4 at Detroit's Olympia, Nick Metz, the brother of Don, got the winner in a 4–3 victory, forcing the Red Wings to put the champagne back in the cooler. Jack Adams, the Wings' manager and coach, lost his temper, raced onto the ice after the game and attacked referee Mel Harwood. The official was badly mauled during the melee and Adams was suspended.

In Game 5, Don Metz scored a hat trick and the Leafs romped to a 9–3 triumph.

It was back to Detroit for Game 6. Toronto goalie Turk Broda was in dazzling form and blanked the Red Wings 3–0. For Game 7 at Maple Leaf Gardens, a full house of close to 17,000 witnessed the final game of the greatest playoff comeback in Leafs history, which ended when Sweeney Schriner scored two third-period goals in a 3–1 Toronto triumph.

Captain Syl Apps won the Lady Byng Memorial Trophy that season, not taking a single penalty, and finished his ten-season career with an average of five minutes, thirty-six seconds in penalties a season. He was my hero. When I was seven or eight, I met him—the first NHLer I ever met—and he gave me his autograph with two extra words, "Best Wishes," atop his signature. My dad said, "Son, Apps is special. He's never uttered a curse word."

I said to my dad, "I'll never forget this day." And eighty-five years later, I recall it clearly.

Bob Goldham, my partner in the broadcast booth for many seasons, rose from a Leaf rookie to playoff hero in that series. "Goldham's game reached new heights in Game 6," wrote scribe Elmer Ferguson. "It was Goldham who fought back savagely, met the Wings surging drives and fought his way out."

Hap Day had gone from villain to victor, capturing his first Stanley Cup as Maple Leafs coach. Many more would follow.

Gordie Drillon was devasted at being benched for much of the series. Goldham said, "He took the benching like a pro but he said he would never play another game for the Leafs."

After the fifth game, a bunch of hoodlums appeared at Drillon's house about midnight. Drillon said, "They tossed stones and put on a wild, hooting demonstration. Even the kids in the neighbourhood got to booing me. And I had been a pal to many of them."

After scoring a career-high twenty-eight goals in forty-nine games for Montreal in 1942–43, he served in the army and never returned to play NHL hockey.

GUS BODNAR'S QUICK START

GUS BODNAR had an extraordinary debut in a Leaf uniform.

"Well, I was thrilled to sign with the Leafs," he told me. "Squib Walker, the famous Toronto scout, offered me a contract, and that's a story in itself.

"He put some bills on a table in front of me. First, green ones, dollar bills, then a couple of twos. And some fives. Then a twenty. He'd look at me as if to say, 'Is that enough?' Well, I was so stunned.

GUS BODNAR

I couldn't speak. So, he put down a brown one. I said, 'What's that?' And he said, 'Gus, it's a hundred.' Fuck me, a hundred-dollar bill! Well, I wasn't going to lose that, so I grabbed his pen and signed. Then he says, 'Well, now, if you're going to be a big NHL star, you'll need insurance.' So he reaches out and starts taking some money back. I wanted to grab him by the wrist. But he took a hundred back for insurance. Geez, he must be turning over in his grave now hearing me talk about him like this.

"I'll never forget my first game," Gus continues, "and my first shift. It was October 30, 1943—against the New York Rangers. I was certainly a nervous young boy coming into Maple Leaf Gardens from Thunder Bay—Fort William, they called it in those days. I was so nervous I couldn't eat the pre-game meal.

"So, the puck was dropped and I took a few strides and scored a goal—in fifteen seconds. The red light flashed and I stood there—stunned. I couldn't tell you anything about that goal except I think it was against the Rangers' Ken McAuley."

Bodnar went on to win the Calder Trophy following a sixty-two-point season.

"Years later, it was against another Ranger goalie I set a record for the three fastest assists. That was in '52, when I was with Chicago. Bill Mosienko scored three goals in twenty-one seconds and I assisted on all three. They came so fast. And the goalie was Lorne Anderson, a kid from Renfrew who never played another game after that one."

"Your fifteen-second goal was a surprise," I told him. "Rookies seldom get to start a game."

"Right. And it was a bigger surprise to assist on Bill Mosienko's three goals in twenty-one seconds in 1952.

"It's still the fastest hat trick," Gus insists.

But if Wayne Gretzky is reading this, he might laugh and say, "Guys, I had ten hat tricks in a season—and I had ten again in another season. I even had hat tricks on consecutive days, against St. Louis one day and Pittsburgh the next, with four goals in each game. That's eight goals in twenty-four hours." But then, Gretz might not say anything for fear it might sound like he was bragging. And Gretzky is not a braggart.

TEEDER AND ULCERS SURPRISE MONTREAL AND DETROIT

IN THE 1944–45 season, Frank "Ulcers" McCool replaced Turk Broda, who'd gone off to war. Rookie Ted Kennedy, who turned nineteen during the season, had a club-high twenty-nine goals and fifty-four points. Toronto collected fifty-two points to finish in third place, and they met the first-place Canadiens in the semifinals. The Habs had lost only eight regular season games and accumulated eighty points.

But the kids—Kennedy and rookie goalie Frank McCool—were a force in the playoffs. Toronto upset the high flying Habs in six games.

Then the Leafs faced Detroit in the final, and the Red Wings were still seething over the humiliation the Leafs had foisted on them in the famous 1942 comeback series.

For the first time in playoff history, two rookie goalies met in a Stanley Cup final. For the Red Wings, eighteen-year-old Harry Lumley was in net; for the Leafs, the twenty-six-year-old McCool.

McCool had been discharged from the army because he suffered from stomach ulcers, but despite his health problems, he would win the Calder Trophy as best rookie. And he didn't allow second-place Detroit, who'd gone 8–1–1 against Toronto that season, a playoff goal until just past the two-minute mark of the fourth game. McCool set an NHL record for most consecutive shutouts in the postseason with three, a mark that has been tied but not beaten to this day. He set another Stanley Cup record, for the fewest goals allowed in the final, with nine. There was even one more milestone: he became the first NHL goaltender to record an assist.

After Game 3, veteran Red Wing forward Mud Bruneteau said in frustration, "The Leafs can't be that good. We'll have to win four straight."

His team almost did. The Red Wings offense finally caught fire in Game 4, with rookie Ted Lindsay (who scored the game-winner at 3:20 of the third period) helping to overcome a Ted Kennedy hat trick.

Wings goalie Harry Lumley excelled in Games 5 and 6, shutting out the Leafs. The series returned to Detroit for a seventh game, the Wings hoping to avenge the "choking" stigma they'd felt since their stunning loss in 1942.

The Leafs won the Cup in the last-chance game by a final score of 2–1. Defenceman Babe Pratt scored the winning goal.

After the game, the Detroit crowd chanted, "We want Lumley!" and the dejected goalie was brought back to take a bow. Lumley would go on to a Hockey Hall of Fame career, while McCool would play just twenty-two more games in the NHL. His ulcers acted up and affected his play.

As the war came to an end in 1945, some of the Leafs who had served overseas were back in the less risky world of hockey. But it took time for them to find their skating legs. In January of 1946, Turk Broda was back from army duty and got his old job back.

The Leafs, missing the injured Teeder Kennedy for most of the season, were not a force in 1945–46. Maple Leaf winger Gaye Stewart led the league in goals, with thirty-seven. Cup hero goaltender Frank McCool held out for a higher salary. The Maple Leafs decided to let McCool twiddle his thumbs, and they leaned on the goalie tandem of Baz Bastien and Gordie Bell. Both gave up an average of four goals per game. By the time McCool signed a contract and Turk Broda returned from overseas, the club was headed for a fifth place finish.

PRATT BANNED FOR BETTING

THERE WAS stunning news on January 30, 1946, when Leaf defenceman Babe Pratt, a Stanley Cup hero, was expelled from the NHL for betting on games. Wagering was commonplace back then. There was even a betting pool in the corridors at Maple Leaf Gardens. I was about seven years old when I attended my first game there and can recall seeing men in the corridors, some laughing, some grousing, as money—plenty of it—changed hands.

I learned later that players of the era—how many, we'll never know—were also wagering. Pratt admitted he only bet on the Leafs, and he appealed his expulsion. On his promise that he would never wager on hockey again, he was reinstated. He missed nine games during his suspension.

Decades later, when Pratt was with our *Hockey Night in Canada* crew in Vancouver, I asked him about his long ago suspension. He became flustered and mumbled a few words. It was obvious he didn't want to discuss it.

An aside: the NHL did a good job of forcing players to give up wagering on games. Today, NHL telecasts are rampant with ads encouraging fans to bet. Even Gretzky and McDavid became involved. How come? How many family members will become addicted to gambling, creating a major drain on family incomes? Even when I watch alone, I mute the sound on these annoying, irritating ads. Shame on the NHL for allowing it.

Another question: How did the NHL of that time justify lifetime suspensions for players caught wagering on games? Billy Taylor, a New York Ranger, and Don Gallinger, a Boston Bruin (and the first Junior B player to make the leap to the NHL), were both suspended for life from the NHL in 1948 for wagering on hockey. None of Taylor, Gallinger or Pratt had a lawyer to plead his case. And NHL president Clarence Campbell showed Taylor and Gallinger no empathy, no mercy. Their careers were over.

MEEKER AND KENNEDY SHINE, RICHARD IS SUSPENDED

ON JANUARY 9, 1947, Howie Meeker was in the hockey spotlight. He was credited with five goals in a single game, the most ever by a rookie. The record was tarnished somewhat when Leafs defenceman Wally Stanowski claimed he—not Meeker—scored two of the goals.

The 1947 Stanley Cup final was a matchup between the Leafs and the defending champion Canadiens, the first all-Canadian final series since 1935, when the long-gone Montreal Maroons defeated the Leafs.

The Maple Leafs won the series, four games to two. The Habs had finished first in the league with seventy-eight points, while the Leafs finished close behind with seventy-two.

Montreal defeated Boston 4–1 to advance to the final while Toronto was ousting Detroit by the same 4–1 count.

HOWIE MEEKER

In the final, Ted Kennedy was the Leafs' leader with three goals, including the Cup winner. His mates included new faces like Bill Barilko, Howie Meeker and Bill Ezinicki, as Toronto sported the youngest NHL team to win the Cup to that time.

Montreal started fast, blanking the Leafs 6–0 in the opener. Canadiens goaltender Bill Durnan reportedly asked, "How did those guys get in the league?" although he later denied saying those words.

The second game was a violent one, with Maurice Richard clobbering Vic Lynn and Ezinicki with high-sticks to the head. Richard earned over twenty minutes in penalties and a suspension for Game 3. The Leafs took advantage and defeated Montreal 4–0.

Games 3 and 4, played at Maple Leaf Gardens, were both won by Toronto, who took a 3–1 series lead. Returning to the Forum, Montreal extended the series to six games. Back at the Gardens, Turk Broda sparkled in goal and the Leafs won 2–1 to skate off with the Stanley Cup.

Well, that last part is not quite true. After the sixth game ended, the Cup was not presented to the Leafs. NHL president Clarence Campbell declined to present the trophy immediately. He was said to be concerned over the threat of fan violence.

Violence, Clarence? At Maple Leaf Gardens? In the 1940s? Come on.

WALLY STANOWSKI THE FIGURE SKATER

I RECALL a Sunday afternoon years ago in Georgetown, Ontario, when the Leaf Oldtimers were playing the Detroit Red Wing Oldtimers. A number of Bob Goldham fans were in the crowd, as Bob grew up in Georgetown and had played pro for both teams.

There were the usual hijinks. Jackie Hamilton, who played for the Leafs at 150 pounds and played for the Oldtimers at 250, tied the puck to his stick blade with some fishing line. Ivan Irwin doused the Red Wings bench with a bucket of water (they thought it was filled with popcorn). Ike Hildebrand lay prone on the ice, kicking his legs up and down like a spoiled child, acting out a temper tantrum because of a referee's call.

Meanwhile, Wally Stanowski, who'd been a Leaf for seven years in the '40s, had quietly slipped away from our bench and disappeared.

There was a whistle, and from the Zamboni entrance, Wally was back, making a grand entrance. Streaking at hockey games was a fad back then, and Wally was the funniest streaker of them all. He'd doffed everything but his long johns and his skates. There he was, figure skating around the ice in his long johns, the big flap at the back swaying this way and that, bare bum exposed for all to see. The crowd howled in glee and applauded his act, as they would for any master showman.

I learned one day it was not Wally's first attempt at fancy skating. He even did it in the NHL.

"When Conn Smythe was mad at me one year," he begins, "I got very little ice time. We were in Boston one night and their goalie, Frankie Brimsek, got hit by a puck and went off to get stitched up. No backup goalies then, so there was a long delay. And Smythe was at the game—just back from a vacation in Florida.

"Coach Hap Day says to me, 'Wally, get out there and skate around. Get warmed up.'

"There was nobody on the ice. So I skated around a bit. Then I spun around and did a little pirouette, and the crowd laughed and applauded. So I did my Sonja Henie move—skating backwards, one leg high in the air. That earned me a big ovation. I finished at our bench and looked for Hap. But he was doubled over laughing, laughing so hard he ducked down behind the bench. He was afraid Smythe would pop up and blister him for allowing such tomfoolery. And Smythe would blister me, too. But the old man didn't show, so I got away with it.

"I performed much better at Madison Square Garden years later," Wally tells us, eyes twinkling. "In 1968, the Rangers brought back all their great players for a reunion game and I was invited. They were closing down the old Madison Square Garden. Before the opening ceremonies, souvenir hunters began tearing loose signs to rest rooms, exit markers, anything they could get their hands on."

"Were you involved at all, Wally?" I ask.

"Yeah, I was. I went looking for the cash register.

"So, who's there but the Rocket—Maurice Richard—a special guest. Somebody said, 'The Rocket will get a huge ovation when he skates out tonight.' And I said, 'Aw, I'll get a bigger one.' You know, just kidding. And someone bet me ten bucks I wouldn't. I said, 'You're on.'

"Well, when I was introduced, I dashed out and did some spins and pirouettes and a couple of figure eights and the place exploded. I thought the roof would fly off.

"And when the Rocket came out, he got a similar ovation. But not so big as mine. The ten bucks went into my pocket."

WALLY LOVED BEING A LEAF

I TOLD Wally I was seven years old when I saw him play at Maple Leaf Gardens, playing with the St. Boniface Seals against the Oshawa Generals for the 1938 Memorial Cup. He and Oshawa's Billy Taylor were the stars of the series. I told Wally this and he chuckled, recalling the series.

"Someone tried to bribe me to throw that series," he said. "True story. I received an anonymous letter stating I'd be paid $100 if I'd throw the game. If I accepted the deal, I was to kneel down and tie my skate laces during the warmup—a signal to the note writer that the deal was on. I reported the bribe but nobody seemed to care about it. And I considered kneeling down just for a laugh but I didn't do it. We won the Memorial Cup by a 7–1 score in the final game.

"Billy Taylor might have kneeled. Years later, he was caught gambling on the outcome of NHL games and drew a lifetime suspension."

I asked Wally to talk about his hockey beginnings in Winnipeg.

"My first skates were called bob skates—with double runners. Most kids started out on those. Then somebody gave me a pair of ladies skates before I got some real skates—hockey skates. I remember they cost $2.95.

"My dad didn't want me to play hockey. 'A waste of time,' he'd say. He wanted me to learn the blacksmith business. That's what he did.

"I loved hockey and I was thrilled to wear the big leaf on my sweater. I always told people, 'Love what you do in life. Do something that you really enjoy.'"

He won four Stanley Cups with the Maple Leafs, and in 1942 he became the first Leaf defenceman to record four points in a playoff game.

Stanowski was the last surviving member of Maple Leafs' 1942 and 1945 Stanley Cup teams.

RICHARD WAS A REBEL

THROUGHOUT THE 1940s and into the '50s, Toronto teams had trouble handling the Canadiens and their temperamental winger Rocket Richard, Montreal's top scorer.

On April 10, 1947, in a Stanley Cup final game at Montreal, Richard slashed Toronto's Vic Lynn, who was knocked unconscious and required six stitches to close a cut over his left eye. Later during the same period, Richard slashed Bill Ezinicki's head for eight stitches. The Rocket drew a major penalty for the first offence, and a match penalty for the second. He was also fined $250.

He was still using his stick in bayonet fashion into the '50s. On October 31, 1951, during a game in Toronto, Richard swung his stick at a rinkside spectator. After the game, he swung it again—at another patron. No disciplinary action was taken.

On December 29, 1954, Richard charged Leafs rookie Bob Bailey (my junior hockey teammate in Stratford back in 1951), butt-ending him in the face and knocking out two teeth. He repeatedly tried to retrieve his stick to renew his attack on Bailey and refused to leave the ice when ordered to by the referee. His actions again drew a fine of $250.

NHL president Clarence Campbell said, "Fines never bothered Richard. For every $250 I fined him, Quebec businessmen would send him $1,000. Richard could do no wrong. I was always the villain."

MAX BENTLEY IS WELCOME

ON NOVEMBER 2, 1947, when Conn Smythe handed Chicago five players in exchange for two Blackhawks—elite forward Max Bentley and throw-in Cy Thomas—the move was soon referred to as "one of the gutsiest and gaudiest in NHL history."

Smythe, the wily Toronto Maple Leaf owner, seldom acted impulsively. He asked his coach, Hap Day, to name the best centreman in hockey who wasn't a Leaf.

"Max Bentley," said Day. "He's the greatest."

King Clancy and others agreed.

So, Smythe sent a full forward line (Gus Bodnar, Gaye Stewart, and Bud Poile—known as the "Flying Forts" because they all hailed from Fort William) and the defence pair of Bob Goldham and Ernie Dickens to the Blackhawks for Bentley. (The Leaf boss wasn't interested in the least in rookie forward Thomas.)

Smythe considered the deal to be the key to future Stanley Cup clashes, with Bentley tipping the odds in favour of his Leafs. Smythe was proven right when the Leafs captured the Cup in each of the next two seasons.

Born in 1920 in Delisle, Saskatchewan, Max Bentley might have become a Boston legend, but the Bruins thought he was too small when he auditioned for them in 1938. They gave him a pat on the head and sent him packing. He was given a look by the Canadiens, but the Habs' team doctor told him he had a weak heart and should give up the game. So, Bentley wound up in Chicago, where his brother Doug had become a fixture. Doug told the Hawks management, "My brother's a better player than I am." Max, Doug and Bill Mosienko played on the famous "Pony Line." With the Leafs, he won a total of three Stanley Cups. Over the course of his career, he also won a couple of NHL scoring titles, along with a Hart Trophy and a Lady Byng.

The Bentley brothers both retired from the NHL in 1954, with one slim point separating their career totals: Max had racked up 544, while Doug retired with 543.

MAX AND DOUG BENTLEY

Max Bentley told writer Jack Batten that when he came to the Leafs from Chicago in 1947, "I thought I knew a lot about hockey but after playing for Hap Day for a few weeks I concluded he knew more about the game than I'd ever know. He was a brilliant coach. And a lot of other players would say the same thing."

One more fact about Bentley: one night, he scored a big goal and became a horse owner.

"That's right," he told Batten, laughing. "But it was two horses—both thoroughbreds.

"We were trailing Detroit by a 2–1 score and this rich man named Hemstead shouted, 'Max, get a goal and I'll give you a horse.'

"I thought he was kidding but when I scored, Hemstead shouted, 'Max, you got a horse!'

"Then Mr. McCullagh, another wealthy guy, came in the dressing room and said, 'Hemstead gave you a horse, did he? Well, I'll give you a better one.' And he did. When I got back home, I raced them and won some money. But then they both got claimed and that ended that story."

COSTELLO CHOOSES THE HOLY LIFE OVER THE HOCKEY LIFE

LES COSTELLO'S hockey career with the Maple Leafs is hardly worth mentioning. But his life after pro hockey is another story. As an NHL rookie in 1948–49, he played in fifteen games and scored two goals with three assists.

His one shining moment was in the 1948 playoffs when, at age twenty, he scored two goals and two assists in five playoff games and helped the Leafs win the Stanley Cup.

He might have played for a dozen years or more had he not made a life-changing decision in 1950—to skate away from pro hockey and enter the priesthood.

As a priest, he would earn as much adulation, love and respect as he ever would have garnered from playing with pucks and sticks. When

LES COSTELLO

he died after an awkward fall on the ice in a hockey game with the Flying Fathers just before Christmas 2002, his pals and parishioners said he had indeed become a great one—as great in his way as Orr or Gretzky or Apps.

His parish was in his hometown—Timmins, Ontario, where he was known as an entertainer and where he devoted much of his time to assisting people who needed a helping hand.

Because he'd befriended so many across the North and beyond, his funeral service was held in the McIntyre Arena. Timmins native Shania Twain said, "Father Les married my parents and he buried them. He has been there for us many times over the years. Whether it was to find my grandmother a second-hand fridge, marry my parents, give our family funeral services—including our beloved Mom and Dad—or just plain joining in on a good joke. The goodness of God is with this very special man and he shares that spirit with everyone around him. We all love him."

The hockey arena in the town of Cobalt, where he also served, is named for Father Costello. You'll laugh, as I did, on approaching it. There's a Father Costello poem above the front doors:

The wind may kiss the clear blue sky,
The rose may kiss the butterfly,
The morning dew may kiss the grass,
And you, my friend—I consider class.

The final three words of the poem are often substituted, depending on the orator's audience.

Perhaps his greatest gift to hockey and society came in 1963, when he and Father Brian McKee founded the Flying Fathers, a team of Catholic priests who played fundraising hockey games all over North America and even in Europe.

They booked a week-long tour of the Maritimes one season, and Father Les called me.

"You're coming with us," he insisted. "We need a right winger. You score three goals and we'll make you a bishop."

I went, and I had a marvelous time. I got a hat trick and earned a nickname: Bishop.

In 1979, Father Costello got lost in the winter woods for over twenty-four hours, and subsequently had to have several toes amputated due to frostbite. The incident didn't stop him from playing hockey—he filled the space for his missing digits with a rolled-up sock.

At one point, a producer decided to make a movie about the Flying Fathers and brought Wayne Gretzky to Hollywood to audition for the role of a young Costello. But the film was put on hold when Gretzky's acting ability was questioned. What? There's something Gretzky can't do?

Father Les was inducted into the Timmins Sports Heritage Hall of Fame in 2014. The Hockey Hall of Fame might well consider a special niche for special people like Father Les.

THREE CONSECUTIVE CUPS

AFTER CAPTURING the Stanley Cup in 1947 against Montreal, the Leafs won again in 1948 and 1949, both times over Detroit.

Max Bentley's superb stickhandling and playmaking became a huge factor in the 1948 final—as were Kennedy's fourteen points in nine games—when the Leafs swept the overmatched Red Wings.

That season was the Stanley Cup debut for Detroit's Gordie Howe—brought up from Omaha, where his salary was $2,500 for the season—and the last for Toronto's Syl Apps, who retired (for the second time) after the '48 series. There was no surprise when tenacious Ted "Teeder" Kennedy replaced Apps as captain.

In 1948–49, Toronto finished a lowly fourth in the standings with a 22–25–13 record, but still fought their way into the final against Detroit and won again in four straight. Ted Kennedy, rookie Sid Smith and goalie Turk Broda were the leaders. And, of course, there was the wizardry of Max Bentley.

Not since Ottawa's fabulous Silver Seven, long before the formation of the NHL, had a team won three straight Stanley Cups. And the

Leafs had won nine straight games in the finals, beating Montreal in Game 6 in 1947, plus the sweeps of the Wings in '48 and '49. No team had yet captured the Cup six times, and no coach had guided his team to three consecutive Cups. Happy Day was a happy guy.

Detroit's Ted Lindsay was not. "I hated those Leaf teams," he snarled.

Guided by coach Joe Primeau, Toronto won again in 1951—four Cups in five years. This Leaf dynasty included a number of future members of the Hockey Hall of Fame, including Apps (1961), Bentley (1966), Broda (1967), Fern Flaman (1990), Kennedy (1966) and Harry Watson (1994). Coaches Day (1961) and Primeau (1963) were also inducted into the Hall as players.

LINDSAY AND KENNEDY: ENEMIES TO FRIENDS

For three NHL seasons in the early '70s, I worked with Ted Lindsay on the NBC telecasts. Ted often talked about an outstanding juvenile team he played on in Kirkland Lake, Ontario: Holy Name.

"We were said to be the best juvenile team in Canada," he says convincingly.

> *But we got robbed in the playoffs when a team owner slipped several Junior A players—ringers—into his team's lineup for the championship game. They won, but they were cheaters.*
>
> *Well, the next season we played in Port Colborne, Ontario—and two of the guys we played against were Ted Kennedy and Don Gallinger. Both would go on to the NHL—Kennedy as captain of the Leafs and a Hall of Famer; Gallinger would get thrown out of hockey for life for associating with gamblers and then lying about it.*
>
> *Kennedy and I hated each other's guts when we played against each other in the NHL. But long after our careers were over, we became associ-*

ated with the Special Olympics. At first, we barely spoke to each other, but one day we had a drink together. That seemed to go all right, and the next year we had another drink, and one or two more the following year. We finally realized we weren't such bad fellows after all and we wound up being good friends. Kennedy earned my utmost respect. But boy, did we hate each other when we played.

This was forty years after we'd clashed as juveniles. And Teeder said to me one night, "You know, Ted, that juvenile team you were on—Holy Name—was the best juvenile team I ever saw. The best in Canada." He even remembered the name of our goalie. I was really sad when I heard that Kennedy passed away in 2009.

THE GARDNER-REARDON BATTLE

I PLAYED many oldtimer games with Cal Gardner, a Leaf from 1948 until 1952, and he seldom mentioned his famous fight with Montreal's rugged Ken Reardon. But hockey historian Jack Batten remembers it well. He and his brother were just kids when they attended a game at the Gardens one night—the night Gardner and Kenny Reardon began hammering away at one another with their sticks.

Batten says:

I recall the date—January 1, 1949, New Year's—and we were in my father's seats that night. As usual, the two teams went at it hammer and tongs, but there was no hint of the fight that lay ahead. Suddenly, Cal Gardner and Ken Reardon collided and began slamming one another with their sticks.

And their encounter was electrifying. They raised their sticks like medieval adventurers threatening

> *their enemies with long wooden staffs. Reardon flailed first at Gardner, as I remember, and Gardner retaliated with quick, chopping strokes. My brother and I, our mouths hanging open in dumb, stunned surprise, rose out of our seats. We were appalled and terrified and thrilled. The episode lasted no more than thirty seconds but I think we felt that we'd been riveted to the spot for an eternity. It was powerfully real, primitive and raw and it was brief and shocking.*
>
> *It ended as suddenly as it had erupted. Reardon and Gardner, both conscious and upright, were led off the ice, banned from the game. My brother and I sat down with the rest of the crowd. It was over, but it was a moment that was impossible to erase from our memories.*

Cal recalled a previous confrontation with Reardon in New York when he was a Ranger.

"There was a brawl and somebody's stick caught Reardon for about eighteen stitches, and he was told it was my stick. The bad blood between us never went away. Years later, when I was player-coach in Springfield and we played Rochester one night, I was told that Reardon offered fifty bucks to any Rochester player who would nail me.

"I never talked to him after our fight at the Gardens and I vowed I never would."

Tell me about Conn Smythe, I prompted.

"Playing for Smythe was full of surprises," Cal said. "Like how he insisted we all use twenty-two-ounce sticks. They were so heavy. And how shocked we were when someone told us he was taping our phone calls."

And the best coach you ever had, Cal?

"That would be Clarence 'Happy' Day. He always insisted his players have 'total dedication' to the Toronto Maple Leafs. He'd point to the symbol on our sweater and say, 'You should be honoured to be a

Leaf. Millions of young players aspire to become Leafs and never make it. You are the select few who made it all the way to the top.'"

SYL APPS RETIRES

AS NOTED above, the Leafs' sweep of Detroit in the 1948 Stanley Cup final marked the end of Syl Apps's brilliant career.

Conn Smythe often rated that 1947–48 club as his strongest, with great leadership down the middle in centres Apps, Ted Kennedy and Max Bentley. My colleague Dick Beddoes would say years later, "Gretzky would be a fourth line centre on that club."

"You sure, Dick?" I replied. "Gretzky's the highest scoring centre in history. I can't picture Kennedy and Bentley—even my hero, Apps—keeping pace with ninety-nine."

Gretzky would take Beddoes's slight in stride. "Somehow Beddoes didn't like me much," he shrugged.

Apps served a mere fifty-six minutes in penalties in his 423-game career. But years later, a Red Wing, Val Fonteyne, made Apps's penalty stats look more like those of legendary ruffian Tiger Williams. Fonteyne played in more than eight hundred NHL games and served a total of twenty-six penalty minutes (that's thirteen minors). He played another 149 games in the World Hockey Association and was assessed just two minors. He played five complete seasons without visiting a penalty box.

Here's to you, Val—the first player from Wetaskiwin, Alberta, to reach the NHL. If you were a knight, you'd be Sir Val.

You'll settle for being Mr. Clean.

But Apps, in his day, was as popular with Leafs fandom as Jean Béliveau became in Montreal. The late Bill Fitsell, an amazing hockey historian from Kingston, Ontario, and one of the founding members of the Society for International Hockey Research, idolized Apps as a youngster—as I did.

Fitsell entered a public speaking competition when he was eighteen. The topic: Who is your hero? After Fitsell gave his talk about all the outstanding qualities of Syl Apps, a young woman spoke about *her* hero—Jesus Christ. Of course, she won the contest. Fitsell phoned Apps to say, "Unfortunately, you lost, but at least you lost out to the best."

Apps earned $8,000 in his final season. A few years earlier, he broke his leg after twenty-nine games and missed the rest of the season. With a $6,000 salary for the year, he wrote a $1,000 cheque to the Maple Leafs because he felt he was earning more than he deserved. The team did not cash the cheque, but the gesture, so Appsian, so startling and extraordinary, added another laurel or two to the sterling reputation of this great captain.

FADING IN THE FIFTIES

HOWE NEARLY DIED, KENNEDY WAS BLAMED

TED KENNEDY was the ultimate Toronto Maple Leaf. While he lacked the skating skills of others, "Teeder" made up for it with his competitive spirit. One might argue that he was the greatest leader in franchise history.

But in Detroit, he was hated for the longest time. And it stemmed from a horrific episode where he was blamed for almost killing a young Gordie Howe.

The incident took place midway in the Detroit Olympia, during Game 1 of the semifinal series between the Leafs and Red Wings on March 28, 1950. Midway through the third period, the Leafs held a 4–0 lead. After Kennedy slipped away from a Howe check, the big right winger slammed headfirst into the boards and suffered a concussion, a broken nose, a scratched eyeball and a broken cheekbone. There were fears that Howe would die of his head injuries.

"I saw Howe lying on the ice with his face covered with blood," said Kennedy. "I knew what a great player he was and how I hoped he wasn't badly hurt. Then Detroit players started shouting that I speared Howe but I knew I hadn't."

Red Burnett of the *Toronto Star* wrote of the incident: "Referee George Gravel saw the mishap to Howe, didn't call a penalty, and that proves, as far as we are concerned, that Kennedy did not hit Howe." Furthermore, the referee's report was enough to convince NHL President Clarence Campbell to exonerate Kennedy fully.

No video or photographic evidence of the collision exists.

Seeing the twenty-one-year-old Howe, already a star in just his fourth season, lying on the ice unconscious, the Red Wings players feared not only for the life of their teammate, but also their Stanley Cup chances.

The second game of the series was as violent a game as has ever been played, with Detroit players taking runs at Kennedy, resulting in numerous bloody fights. A fan even got involved, pinning Kennedy's arms for a few seconds.

The rivalry threatened to spread beyond the arena. Conn Smythe accused the Red Wings of having tried to injure players in the past. Detroit general manager Jack Adams responded by threatening to sue for damaging reputations. The sum of $75,000 was mentioned.

The series went the full seven games, with Detroit winning the deciding match in overtime by a score of 1–0. The winning counter was ugly—a fluke goal from Red Wing defenceman Leo Reise.

The Wings went on to edge the New York Rangers in the final. Howe underwent emergency, life-saving surgery and not only returned to the NHL the following season, but dominated the league scoring race over the next four years. In 1950–51, he won his first scoring title with an NHL-record eighty-six points—twenty more than runner-up Maurice "Rocket" Richard. He equalled that mark in 1951–52, beating linemate Ted Lindsay by seventeen and picking up his first Hart Trophy as Most Valuable Player. In '52–53, he raised the bar with an unheard-of ninety-five points, twenty-four more than Terrible Ted. And in '53–54, Howe outscored the Rocket by fourteen.

THE TURKEY MAN

GOALTENDER WALTER "Turk" Broda was one of the most popular Leafs in the team's long history. Among Toronto goalies, he was an icon on a par with Johnny Bower.

WALTER BRODA

But there was a time in November 1949, when Conn Smythe felt that Broda's expanding waistline was affecting his game. Smythe demanded a remedy: that Broda drop seven pounds.

"And he'd better lose those pounds before our next game," Smythe declared. "I mean it. If not, I'll find another puck stopper who'll gladly take his place."

Smythe promptly recalled skinny Gil Mayer from the Pittsburgh farm club. Mayer had been swallowing milkshakes there, trying to gain weight.

Broda took Smythe's threat seriously and lost four pounds the very first day. For the next few days, all of Canada got caught up in his "Battle of the Bulge." There were photos of him emerging from a steam bath, shots of him nibbling on celery sticks, shots of him lifting weights.

On Saturday afternoon, before the Leafs' game with the New York Rangers, his fans held their breath when he stepped on the scales. The needle stopped just shy of 190 pounds. He'd made it—and the flash bulbs popped.

A tremendous ovation awaited him when he skated onto the Gardens ice. He played superbly, shutting out the Rangers. He and Smythe and everyone else but the members of the visiting team went home happy.

It didn't take long for the roly-poly Broda to establish himself as one of the game's best puck stoppers and one of hockey's most popular players. From 1936 to 1952, he played in 629 games for the Leafs and recorded sixty-one shutouts. He played in 101 Stanley Cup playoff games, a record at the time, and chalked up thirteen playoff shutouts, another record. He won the Vézina Trophy twice, with a 2.06 goals-against average in 1940–41 and a 2.38 average in 1947–48.

His work in the playoffs was often spectacular, and he is frequently named by oldtime scribes (like me) as one of hockey's greatest "money" goaltenders. In the 1949 Stanley Cup final against Detroit, Broda allowed just five goals in four games as the Leafs swept the Red Wings aside for their third straight Cup triumph. In 1951, at age thirty-seven, he allowed just nine goals in eight games as Toronto won the Cup again.

On December 22, 1951, during Broda's final season, Conn Smythe held a night for him. Only one other Leaf, King Clancy, had been so honoured. In retirement, Broda turned to coaching and found his mentoring niche in junior hockey. His Toronto Marlboros won two Memorial Cups in the 1950s. He yearned for a crack at coaching at the NHL level, and three times the Leafs position came open. Three times he was passed over, in favour of Howie Meeker, Billy Reay and Punch Imlach.

In his fifties, his health began to fail. His final thrill in hockey was being named to the Hockey Hall of Fame in 1967. Five years later, he died of a heart attack.

He's the Leafs' all-time leader in wins, shutouts and games played in net. In 2016 his No. 1 sweater was retired. A year later, he was also among those named to the NHL's list of the 100 Greatest Players of All Time.

Sportswriter Rick Boulton tells the story of one of Broda's daughters and some of her friends returning from a rock concert one night, a few weeks before Turk passed away. "Mr. Broda," said one of the teenagers, "you never heard such a noise at Maple Leaf Gardens."

"Oh yes, I have," he grinned in reply.

BILL BARILKO: TRIUMPH TO TRAGEDY

THERE WAS one shining moment for the Leafs early in the 1950s.

On April 21, 1951, Howie Meeker set up one of the most memorable of Stanley Cup-winning goals. At 2:53 of sudden-death overtime in Game 5, with the Leafs leading the Canadiens three games to one, Meeker sent a pass from behind the Montreal goal to defenceman Bill Barilko, who scored with a diving shot, giving Toronto a 3–2 victory and its fourth Stanley Cup championship in five years.

Seldom have Maple Leaf players achieved instant hero status. But Barilko did, his memorable moment coming before a full house at Maple Leaf Gardens. Too bad televised hockey was still a year away in Canada. The most famous photo of his winning goal, snapped by lensman Nat Turofsky precisely at the moment when the puck entered goalie Gerry McNeil's net, has been reproduced possibly a million times. Turofsky's shot and Ray Lussier's photo of Bobby Orr's "flying through the air" goal that clinched the 1970 Stanley Cup for Boston are two of the most famous playoff photos of them all.

Barilko raced in from the Montreal blue line and, while airborne, whacked the puck by a startled McNeil. The red goal light flashed and the Leafs had captured the Stanley Cup. While McNeil cursed himself for falling too early, the Leafs began to celebrate. Barilko's overtime blast ended a final series in which all five games required an extra period—a hockey oddity.

Following the Leaf celebration on the ice, Montreal sportswriter Red Fisher visited the Habs locker room where little Gerry McNeil, who had turned in one of the greatest goaltending displays in Cup history, had pulled off his jersey. "He sat there in his steaming underwear," Fisher wrote. "Tears trickled down his cheeks as he fumbled with the straps on his goal pads. In twenty minutes he failed to undo a single buckle."

Danny Lewicki, a nineteen-year-old Leaf rookie, recalls the excitement in his 2006 autobiography, *From the Coal Docks to the NHL: A Hockey Life*:

"The roar of the crowd was deafening. I have never heard such pandemonium. What an unbelievable series! The next hour was a blur. We skated around the ice in glee. I hugged so many people and shook so many hands that I was sore. We went into the dressing room to change and the Stanley Cup was there, carried in by Ted Kennedy. They brought the Cup in and then they just whisked it out. I didn't even get a chance to touch it, much less drink from it."

Later, Bill Barilko's mother, Faye, using a soup ladle, helped hockey's newest celebrity sip champagne from the bowl of the Stanley Cup. In 1924, she left behind the hunger and poverty she had known in her hometown, in what is now Belarus, to begin a new life in Canada—in the Northern Ontario mining city of Timmins. Losing her husband in 1946 had been a terrible shock, but on this night she was ecstatic. Her twenty-four-year-old son was the talk of a nation.

A few weeks later, back home in Timmins, she would suffer another devastating loss.

Her daughter Anne told me the story.

> *One weekend, against Mom's wishes, my brother Bill and a dentist friend, Dr. Henry Hudson, flew off on a fly-in fishing trip to some far-away northern lake. Later, Mom would say, "Oh, I made such a terrible mistake that day, letting Bill go without kissing him goodbye, pretending I was asleep when he looked in my bedroom that morning, being angry and not telling him I loved him."*
>
> *Bill and Dr. Hudson flew north to the rivers that flow into James Bay. Two days later, with the plane's pontoons loaded with fish—as much as 150 pounds of extra weight—they started back. Witnesses said Dr. Hudson had difficulty getting the Fairchild into the air. He finally managed it, but it never arrived back in Timmins. Somewhere along the way, the plane went down without a trace.*
>
> *A massive search was organized. Hundreds of search planes flew over thousands of acres of dense bush. None reported any sightings.*
>
> *Then, in 1962, helicopter pilot Gary Fields spotted the reflection of the sun glinting on something strange—a piece of metal, perhaps—buried in the bush about fifty miles north of Timmins. He marked the spot with some toilet tissue thrown into the tree branches. A few hours later he led a search party into the area and located the missing Fairchild. The skeletal remains of Bill and Dr. Hudson were found inside.*

The Barilko family erected a gravestone in Timmins in 1960. On the tombstone is a picture of Barilko in a Maple Leafs uniform.

In 2002, the *Toronto Star* named his 1951 Cup-clinching goal as one of the ten sporting moments that fans would never forget.

DEATH THREAT ON HOWE AND LINDSAY WAS A HOAX

IN 1952, the Detroit Wings swept the Leafs in the Stanley Cup semifinals in four games. Two years later, it took the favoured Red Wings just five games to bounce Toronto. In 1955, Detroit once again swept the Leafs on their way to their fourth Stanley Cup in six years. And in 1956, the Wings won the first two games of their semifinal showdown with the Leafs. In Game 2, Gordie Howe knocked the Leafs' leading scorer, Tod Sloan, out for the year with a vicious, but clean, body check that broke Sloan's shoulder.

An angry Leafs fan telephoned local newspapers before Game 3 with a death threat, claiming he was going to shoot both Howe and Ted Lindsay.

The death threat ultimately proved to be a hoax, but the two Detroit stars, while not frightened, were annoyed by it. Howe was angered because the news upset his mother back in Saskatchewan. Lindsay was equally incensed.

The Leafs held a 4–2 lead halfway through the third period of Game 3. Howe closed the gap at 9:11, and Lindsay tied it up a few minutes later. The game would go into overtime, with Lindsay scoring the game-winning goal, on an assist from Howe. The Wings now had a daunting 3–0 series lead.

In celebration of the goal, Lindsay inverted his stick, cocked it like a rifle and skated around the ice of Maple Leaf Gardens, pretending to shoot at the audience.

"Society has changed so much, I might not do that today," Terrible Ted told me one day thirty years later. "Somebody might shoot back—with real bullets.

"But if I ever wanted a couple of goals in my life, that was the night to get them."

SMYTHE WANTED LUMLEY

IN 1952, the Leafs traded their Vézina Trophy–winning goaltender, Al Rollins (along with Cal Gardner, Gus Mortson and Ray Hannigan), to Chicago for goaltender Harry Lumley, who'd started his career in 1943 as a seventeen-year-old with Detroit, giving up thirteen goals in his first two starts. The nervous rookie was the youngest NHL goalie ever.

"I wanted Lumley," said Conn Smythe in 1952, "because he sells tickets and wins games."

Sells tickets? Surely Smythe knew there were seldom any spare tickets for sale.

I recall admiring Rollins (and his 2.19 goals-against average) at the time, but must admit Lumley did well in a Leaf jersey, winning the Vézina by one goal with a 1.86 GAA in 1953-54 and losing it by a goal to Terry Sawchuk a year later. His thirteen shutouts in 1953-54 were a modern NHL record that stood until Chicago's Tony Esposito recorded fifteen in 1969–70.

ROLLINS BECAME A ROCK STAR IN CHICAGO

BORN IN Vanguard, Saskatchewan, in 1926, Al Rollins was a member of an exclusive club of NHL goalers. He and Jacques Plante and Dominik Hašek are the only keepers to have collected a Stanley Cup championship, a Hart Trophy and a Vézina Trophy. For Rollins, the Cup and the Vézina came as a Leaf in 1951, when he held a sparkling goals-against average of 1.75. It was the end of a Leaf dynasty that saw them win four Cups in five seasons.

The following year—1953—the Leafs found themselves without a playoff berth for only the second time since the opening of Maple Leaf Gardens. By then, Rollins had been traded to Chicago, where he enjoyed his MVP season in 1953–54, despite a horrible last-place finish by his team.

I can see you, reader, shaking your head in disbelief. "How valuable could he have been?" you ask. "Wouldn't they have been finished in the basement without him? Rollins played in sixty-six games for the Hawks, winning only twelve, while posting a GAA of 3.21. The Hawks that year gave up the most goals in the NHL and scored the fewest.

BÖRJE SALMING

Still, Rollins won the Hart. He was the only Chicago player smiling when the season ended. Obviously, voters felt he'd been sensational in all his losses.

In 1956, the Leafs lost four games to one in their playoff series against Detroit. And after four seasons in Toronto, Harry "Apple Cheeks" Lumley was traded back to Chicago. Why trade for Lumley in the first place, giving up a lot, only to trade him back to Chicago? The deal made no sense.

Lumley didn't like it, either. He wanted no part of the struggling Black Hawks and refused to sign. He played instead with the Buffalo Bisons of the American Hockey League for most of the next two seasons. He was brought back to the NHL by the Boston Bruins in 1957.

Lum was late getting to the Hockey Hall of Fame, inducted twenty years after he retired.

PRIMEAU RETIRES, CLANCY TAKES CHARGE

BY 1952, the grand invention called television had become immensely popular and *Hockey Night in Canada* on Saturday night was "must see" entertainment from coast to coast. While the first period was not broadcast, fans were thrilled to see the rest of the action.

The Leafs finished the 1951–52 season in third place, and were swept by their Detroit rivals in the semifinals. In 1953, they finished out of the playoffs, their first exclusion since 1946.

Coach Joe Primeau resigned at the end of that season. He had a thriving cement block business that needed his attention. Cement blocks don't fall down and give pucks away, make excuses and gripe over benchings and bonuses.

Primeau made a wise decision. What's more, his pal King Clancy was ready to try his luck behind the bench.

On March 25, 1953, Clancy became the new head coach of the Leafs.

"I'm overjoyed," said the popular Clancy. "I never dreamed I'd ever be coaching the Leafs. It's wonderful to hear that I got the job."

But it was only wonderful for a while.

The Maple Leafs made the playoffs in 1954, but they lost to the Detroit Red Wings in the semifinals. The '54–55 season saw the Leafs finish in third place with a record of twenty-four wins, twenty-four losses, and twenty-two ties for seventy points. This time, they were swept in the semis by Detroit, who went on to win the Cup.

The third time wasn't the charm. The Leafs dropped to fourth place in '55–56, with a losing record of 24–33–13. And in the postseason—you guessed it—they lost to Detroit in the semifinals.

And with that, Clancy was relieved of his coaching duties and given the title of assistant general manager.

SID SMITH PASSES THE TORCH

WHEN TEEDER Kennedy retired in 1955, Sid Smith was elected to succeed him as captain. At the age of thirty, Smith was amongst the eldest of the Leafs.

Coming off a season in which he led the team with thirty-three goals and fifty-four points, Smith ended the '55–56 campaign having played in only fifty-five of seventy games, scoring just four goals and twenty-one points. He resigned the captaincy after one season, and the job was passed on to veteran blueliner Jimmy Thompson. Smith rebounded in 1956–57, playing all seventy games, potting seventeen goals and racking up forty-one points.

By the fall of 1957, the Maple Leafs were six seasons removed from their last Stanley Cup. Young players were proudly pulling on blue and white jerseys, confident they'd be wearing them for years. Tim Horton, George Armstrong, Bob Baun, Carl Brewer, Bob Pulford, Dick Duff and Frank Mahovlich were rising stars, and Smith and Tod Sloan were the only two Leafs over the age of thirty. Three weeks into the 1957–58 season, Smith retired. At that time, only three active NHL players—Gordie Howe, Maurice Richard and Ted Lindsay—had scored more career goals than Sid.

Smith was also a two-time winner of the Lady Byng Trophy for sportsmanship and gentlemanly play, in 1952 and 1955. He had been selected to the NHL's Second All-Star Team in 1951 and 1952, and the First All-Star Team in 1955.

Smith became a player-coach with the Whitby Dunlops, winning a world championship and an Allan Cup (as senior hockey champions of Canada).

Smith, who played dozens of fundraising games over twenty years with our NHL Oldtimers, was a delightful teammate who began his career in Toronto's Christie Pits area. Every winter, today's young skaters in the neighbourhood skate on the Sid Smith Artificial Ice Rink, formerly the Christie Pits Rink, which was renamed in his honour in 2018.

Smith died in 2004.

DALY WAS A DELIGHT

WHEN I asked Sid Smith about Tim Daly, he laughed and said, "Oh, he was a real character who delivered lines that ended in laughs. During the Korean War, Daly got confused one day. In the dressing room he came up with the line, 'I wish some of you guys had the courage of our brave troops fighting over there in Kenora.'

"Another time Daly spent the afternoon at the movies. When he showed up in the dressing room, I asked him what he'd seen. 'It was a John Wayne movie called *Unconcurred*,' said the trainer.

"I'd never heard of the movie, but I knew of one with a similar name.

"'Tim, was the movie *Unconquered*?' I asked.

"'Sumpin' like that,' admitted Daly."

MEEKER PUNCHES HIS BOSS

AFTER EIGHT seasons with the Leafs, and a couple games with their farm team in Pittsburgh, Howie Meeker returned to Toronto as head coach for the 1956–57 season. But when the Leafs finished fifth in the old six-team NHL, he expected to be fired. Instead, he was moved up a notch, to general manager. But before the 1957–58 season had even begun, he was fired. Howie was so outraged, he jumped up and punched his boss, Stafford Smythe, right between the eyes.

Meeker was elected to the media section of the Hockey Hall of Fame in 1998 for his broadcast work over thirty years, receiving the coveted Foster Hewitt Memorial Award.

He might not have won that award if the voters had ever inhaled the stinking smoke from his cigars. One night, he got his comeuppance. On camera, he lit a stogie—and it exploded!

Meeker wasn't around long enough to keep the Leafs from an alarming tailspin. In 1958, they finished in sixth place, with their lowest point total of the decade, and were playing for their fourth coach of the decade, the affable Billy Reay. The players, looking for a little good humour, relied on their trainer and standup comedian, Tim Daly.

DAY WALKS AWAY

HAP DAY had had enough of the pressures of coaching and managing. After letting go of the coaching reins in 1950, he was promoted to assistant general manager, and then GM in 1955. But his self-esteem suffered because Conn Smythe made most of the major decisions, and Day was never comfortable in a subservient role. So, he walked away from the Leafs—and from hockey in general.

"I was glad to get away from it," he said at the time. "I would have dug ditches rather than stay with the game."

Hap was twice offered the presidency of the American Hockey League, but by then he'd cut most of his ties to the game. He retired to St. Thomas, Ontario, where he owned a company called Elgin Handles. It made handles for hammers and axes, and did not make hockey sticks. Perhaps Day was so sour on hockey by then that he never considered making sticks.

BRIAN MCFARLANE AND HOWIE MEEKER

Day was one of the toughest coaches ever to handle the Leafs. His training camps were described as prison camps. Pity the poor Leaf who made a mistake in practice. His players might have cursed him—behind his back, of course—but they agreed that he knew what he was doing at all times and was able to get the best out of them. What better endorsement can a coach receive? In nine seasons behind the bench, he captured five Stanley Cups—a league record at the time. He was inducted into the Hockey Hall of Fame in 1961.

GEORGE ARMSTRONG: NATIVE SON

IN THE days when racist barbs were common in sports, George Armstrong, the captain of the Leafs, was often taunted about his Indigenous heritage. He was, after all, half Ojibwa and a proud honorary chief of the Stoney Tribe, named "Big Chief Shoot-the-Puck."

During one game, Armstrong heard one too many insults about his Indigenous roots. After the contest, he skated over and addressed the loudmouth fans.

"You guys aren't so smart. Think about this: when you white people came to this country, the Indians knew how to run things. We paid no taxes. We had no debts. The women did most of the work and we menfolk spent all our time hunting and fishing. How can you beat a system like that?"

Army didn't like signing autographs. But a kid asked him to sign a cap one day, and Army agreed. The kid said, "Now will you sign my shirt?" Army said, "I bet you'd like me to sign your ass."

"You bet," said the kid. "Would you?"

Army told the kid to turn around and drop his drawers. He took a black marker and wrote across the kid's bare butt: Johnny Bower.

Armstrong played twenty-one seasons in Toronto and was team captain for more than ten years, longer than any other Leaf. Throughout his career, he was associated with champions. He played on a Memorial Cup winner, an Allan Cup winner, a Calder Cup winner with the Pittsburgh Hornets, and four Stanley Cup-winning teams.

In 1975 he became the first Indigenous player to be inducted into the Hockey Hall of Fame.

PUNCH IN COMMAND

THE MONTREAL Canadiens dominated the latter half of the 1950s with an unmatched record of five consecutive Stanley Cups.

During that half decade, Toronto's Conn Smythe was ready for retirement, with his son Stafford waiting eagerly in the wings. Backstage, plotting how to muscle his way into a prime spot in the organization was a man named Harold E. Ballard.

And amidst them all was a hockey guy nobody knew much about.

A relative unknown, George "Punch" Imlach was hired as coach and assistant general manager of the Toronto Maple Leafs in 1958. The latter part of his job description puzzled everybody—including Imlach—as he had nobody to assist. The club had no general manager at the time. King Clancy was in the executive suite, but he, too, bore the title of assistant GM. And Clancy had no ambitions to become anything else.

Newcomer Imlach and old-timer Clancy both might have been assisting Billy Reay, who had coached the Leafs to a dismal last-place finish in his rookie season in 1957–58. Conn Smythe had been impressed with Reay and offered him the GM's job, but Reay turned him down.

What was he thinking?

"I'd rather be the team coach," explained Reay. "I've got something to prove here."

It was the worst decision Reay ever made.

When Imlach was offered the manager's position, he grabbed it and quickly fired Reay. Reay remained tight-lipped following his dismissal, but—as Trent Frayne wrote, "it's no secret that he has remained somewhat unkindly disposed towards his executioner."

I wondered at the time—and still wonder—why the Leafs didn't pass on Imlach and hire somebody within their organization to manage and coach the team. Conn Smythe had done well, hiring qual-

PUNCH IMLACH

ity men like Dick Irvin, Hap Day and Joe Primeau. But he had lost his clout. Son Stafford, his pal Harold Ballard, and John Bassett were the decision makers. What a lucky break for Imlach.

The Leafs plucked Imlach from the Boston organization. He'd started as a bank clerk in Toronto, served in the army, then got involved in hockey in Quebec City, where he was player-coach and part owner of a senior team, the Aces. He helped groom his team's best player, Jean Béliveau, for the NHL. Next, he spent a year with the Bruins' farm club in Springfield, trying to get along with the cantankerous Eddie Shore. It was a challenge. For almost one full season they barely talked. Both were stubborn, opinionated hockey men.

A few of the Leafs players had never heard of Imlach. One day, he even had to prove his identity before he was allowed to enter the Gardens. The Leafs had no inkling what an impact he would soon have on their lives and careers.

When Toronto won only five of its first sixteen games in 1958, Imlach solidified his future by moving up to general manager. Some say he was spotted turning cartwheels in front of the building and showing his contract to strangers after accepting an offer of $25,000 per season and a company car. When he calmed down, he decided he had no choice but to fire Reay, even though the coach was a favourite of team owner Conn Smythe.

He stepped in to coach as well, at least on an interim basis, and after a 2–1 loss to Chicago, the Leafs embarked on a six-game undefeated streak. Imlach told reporters, "Guys, my last-place team is now inspired and we will make the playoffs."

Sure, Punch. You're a funny little guy, aren't you? Everyone scoffed at the words of this cocky little optimist.

The new manager-coach said he was pleased with his goaltending. Old Johnny Bower, acquired from Cleveland in the off-season, was proving to be a standout at age thirty-three. Reporters chuckled when Bower confessed he'd never worn real goalie skates until he got to Cleveland. When he first showed up there, he was clutching a pair of tube skates that a former pro—a forward—had given him when he played amateur hockey.

Imlach bolstered his defence by turning Carl Brewer pro and picking up Allan Stanley from Boston in return for Jim Morrison. When the Bruins placed Larry Regan, a former rookie of the year, on waivers, Imlach claimed him. He traded minor leaguer Willie Marshall to Hershey for Gerry Ehman, who had scored forty goals for him in Springfield.

Despite his canny moves, by mid-March Imlach's Leafs were still long shots for a playoff berth. Time was running out and they were nine points behind the fourth-place New York Rangers. When I interviewed Rangers coach Phil Watson and asked, "Is there any chance the Leafs can overtake your club in the race to the playoffs?" Watson scowled and said, "Young fella, there's no way that's gonna happen. No way! You can tell Imlach his club will never put my team out of the playoffs."

The NHL offices, then located in Montreal, began releasing possible playoff matchups for the media. Someone there must have agreed with Watson that it was preposterous to even consider the Leafs for any postseason activity, for there was no mention of Toronto in any of the groupings.

IMLACH'S BIGGEST THRILL

WITH A little over a week left in the regular season, the Leafs met the Rangers in back-to-back games. On Saturday, March 14 at the Gardens, Toronto blanked New York 5–0 and then held on the following night to win a 6–5 thriller back in New York. Now Toronto was only three points behind Watson's club with three games left to play.

The following Thursday, the Leafs went into the Montreal Forum and defeated the Canadiens 6–3. They were only one point back of New York, the Rangers having lost to the Bruins the previous night.

On the last weekend of the schedule, the Rangers regrouped on Saturday night and beat Detroit 5–2 to re-establish a three-point cushion over Toronto. But the Leafs downed Chicago 5–1 on home ice, which meant the race would go down to the final Sunday—with Toronto at Detroit and New York hosting Montreal.

At the old Detroit Olympia before game time, Imlach's heart almost flipped when he learned that the Rangers had jumped into an early lead over Montreal in their clash at Madison Square Garden. But his confidence returned when a follow-up report indicated the Habs were leading 2–1 after goals by Moore and Béliveau.

His next jolt came after the puck was dropped in Detroit. Two Red Wings, Norm Ullman and Marcel Pronovost, scored first-period goals against his Leafs to open up a 2–0 lead. By then the final score had come in from New York: Montreal 4, Rangers 2. Punch rejoiced. There was still a chance. A Toronto win would cap one of the most incredible seasons in hockey history.

While he paced nervously outside the dressing room after the first period, Imlach was approached by Stafford Smythe, who looked dejected. "Well, our boys gave it everything they had," said Smythe. "They've got nothing to be ashamed of."

"Stafford, don't be a dope," snarled Imlach. "You watch. We're not going to lose this game."

Regan scored a pretty goal early in the second period, and then Bob Baun batted one in—his first goal of the season. Ullman scored his second of the game to put Detroit ahead again, but Brewer quickly tied it with a blast. Then Regan, enjoying the best game of his career, put the Leafs ahead 4–3. But Wings defenceman Marcel Pronovost made a nifty rush and fired the puck off Bower's glove into the net. With twenty minutes to play, the score was tied 4–4.

In the third period, Regan displayed some of the slick stickhandling he'd shown some of us as kids on the outdoor ice of McNabb Park in Ottawa. He set up Dick Duff for his twenty-ninth goal of the season as the Leafs took a 5–4 lead. The insurance marker was engineered by another smooth stickhandler, Billy Harris. Harris slipped the puck to Baun, who fired it toward the Detroit net. Harris deftly tipped it out of the air and into the cage to complete the scoring. Toronto 6, Detroit 4. The Leafs were in the playoffs, edging the Rangers by a single point. It was an amazing finish.

PUNCH'S BEST WAS YET TO COME

"THEY CALLED us the Cinderella Leafs because we got off the floor and started winning and we refused to quit," Imlach told the media. "People love that sort of thing."

Imlach predicted his Leafs would win the first round against Boston, and they did, even after falling behind 2–0 in games.

They fought back with two wins on home ice, and it was Johnny Bower, described by the scribes as "a miracle man," who was instrumental in the Leafs third straight win by a 4–1 score in Boston. "You know, I almost benched the guy in favour of Ed Chadwick," Imlach told reporters after the game.

The Bruins avoided elimination with a 5–4 triumph back at the Gardens, but two nights later, in Game 7, Gerry Ehman scored the winner in a 3–2 squeaker. Ehman scored six goals in the seven-game series.

Imlach's team had made it to the final.

But Punch's crystal ball let him down in the final against Montreal. His team came close, a real threat to the mighty Habs, who were establishing a streak of five consecutive Stanley Cup triumphs. Montreal won the first two games at the Forum by 5–3 and 3–1 scores. Back in Toronto, the Leafs captured Game 3 by a 3–2 margin, and might have won the follow-up game but for a twist of fate. George Armstrong's hard shot went right through the webbing in Jacques Plante's net and the goal judge's light failed to go on. Had the Leafs won that game (they lost 3–2) they would have returned to the Montreal Forum tied 2–2 in games instead of down 3–1. The Habs won Game 5 with Ralph Backstrom enjoying a four-point night, and two nights later the Habs captured another Stanley Cup by a 5–3 score.

Marcel Bonin, using a pair of gloves borrowed from Maurice Richard, led all players with ten playoff goals. He had scored thirteen goals and forty-three points in fifty-seven regular season games.

By the end of the 1958–59 season, Imlach was a fixture in Toronto, hugely popular. He would lead his Leafs to the Stanley Cup four times in the 1960s. But even after those stirring triumphs, he would often look back with pride on that first season and the dramatic victory over Detroit that won his team a surprise playoff berth.

"It was the greatest thrill I've ever experienced in hockey."

THE GLOW OF THE SIXTIES

KEON MAKES HIS DEBUT

AFTER JOINING the Maple Leafs in 1958, Punch Imlach kept building a winning roster, one that would be in the Stanley Cup hunt long into the future. By the mid '60s he could boast, "Well, look at that. Three Stanley Cups. And maybe I'll bring you a couple more."

In 1960–61, three players won Imlach's approval and found places on his roster. Hard-shooting defenceman Larry Hillman played in sixty-two contests. Right winger Bob Nevin was promoted from Rochester and found himself performing on a line with Red Kelly and Frank Mahovlich. And on October 6, 1960, Dave Keon pulled on his number fourteen jersey and skated in his first NHL game. Keon would quickly become a fan favourite and would carry off the 1961 Calder Trophy as top rookie following his forty-five-point season. A skating wizard, Keon would lead Toronto in scoring on three occasions, and would often shut down the opposing team's star player.

The pieces hadn't quite come together yet. In the 1960 playoffs, Toronto finished second but were upset by Detroit in the semifinals. In the other series, the Chicago Black Hawks, led by Bobby Hull, Stan Mikita and Glenn Hall, ended the Montreal Canadiens' awesome five-year reign as champions before going on to win the Cup final over the Red Wings.

ANOTHER CLASSY CAPTAIN

LIKE OTHER Toronto captains before him, such as Ted Kennedy, Syl Apps and George Armstrong, Dave Keon could do it all. He was a gifted goal scorer, a tireless skater, a relentless checker, a superb playmaker and a leader who avoided the penalty box.

In 1960, he jumped from junior to the NHL and won the Calder Trophy as Rookie of the Year in 1961. In his second season, he played on a Stanley Cup winner, his biggest thrill. His second biggest was capturing the Cup a fourth time in '67 and being named MVP of the playoffs. He remains the only Leaf to win the Conn Smythe Trophy.

"It was a wonderful time to be a Leaf," he says, "playing in the '60s and winning four Stanley Cups."

One of only five Leafs to play more than one thousand NHL games in the blue and white, Keon set team records with 365 goals and 858 points. Both marks were later erased by another great captain, Darryl Sittler. And then by Mats Sundin, the first European player to be captain. Mats led the Maple Leafs in scoring in twelve of the thirteen seasons he played in Toronto and stands as the all-time Leaf leader in goals (420) and points (987).

Keon was twice awarded the Lady Byng Trophy for his gentlemanly play. When Bobby Hull was barred from Team Canada in 1972 because he had jumped to the WHA, there was a storm of criticism—which overshadowed the anger of Keon fans who felt that this great little player who excelled in "European style" hockey, should have been selected. Jim Proudfoot, writing in the *Toronto Star*, said, "Keon was the most talented individual omitted from Team Canada."

He was elected to the Hall of Fame in 1986, and in 2016 the Maple Leafs recognized him as the best player in club history.

KELLY BECOMES A LEAF

THROUGHOUT THE 1950s, Leonard "Red" Kelly of the Detroit Red Wings was arguably the NHL's top rushing defenceman. He was

RED KELLY

a fixture in Detroit, a Norris Trophy winner, a three-time winner of the Lady Byng Trophy, and his name had been etched on the Stanley Cup four times.

During the 1959–60 season, Kelly suffered an ankle injury that slowed him down. His boss, Jack Adams, concluded that the popular redhead was growing old, and now would be a good time to trade him. The New York Rangers were eager to deal and coughed up Bill Gadsby and Eddie Shack for Kelly and Billy McNeill.

But Kelly refused to report to New York and announced his retirement. Two days later, he went to work with a firm in Detroit.

NHL president Clarence Campbell called him. "I hope you know what you are doing, young man," he admonished Kelly. "If you don't report to New York, I may have to blackball you from hockey forever."

"Go ahead and blackball me, Mr. Campbell," said Red. "I've had a dozen good years in the game and I've already got a new job outside of hockey. I'm good with that." He hung up.

"Eddie Shack's reaction to the trade was quite different," Red said. "When Eddie learned that he was coming to Detroit, he called Ranger coach Phil Watson every dirty name in the book. A parting shot. The next day, he was told he had to go back and play for Watson. Shackie must have wished he'd duct-taped his mouth shut that time.

"Then I got another call, this one from King Clancy of the Leafs. 'Red, we've got permission from Mr. Adams to talk to you. How about coming to Toronto for a meeting with Punch Imlach?'"

Red agreed to fly to Toronto. He was curious to know what Imlach had in mind.

Later the next day, Kelly agreed to the generous offer Imlach placed on the table. When Imlach told Red he wanted him to switch from a defenceman to a centreman, Red said, "Sure, I can do that. It's something Jack Adams never thought of."

Imlach phoned Adams, who agreed to take journeyman defenceman Marc Reaume for Kelly. Adams hung up, failing even to wish Kelly good luck.

The acquisition of Kelly was front-page news. At the Gardens, he posed for photographers wearing jersey number four. His wife, Andra, carrying Red's skates, flew in from Detroit for the game that night against Montreal. She told me, "I couldn't believe the reception Red got from the Toronto fans. I was newly married and knew he was a big hockey hero in Detroit. But I didn't realize how popular he was with Toronto fans."

The redhead went on to help the Leafs win four Stanley Cups. He even found time to combine hockey with politics, serving two terms as a member of Parliament for the riding of York West. In the second election, he beat out a young man named Alan Eagleson.

"Why did I leave politics? Well, I came home one day and my daughter Casey, who was about four years old, saw me when I stepped out of a cab. She said to Andra, 'Mommy, here comes Red Kelly up the walk.'

"That made me blink. Casey didn't even call me Dad. And I thought, 'My kids will be all grown up and not even know their father if I continue to hold two jobs. So I decided to stick to hockey.'"

Every Leaf fan applauded his decision.

The trade that brought Red Kelly to Toronto was perhaps the best deal in Leaf history. Kelly would switch positions, from defence to centre, and lead the Leafs to four Stanley Cups, matching his Detroit haul.

BILLY HARRIS ON OLMSTEAD AND IMLACH

THE LATE Billy Harris, a popular member of the Toronto Maple Leafs from 1957 to 1965, enjoyed reminiscing about the '60s and the three Cup winners he played on. Prior to his death at age sixty-five in September 2001, he talked candidly about the players—and his coach—from that era:

> *If we don't get Bert Olmstead from the Canadiens in '58, I don't think that we would have won the Stanley Cup in '62. We got great leadership from Bert. We learned what pride was all about and*

how important it was to win a Stanley Cup when you have an opportunity.

Béliveau once called Olmstead a "hard-rock left-winger" who could hammer an opponent senseless and seconds later chew you out on the bench because you were three inches out of position on a play. And Conn Smythe often said that Olmstead had the qualities to be the next Maple Leaf coach.

Well, after we won the Stanley Cup in 1962, Punch Imlach dropped Bert's name from our protected list. I think that Punch felt very insecure. He was afraid Bert might replace him, so he got rid of him.

Punch's treatment of people was often bizarre. I think Punch got about maybe fifty percent of the potential out of Brewer and Mahovlich. You can't treat sensitive people like those two like Punch did and expect them to give you one hundred percent.

The players felt they had to back Punch—or else. So, if there had been a better relationship between Imlach and Mahovlich, Frank might have scored sixty or seventy goals a season for the Leafs.

Punch confronted media guys and told them, "You have no right to say this. You have no right to say that." Punch kept a diary on people. Maybe he wouldn't hear a broadcaster's comments, but someone—his wife, Dodo, maybe—would tell him what was said. But Punch, if you said something or wrote something that he didn't like, you'd hear from him. He had that kind of clout, especially with success.

HARRIS ON HIS TEAMMATES

"I MARVEL that Kelly could play hockey and serve as a member of Parliament," Billy Harris said.

Red was able to commute to Ottawa, do his job as a member of Parliament, and be at practice the next day. During games, Kelly and Timmy Horton would sleep between periods. Johnny Bower would give them a signal by whacking his stick on the floor when Imlach came around the corner. Kelly was amazing. It's unheard of, a hockey star who combined a parliamentary career with being a professional athlete.

Timmy Horton was my closest friend. Unfortunately, Tim was killed in a terrible car accident in 1974 during his final season with Buffalo. No team can replace a Tim Horton. He was so reliable—his leadership, his work ethic, all of those things. Timmy had a lot of respect for Punch and Punch had a lot of respect for and got along well with Tim Horton.

From that interesting group, from that mix, the Leafs became Stanley Cup champions.

Let me add how amazing it was that Johnny Bower came up from Cleveland at age thirty-three or forty-three or whatever he was. And he stayed around long enough to win four Stanley Cups and become a Hall of Famer. If you're ever asked to pick a guy that you'd like to have in goal in the seventh game of a Stanley Cup final—pick Johnny Bower.

Here's another thing about Johnny. Every goal that was scored on Johnny, he blamed himself. He didn't point fingers or grimace at teammates. That has a tremendous impact on how your teammates play in front of you.

Rocket Richard of the Canadiens gave him the most trouble. Johnny would say, "That bugger scored more goals on me than any other player.

> *And the Rocket would rub it in. He'd say, 'Hey, John-nee, look out for number two.' I wondered what he meant when suddenly he whipped another one in. And by golly, a few minutes later he fired a third goal past me—'number t'ree.' He'd laugh as he skated past my net. People loved to see him score, but not me. I was so happy when the Rocket retired."*
>
> *Then there was Terry Sawchuk in 1967. What a contrast between the two goaltenders! Johnny Bower loved to practice; Terry Sawchuk hated to practice. But Sawchuk held a record that nobody thought would ever be broken—103 shutouts. When you think of Sawchuk and Bower, you're thinking of two of the greatest!*

As noted above, Billy Harris left us in September 2001 (age sixty-five), Tim Horton in February 1974 (age forty-four), Red Kelly in May 2019 (age ninety-one) and Terry Sawchuk in May 1970 (age forty).

An update: The current record for career shutouts by a goaltender is 125, by Martin Brodeur, who played for the New Jersey Devils and St. Louis Blues from 1993 to 2015. Brodeur also recorded twenty-four playoff shutouts, another record.

NOT EVERYONE RESPONDED TO IMLACH

DURING PUNCH Imlach's climb to the top in Toronto, he had difficulty dealing with sensitive players like Frank Mahovlich and Carl Brewer. While others accepted Punch's George Patton-like approach to the game, the Big M and Brewer did not.

Entering March of 1961, Mahovlich and Bernie "Boom Boom" Geoffrion of Montreal were each within striking distance of a fifty-goal season. Geoffrion reached the milestone when he scored on Toronto's Cesare Maniago on March 16 at the Forum, earning a wild ovation.

Mahovlich, who had potted forty-five through sixty-two games, faded down the stretch and ended up with a team-record forty-eight.

In their final game of the 1960–61 season, the Leafs played to a 2–2 tie with the New York Rangers, and defenceman Bobby Baun was injured—Camille Henry's skate cut him in the throat and mouth in the second period. He was back in action for the third, but after the game there was a frightening moment when he began gasping for breath and hemorrhaging. He was rushed to a nearby hospital, where an emergency operation was performed to ease his breathing. Baun missed a couple of playoff games as the result of the injury, and the Red Wings beat the Leafs 4–1 in the semifinals.

CARL BREWER'S MAGIC GLOVES

ONE NIGHT during the 1959–60 season, Leafs defenceman Carl Brewer said a few unkind words about referee Eddie Powers, who overheard every adjective and sentenced Brewer to the penalty box to cool off for ten minutes. The period ended with Brewer still serving his time, but when the penalty timekeeper got up to leave the box, he got a big surprise: Brewer had locked the penalty box door and refused to let him out. Meanwhile, Powers and his two linesmen were blocked from getting to their dressing room—the only way there was through the penalty box. Hot words were exchanged, and a scuffle ensued. Brewer's behaviour was noted in the referee's report to league headquarters, but there would be no further punishment, aside from the twenty-five bucks Brewer had to fork over for drawing a misconduct.

After a battle on Toronto ice a few years later, referee Vern Buffey spotted a pair of unusual gloves on the ice, dropped there by one of the combatants. He noticed the palms had been removed, and when Brewer skated over to retrieve them, Buffey had the answer to a long-standing mystery: How had the defenceman been able to throw opposing forwards off stride and toss them around like a rag doll?

For the following season, there was a new rule in the book. Players could no longer perform with palmless hockey gloves.

Had Brewer not been such a rebel, he might easily have been considered for induction into the Hockey Hall of Fame. His resumé includes: second in Calder Trophy voting as Rookie of the Year; member of three Stanley Cup teams; runner-up for the Norris Trophy; named to four postseason All-Star teams. But over a span of twenty-two years, the mercurial Brewer only appeared in 604 NHL games, and he retired from the game three different times.

His major contribution to hockey, and every player should thank him for it, was his stubborn resolve in battling the league over millions of dollars in pension money that had not been paid to retired NHL players. It was a battle the players eventually won.

BAUN AND HORTON WERE LIFELONG FRIENDS

AT HIS first Leaf training camp in 1956, sturdy defenceman Bob Baun was teamed with sturdier Tim Horton, who would become his friend for life. Horton was recovering from a devastating on-ice collision with Detroit's Bill Gadsby, one that left him with a broken leg and a broken jaw. There were fears he'd never play again, but they were soon put to rest. He ended up playing for twenty-four seasons with four different teams.

Baun signed his first contract with Punch Imlach for $8,000 a year, plus a $4,000 signing bonus—having negotiated a much better deal than most of the other young junior stars. He knew how to sell himself. Even as a teenager with the Marlies, he drove to the Gardens in a Cadillac.

Defenceman Carl Brewer joined the Leafs in 1957, and his play surprised Baun. "I remember when Brewer could hardly skate, and suddenly, he came streaking out of nowhere, blowing past everybody. Carl was a gifted athlete."

These defencemen, along with Alan Stanley and later Marcel Pronovost (1965), gave Imlach the solid wall he needed on his blue line in the '60s.

Baun told me, "When I think back on those teams we played on, I think we underachieved. If we'd had a strategist like Toe Blake behind our bench instead of Imlach, if there had have been a coach who could keep the Leafs in the right frame of mind, there would have been no limit to our success."

Bobby Baun, like Paul Henderson, is best known for one game. Baun suffered a hairline fracture of his fibula in Game 6 of the 1964 Stanley Cup final, but returned to the ice to score the game-winning goal against the Red Wings. Toronto would win the Cup in Game 7.

Baun was an excellent stay-at-home defenceman, a five-time All-Star, four-time Stanley Cup winner, and the NHL leader in defensive point shares in 1960–61. Yet he was overlooked by the Hall of Fame selection committee.

But it's not too late, guys.

CROWD-PLEASING CLASHES

THE 1961–62 edition of Toronto's NHL squad finished in second place, trailing the Habs by thirteen points and holding a ten-point cushion over third-place Chicago.

In the semifinals, playing against fourth-place New York, Toronto captured the first two games (4–2 and 2–1) on home ice. In New York, the Rangers edged Toronto in Games 3 and 4 (5–4 and 4–2).

Back in Toronto, Red Kelly banged the winner past Gump Worsley at 4:23 of the second overtime period, giving his team a 3–2 victory. Toronto required one more win to advance to the Stanley Cup final. They got some help because of an annual scheduling conflict at Madison Square Garden, where—guess what?—a circus was in progress. The key contest was shifted north of the border to Toronto.

The Leafs exploded for seven goals; the Rangers managed one.

The Leafs were joined in the final by the defending Cup champions, the Black Hawks, who'd been busy deflating Montreal fans by ousting their beloved Habs four games to two.

The Stanley Cup final began in Toronto, with the Leafs jumping ahead by 4–1 and 3–2 scores. In Chicago, Imlach's gang could muster just one goal in two contests. Goalie Glenn Hall was almost perfect with a 3–0 shutout followed by a 4–1 win. Leaf goaltender Johnny Bower, injured in Game 4, was replaced by Don Simmons.

Back in Toronto for Game 5, Bob Pulford's hat trick was a highlight in an 8–4 thumping of the visitors. Toronto unloaded forty-four shots on Hall.

On April 22, 1962, the two clubs battled to a scoreless draw over the first forty minutes of play. At 8:56 of the final frame, Bobby Hull sidestepped a Leaf defender and rifled a twenty-foot shot past Simmons.

Less than two minutes later, after taking a pass from the Big M, Bob Nevin buried the puck past Glenn Hall.

The game winner was delivered by Dick Duff at 14:14.

Tim Horton recalled the finish. "I burst out of the Leaf zone on a power play and threw the puck over to George Armstrong, who went in deep. Army slipped it back to me and I sent it over to Dick Duff, who scored a great goal to win the game and the series."

Horton's assist gave him sixteen playoff points—a new NHL record for points by a defenceman in the postseason.

Horton's regular-season play in 1961–62 had also been superb, and yet, the First Team All-Star berths were captured by Montreal's Doug Harvey and Jean-Guy Talbot. Second-team positions were awarded to Tim's teammate Carl Brewer and the Black Hawks' Pierre Pilote.

Can hockey be unfair? Yes, at times.

Horton would surely have been named the winner of the Conn Smythe Trophy as playoff MVP in 1962, but the award didn't exist yet. It was introduced in 1965.

What's more, Horton's name might well have been associated with the team of the century—1972's Team Canada. Horton turned down an invitation to play because of his loathing for Alan Eagleson, the lawyer and player agent who organized the series.

I recall Tim Horton as a man of great strength, with fierce loyalty to his team, the backbone of a club that won four Stanley Cups.

In the early '60s at Maple Leaf Gardens, each week brought new thrills, produced by players representing six clubs with lengthy traditions, players whose names and numbers were familiar to millions of Canadians. Everyone knew the NHLers of the '60s!

Early in the decade, there were no curved sticks in the Leafs' stick rack, no assistant coaches, no names on the backs of jerseys, no instant replays, no helmets, no mouth guards to chew on, no talk of adding franchises and no idea that European players would one day become regulars on every roster. There were no women in press boxes or the broadcast booth, and any player who even thought of hiring an agent would soon find himself playing for Kalamazoo or Calabogie. He didn't even dare bring his father into the room for the signing. He'd simply hear a manager say, "Sign here, kid. You're lucky we like you."

Most NHL goalies were reluctant to follow Jacques Plante's lead and don facial protection, as he bravely did in 1959. Goalies feared that coaches like Punch Imlach and Toe Blake would question their courage if they hid behind a mask. In time, common sense prevailed and all puck stoppers began to wear masks—all but one holdout, Gump Worsley. Eventually, in his final season, he too succumbed.

In four of the first seven seasons of the 1960s, the Montreal Canadiens finished atop the NHL standings. The Habs' success rankled the other clubs, especially the Leafs. Clashes between Toronto and Montreal guaranteed incomparable, crowd-pleasing hockey. Bower against Plante, Keon and Kelly versus Béliveau and Richard, and the genius of veteran coach Toe Blake pitted against canny newcomer Punch Imlach. One night, Punch started five defencemen against the Habs.

For a game at the Forum, in a blatant display of nepotism, Punch started his own son Brent at centre ice, facing Jean Béliveau! Béliveau was so startled he forgot to score a goal. Brent was not quite NHL calibre and played only three NHL games. But he wore the number nine on his jersey, a numeral favored by superstars like Howe, Bathgate and Hull. Young Brent was kidded by other Leafs. One day, Bob Pulford said to him on the team bus, "Your dad's a miserable son of a bitch."

Brent said, "I know. But you're lucky. I've got to go home to him every night."

Like his dad, after his playing days, Brent became a general manager—but of a baseball team, the Vancouver Canadians of the Pacific Coast League.

In the 1960s, everything stopped on Saturday night for *Hockey Night in Canada*, with a cast that included Foster and Bill Hewitt, Jack Dennett, Eddie Fitkin and Ward Cornell.

As one who was lucky enough to join those TV pioneers, I recall the beginning of the decade, when a player who scored twenty goals in a seventy-game season was a star. It wasn't until 1968–69, after the NHL had doubled in size, that three of hockey's best scorers—Phil Esposito, Bobby Hull and Gordie Howe—surpassed the one-hundred-point barrier.

BAUN GETS BOMBED

BEFORE A home game at the Gardens in 1962, someone threw a small bomb from the stands at the Leafs bench while "God Save the Queen" was playing prior to the opening faceoff.

The bomb exploded near Bobby Baun at one end of the Leafs' bench, briefly blinding the defenceman, and linesman Matt Pavelich, too.

"The blast knocked me off balance," Baun said. "Both the linesman and I couldn't see for a minute or so. It exploded at the top of the gate."

There were holes in Pavelich's sweater, and the front of his sweater was seared.

Police detectives classified the device as a "homemade bomb." But they never found the perpetrator.

A MILLION FOR MAHOVLICH

ON OCTOBER 5, 1962, everyone who was anyone in the National Hockey League convened in Toronto for the annual All-Star Game, set to be played the following night (in those days, the game was played just before the regular season got started). In his suite at the Royal York Hotel, Chicago Black Hawks owner Jim Norris made an offer that would have rocked the hockey world if it had gone ahead: he offered the Toronto Maple Leafs a million dollars for star left winger Frank Mahovlich.

Leaf vice president Harold Ballard almost fell over backwards. "A million for a hockey player, Jim? That's nuts. You've got him. He's yours."

Norris stood up and peeled ten $100 bills from a roll in his pocket and handed them to Ballard.

"A down payment," he said. "I'll get the rest of the money to you tomorrow morning."

"This will knock the World Series off the front pages tomorrow," team president Stafford Smythe chortled. But his general manager, Punch Imlach, was not a happy witness to the proceedings. He grabbed his hat and headed for the door in disgust.

"Ballard shook hands on the deal. I'd never do that," Imlach griped, slamming the door behind him.

But the next morning—oh my. How things had changed. When Chicago GM Tommy Ivan flashed a cheque for a million bucks, nobody in the Leaf front office would take it. The Leafs brass had been loudly admonished by former owner Conn Smythe: "You fellows are making total fools of yourselves." Nursing foggy memories of what had actually happened at the hotel, they rebuffed Ivan.

Scott Young's take on the shenanigans cost him dearly. At the time, *The Globe and Mail* columnist held a second job as a host on *Hockey Night in Canada*. After he mocked the deal in his column, he was told he was no longer welcome on the hockey telecasts. Seems the Leafs (surprise, surprise) had the final say on who worked on TV and who didn't.

Chicago had wooed Mahovlich years earlier. In 1953, when he was a teenager, they offered him a contract that included cash and a five-acre fruit farm near Niagara Falls. The Leafs, who offered cash and a scholarship to St. Michael's College School, won the bidding war, confident that Mahovlich would be a future superstar and lift fans from their seats at Maple Leaf Gardens. He did that and more in his first season, outscoring an even more colourful rookie, Chicago's Bobby Hull, for the Calder Trophy. Someone called him the Big M—and it stuck.

But the Big M's clashes with the Big I caused him to suffer mental anguish and depression. No surprise there—how insulting is it when your boss always mispronounces your name? He wasn't Frank Maholovitch.

Following the farce, Mahovlich's flashes of brilliance became less frequent. He became moody and suffered two nervous breakdowns. On March 3, 1968, Imlach traded Mahovlich, Pete Stemkowski, Garry Unger and the rights to Carl Brewer to Detroit for Norm Ullman, Paul Henderson and Floyd Smith. The heart of the trade was, of course, Mahovlich (295 goals in eleven seasons) for Ullman (298 in thirteen seasons). Once he arrived in the Detroit locker room, Mahovlich felt a huge weight slide from his shoulders.

"Frank fit right in," said Gordie Howe. "I think if the fans in Toronto had cheered him more instead of booing him, the pressure might not have floored the guy."

Mahovlich was traded to Montreal in 1971, where Sam Pollock made sure he fit in again. The Big M set a new playoff scoring record in 1971, with twenty-seven points.

In 1972–73, Mahovlich led the Habs with a career-high ninety-six points and added another twenty-three during the Habs' successful playoff run, the sixth and final time the Big M's name was added to the trophy. In '73–74, he put up ninety-three more points. He averaged more points per game (1.18) in his last three and a half years in the NHL than he did in his first fourteen and a half (0.86). Now, that's a fascinating fact.

The Big M served his country on and off the ice with class and dignity, including a major role (alongside his brother Pete) in Team Canada's 1972 victory over the Soviets. He should have been a Maple Leaf forever, but found well-deserved peace and happiness elsewhere.

I knew Mahovlich as a man who asked interesting questions. Like the time I played on a line with him in oldtimer hockey and mishandled three of his passes. He leaned into me on the next faceoff and said, "Which team are you playing for tonight—theirs or ours?"

Enshrined among the game's immortals in the Hockey Hall of Fame in 1981, Frank Mahovlich was appointed to the Canadian Senate in 1998.

FRANK MAHOVLICH AND RED KELLY
AFTER THE 1967 STANLEY CUP

ONE OF THE BEST TEAMS EVER

"WHY MESS with a good thing?" Punch Imlach told the media as he looked forward to the 1962–63 NHL season. "So, I'll make just one or two changes to my roster."

In the off-season, he acquired defenceman Kent Douglas from Springfield of the American Hockey League for five players. And in the intra-league draft, he lost Bert Olmstead, who was claimed by New York.

The crafty Olmstead is often credited as being the player who taught his Leaf teammates how to win. Punch had diagrammed a play on the chalkboard one day when Bert jumped up and said, "That's not the bleepin' way to do it. Here's how it should be done. Gimme the chalk." And Imlach stood back and listened.

Olmstead's tutelage is one reason the '62–63 Leafs were ranked tenth on *The Hockey News*'s list of the best teams in NHL history. Scotty Bowman, in his recent book, has them at number three.

Adam Proteau wrote in *The Hockey News* in 2013: "If you were looking for a hockey team that employed future Hall of Fame players at every position—and more importantly, got crucial contributions from the top of the lineup to the bottom—the 1962–63 Toronto Maple Leafs would represent your ideal choice."

Nothing fazed the Leafs that season. After a win over Chicago early in the year, a plane carrying the team back to Toronto was struck by lightning, but the flight arrived safely.

Imlach was asked during the preseason who his most important player would be.

"I think Dave Keon," Imlach said. "He's our best man, the top centre and the most consistent player in the business." Keon had yet to celebrate his twenty-third birthday. Right winger Bob Nevin was only twenty-four and Eddie Shack was a twenty-five-year-old left winger whom the fans adored for his on-ice antics and overall zest for the game.

Led by the scoring prowess of Mahovlich—his thirty-six goals put him two behind Howe for the league lead—Toronto fought off Chicago in the final month to earn first place by one point with a

35–23–12 record. For the first time in fifteen years, the Leafs won the Prince of Wales Trophy as top team in the NHL. And their opponents in the first round would be their archrivals, the Canadiens.

Toronto had no problem eliminating the Montreal Canadiens, taking the semifinal series four games to one. How often does that happen?

The Leafs won the first three games of the series before Montreal could reply with a 3–1 victory in Game 4. But the Leafs stormed back in Game 5 with a 5–0 shutout victory.

The Leafs and the Detroit Red Wings opened the Stanley Cup final on April 9 at the Gardens. Toronto won the first two games by identical 4–2 scores.

In Detroit, the teams split Games 3 and 4, putting the Leafs in a good place. They could win Lord Stanley's mug back on home ice.

On April 18, 1963, Detroit and Toronto faced off in a do-or-die contest for the visitors. Toronto centre Dave Keon scored a short-handed goal to give the Leafs a 1–0 lead. The Wings pulled even on Alex Delvecchio's marker.

The game-winning goal for Toronto came at 13:28 of period three. Leaf defenceman Kent Douglas fired the puck at the Detroit goal. His shot struck Eddie Shack's stick, was deflected and flew past goalie Terry Sawchuk.

Another Cup, another lengthy celebration saluting one of the best teams ever.

That season, the league raised the payout to the Cup-winning team to \$63,000 (\$36,000 for winning the final and \$27,000 for prevailing in the semifinals). Each player on the Stanley Cup champions would be \$3,600 wealthier.

"That was a lot of cash back then," Dick Duff said. "We wanted to win, anyway, but that incentive didn't hurt."

EAGLESON GETS INVOLVED

IN THE early part of the decade, a young, talkative lawyer named Alan Eagleson became involved with several of the Leafs—Bob Baun, Bob

Pulford, Carl Brewer and others—through the formation of something called the Blue and White Investment Club.

Eagleson later became a player agent and represented Carl Brewer for a time. Then, he landed Bobby Orr. Years later, both players would turn their backs on Eagleson, saying they distrusted and reviled the man. However, Pulford was close to the Eagle and stayed in his corner. He challenged me one night after a remark I made at a hockey banquet.

"Eagleson never did anything wrong," he shouted for all to hear. "Never. I was in those meetings. He did nothing wrong."

"Really?" I shouted back. "If that's true, Pully, why did he confess to a lot of wrongdoing in a Boston courtroom? Why did he serve time in jail?"

Eagleson really charmed the players. Initially, they were his buddies. But when he took over as executive director of the NHL Players Association he became just as dictatorial as managers like Punch Imlach. And the members of the association started to feel they were viewed as simply a bunch of dumb hockey players. Ted Lindsay, who courageously started the first version of the NHLPA in 1957 at great cost to his own career, was no fan of Eagleson. "The guy stole from us and went to jail for a few months," he told me one day. "He should have served real jail time for about seventeen years."

A TRADE BRINGS BATHGATE

ANDY BATHGATE was named New York's captain in 1961 and wore the *C* until he was sent to the Maple Leafs in a seven-player trade in February 1964.

The right winger had won a Hart Trophy as league MVP, and Punch Imlach was willing to give up several young players to get him. Too many, perhaps. In exchange for Bathgate and centreman Don McKenney, the Leafs gave up Dick Duff and Bob Nevin from their own roster, as well as young minor leaguers Arnie Brown and Bill Collins, and defence prospect Rod Seiling of the Toronto Marlboros.

Ironically, on the day of the Bathgate trade, the Rangers were playing the Leafs in Toronto. So, the players involved joined their new teams simply by switching locker rooms.

Nevin said, "King Clancy called that afternoon. He said, 'Bob, when you come down to the Gardens tonight, go to the Rangers dressing room. We just traded you. Good luck.' I thought, 'Holy cow.' I was twenty-five years old and we had won the Stanley Cup two years in a row and I thought I was going to be with the Leafs for quite some time."

Seiling said, "Oh, it was a huge shock. I was only eighteen years old and you don't expect to be traded when you're eighteen. I heard about it on the radio, not from the Leafs."

Bathgate had nine points in fourteen playoff games for Toronto that year and scored the goal that brought the Leafs a third straight Stanley Cup. But Bobby Baun was not impressed with the trade.

"We gave up too much," he said. "Nevin and [Dick] Duff had been carrying our club on their backs. Bathgate was not a good fit for us and McKenney was a nice guy but not nearly in the class of Duff and Nevin."

As for Bathgate, Punch told me, "Any time you can get a Hart Trophy winner, you grab him. Simple as that."

But really, it wasn't that simple. Bathgate was thirty-two and had his own style. Yes, he and McKenney helped Imlach win a Stanley Cup in 1964. But the Leafs were weakened. Nevin alone was of great value. And when Bathgate sniped at Imlach a year later, claiming his hard practices left the players limp for the game that followed, his comments earned him a ticket to Detroit.

Bob Nevin was giving New York outstanding hockey long after Bathgate and McKenney were gone.

Baun's face would light up when he was asked about the Leafs' defence pairings during the period when the Leafs skated off with four Stanley Cups: Carl Brewer and Bob Baun, Allan Stanley and Tim Horton. "There wasn't a team around that could come up with four as good as we were," he said proudly.

"And the fans loved Eddie Shack," he continued. "Eddie was a born entertainer and a wonderful friend. Sometimes you wouldn't want to be on the ice with Shackie because he'd smack into you and hurt you. Eddie didn't have much education, but he knew all of the four-letter words—and he was loud. Really loud."

BAUN'S BIG MOMENT

LET'S TAKE a closer look at Bob Baun's biggest playoff moment: the 1964 final series with Detroit. Game 6 in Detroit found the Leafs in a must-win situation. Baun bravely stepped in front of a Gordie Howe slapshot and felt a sharp pain as the puck caromed off his leg. Moments later, he turned from a faceoff and heard something pop in his leg. He fell down and there was a delay while he was carried off on a stretcher. In the dressing room, the team doctor froze his leg and he rushed back to play some more.

The game was tied after sixty minutes. Then, in overtime, Baun slapped at a puck rolling out to the point. The puck fluttered toward Red Wing defender Bill Gadsby, bounced off his stick and dribbled into the net behind Terry Sawchuk. The red light flashed. The Leafs won the game on Baun's bizarre goal.

Baun's biographer, Anne Logan, ranks his winning goal right up there with Paul Henderson's classic winner against the Soviets in '72. I'd say that's a bit of a stretch, Anne. Two days later, back on home ice, the Leafs won the Stanley Cup. Only then did Baun agree to have X-rays taken of his leg. They revealed that he'd been playing with a hairline fracture of the fibula.

In that same series, Red Kelly played on a leg that was perhaps just as painful. After the '64 Cup win, both Baun and Kelly were in agony. Kelly went from the hospital to home to the airport the next morning because his vote was needed in the House of Commons that day. Baun probably took a couple of stiff drinks and a handful of Tylenol.

Playoff hockey had given Baun and Kelly something in common. Both placed infant sons in the bowl of the Stanley Cup. And both kids either peed or pooped in it.

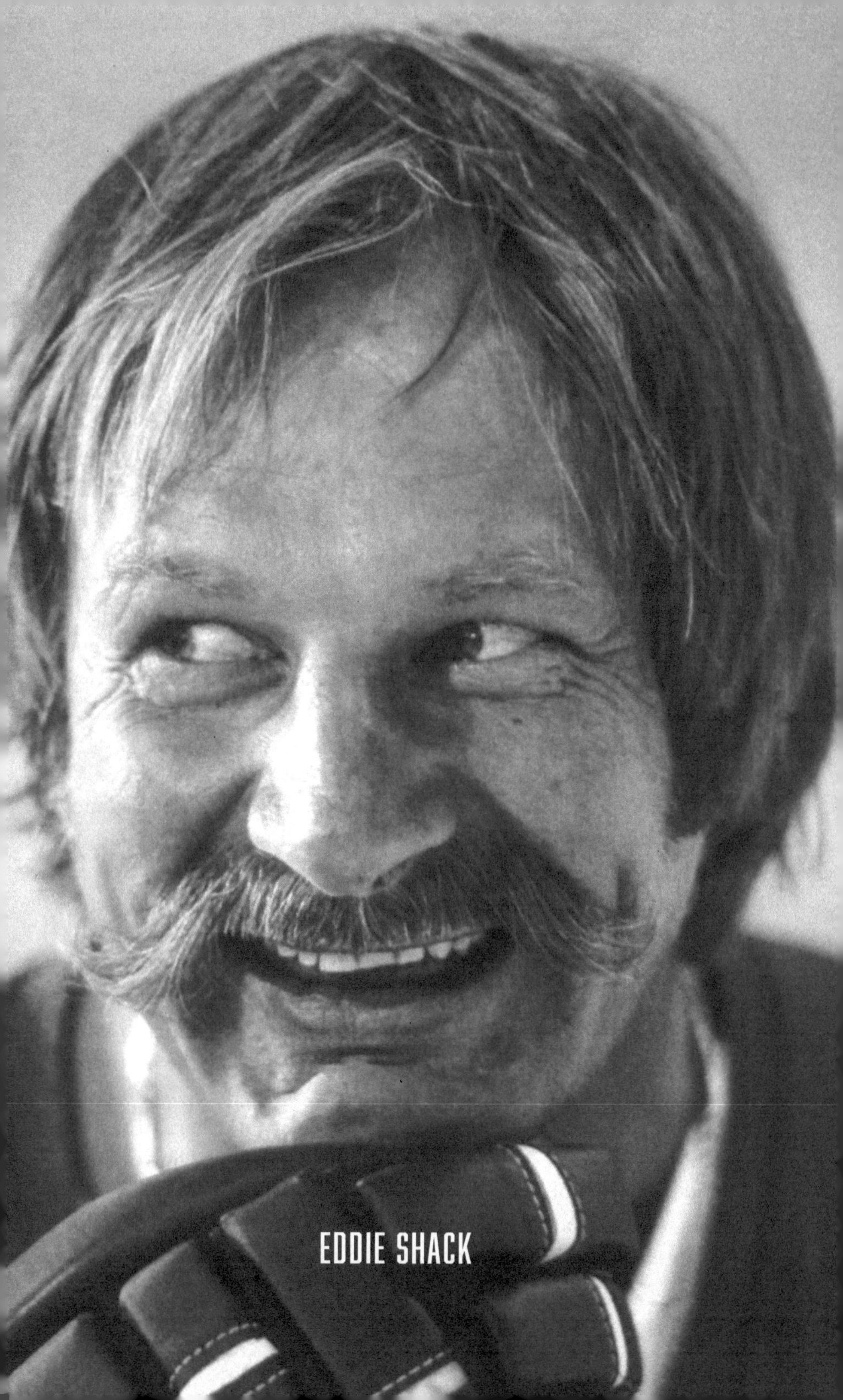

EDDIE SHACK

There was great joy in 1967 when the Leafs won the Cup again—over archrival Montreal. But no joy in the Baun household. Baun had been replaced by Larry Hillman on defence and he felt like an outsider. He was the only Leaf missing when the team was paraded up Bay Street to City Hall. People noticed and chanted, "Where's Baun? We want Baun."

Within weeks, there was an expansion draft. The NHL had doubled in size—six teams to twelve. Baun was left unprotected by the Leafs and was picked by the California (soon to be Oakland) Seals. Seals GM Frank Selke Jr. offered him $37,500—it was said to be the best contract extended to any NHL defenceman.

In May 1968, Baun was traded to Detroit. It's said that Red Wings owner Bruce Norris wanted to see how tough Baun was. At their very first meeting in a Montreal restaurant, he started a wrestling match with Baun. One can imagine the incredible sight, with tables and food flying in all directions. Norris was a huge man—six foot five—and often drunk. And not a pleasant drunk. What a way to meet your new boss.

"How did it end?" I asked Baun.

"With my new boss flat on his back," he answered, laughing.

The following year, Carl Brewer joined the Red Wings at a fancy salary, and it became Baun's job to keep some distance between Brewer and Gordie Howe. Howe wanted to pummel Brewer almost every day, possibly because the defenceman was making twice as much money as he was. And it took Baun to tell Gordie so. Thanks to Baun, who ordered Gordie to demand a huge raise, the Wings doubled Gordie's salary.

Winding down an impressive career, Baun found himself back in Toronto, playing where he loved to be. He was awarded the J.P. Bickell Memorial Award as the outstanding Leaf player in 1970–71.

Around that time, Leaf owners Harold Ballard and Stafford Smythe were awaiting trial on charges of income tax evasion. Smythe died suddenly in October 1971 before standing trial. Baun said Stafford's wake was a fiasco, with Ballard trying to pull Smythe out of the coffin. This was the same Ballard who, as a head table guest at a major banquet in Toronto, had to take a leak. Instead of going to the men's room, he simply lifted the skirt of the table and peed all over the hotel's carpet. The master of ceremonies, Dave Hodge, was a witness to that.

"Stafford was not a boor," said Baun, shaking his head. "I was truly saddened by Stafford's sudden death."

Early in the 1972–73 season, Baun suffered another injury—he was nailed by Detroit's Mickey Redmond and fell on his neck. Doctors told him he might be paralyzed if he continued to play—especially with the fearless approach he brought to each game.

Three years later—after a disastrous cattle farming venture that left him bankrupt, Baun came back to hockey, this time in the WHA as coach of Johnny Bassett's Toronto Toros—for $80,000 a year, plus a car and life insurance. No NHL coach was making more at the time. But he didn't really enjoy coaching, so he quit the Toros and got into selling homes, then cars, then insurance.

Not surprisingly, he began to prosper again. He was able to lend Tim Horton $10,000 that helped get Tim into the donut business. Nobody felt more sorrow than Baun when Horton was killed in a high-speed car accident after a game at the Gardens in 1974.

In 1984, Baun opened a Tim Hortons in Pickering, and it became the most successful franchise in Canada for four straight years. He opened a second location nearby that did almost as well.

If one hockey memory stands out, it was that long, looping, shot that changed direction one night in 1964 to win a playoff game in overtime. It was the night Bobby Baun became a hockey legend.

CHERRY'S SHOT WITH THE LEAFS WAS A MISFIRE

IN 1964, an American Leaguer struggling to land a spot on Toronto's roster was a defenceman with grit and determination. His name was Cherry—Don Cherry.

Cherry had been called up by the Boston Bruins in the 1955 playoffs, and made it into a single game. He played well, but he never got another chance. For decades after, it would be a bitter disappointment.

DON CHERRY

For a decade as a pro, he bounced around the minors, his NHL rights passing from Boston to Detroit, to Montreal, and finally Toronto. He was with the Leafs' Rochester farm club in '64, and the two teams were holding training camp in Peterborough, Ontario. One day, Cherry was tapped to scrimmage with the big club. He spotted Ron Ellis, a highly touted Leaf rookie, cutting across the ice and walloped him. If Grapes thought he had a shot at making the team, he would soon find out otherwise.

"Get that fifty-cent hockey player off the ice with my million-dollar player!" Leaf coach and GM Punch Imlach screamed.

Imagine if some clairvoyant had tapped Cherry on the shoulder at that point and said, "Son, someday your name in hockey will be as big as those of any of the greats of the game. You'll win a trophy as NHL Coach of the Year. Then you'll spout your opinions on TV and radio, and millions will hang on your words. You'll make a fortune. Your fans will even know the name of your dog. They'll name you as one of the ten greatest Canadians. And you'll have a wardrobe that will light up the warehouse you'll need to store it in."

Cherry would have said, "Sure. Sure. What have you been smoking, pal? I'm a minor leaguer. Looks like I'll always be one."

SHACK BETTER THAN THE BIG M AND GOLDEN JET?

IT WAS June 21, 2009, the eve of the Canadian Association of New York's annual hockey banquet at the posh Waldorf-Astoria Hotel. A select group of head-table guests had been invited to a reception at an equally posh restaurant, where I was about to interview many of them. But Eddie Shack couldn't wait for an introduction. He jumped up, grabbed a microphone, and look out! The Great Entertainer was off and running.

"I want you folks to know I played my junior hockey up in Ontario and I was a better junior than Bobby Hull. And I was better than Frank Mahovlich." Someone at the Mahovlich table chuckled. "Hey Frank, you know I was a better player than you. And if I wanted to, I could kick the shit out of you any old time.

"Then I get to the NHL with the Rangers and I get a goddamn coach named Phil Watson. And they shit on me here in New York. That really hurt me."

Eddie turned to Red Kelly and shouted. "Red, remember when I was traded for you in 1960 and you refused to come to New York. How come?"

Red shouted back, "My mother-in-law lived in New York, Eddie."

Everybody laughed, Shack louder than anyone.

"Listen, I got out of the butcher shop in Sudbury, didn't I? And I and made it to the NHL, didn't I? But I never played very much under Imlach. If he did call for a line change, he'd shout, 'Harris and Shack and whoever the Christ wants to go with them.'

"But I scored twenty-six goals for the Leafs one season. I didn't hear Imlach squawk about that. And I scored twenty or more goals with five other clubs after the Leafs got rid of me. How many guys have done that? But I'll never forget those Leaf teams and the Stanley Cups that we won. I loved that Leaf sweater, number twenty-three, and I loved playing in Toronto. I loved everything but playing against John Ferguson. I'd call him 'Shithead' and he'd get so mad he wanted to kill me. That wasn't fun, but I'll always love the Leafs."

When Shack sat down, I told the audience, "Shack and I have had our differences, but of all the guys I've met in the NHL there was no greater entertainer than Eddie Shack."

LEAFS LAUGH LAST IN THE CENTENNIAL YEAR

IT WAS Canada's Centennial year, 1967, and the Montreal Canadiens planned to celebrate the momentous occasion with a Stanley Cup triumph. The attention of the world was on Montreal that summer, as the city was hosting the world's fair, Expo 67. How fitting that Montrealers would bask in the glow of having won Lord Stanley's gift to hockey. They had the players to do it.

But it was not to be. The Toronto Maple Leafs—those spoilsports—easily the oldest team in the league, ruined all those best-laid

Expo plans. It's true that the Leafs appeared to be in for a thrashing when they faced rookie goalie Rogatien Vachon and the Habs at the Forum. But Punch Imlach was defiant. He squawked, "Don't tell me they're starting some Junior B goalie against us." Game 1 was a slaughter, a 6–2 Habs victory. Mrs. Imlach, watching on TV, became so angry at the Toronto broadcast crew's description of the shellacking that she was tempted to kick in her TV set.

The Toronto writers were much more caustic. One said it was like a battle between jet fighters and Sopwith Camels. Vachon said, "Maybe Punch will call me a Junior A goalie now."

Terry Sawchuk was banged up so badly in the opener that Johnny Bower started Game 2 for Toronto. Amazingly, he shut out the Habs 3–0 and showed great poise, even though he was belted three times by John Ferguson, who stampeded through his crease like an angry bull.

Back in Toronto for Game 3, Bower ignored his swollen nose (whacked by Ferguson's stick) and stopped sixty shots in a game that went into sudden-death overtime. The overtime was packed with thrills, drama, pressure and close calls. Finally, Bob Pulford slipped the game winner behind Gump Worsley at 28:26 of extra time.

Bower drew the starting assignment in Game 4, but a pulled muscle in the warmup sent him limping off and forced Sawchuk to come in cold. But the old warrior played poorly and once again gave up six goals in a 6–2 loss.

For the second time in the series, Leafs fans and members of the media tumbled off the bandwagon. Critics declared the Leafs finished—game old codgers but shooters of last bolts.

Bower, it turned out, was through for the year, and Sawchuk looked like a survivor of a train wreck. The Habs couldn't wait to start peppering the man they'd beaten twelve times in two games. But Sawchuk, who had recorded his hundredth career shutout earlier in the year, played near-perfect hockey in Game 5. He allowed just one goal—a deflection—and skated off with a 4–1 victory.

For Game 6, Imlach dressed Bower as the backup, even though the future Hall of Famer could barely walk. Imlach didn't plan to use him—he had a third goalie, Al Smith, half-dressed and waiting in the

Leafs dressing room—but he wanted Bower to share in the glory if the Leafs should win the Stanley Cup that night. He was also thinking of the expansion draft, and how it would rob his team of many of his favourite players. It was the end of an era for his Leafs, and he was determined it would end with memories that would last a lifetime.

Once more, Sawchuk reached back and found a way to match some of his best playoff performances from the past. Ron Ellis and Jim Pappin scored for the Leafs. Dick Duff, the ex-Leaf, spoiled Sawchuk's shutout bid.

With the Leafs leading 2–1, the game came down to the final minute of play. There was a faceoff to the left of Sawchuk in the Leafs zone. Imlach surprised everyone by sending out his oldtimers in this crucial situation. There were Allan Stanley, Tim Horton, George Armstrong, Red Kelly and Bob Pulford in front of Sawchuk. Stanley was told to take the faceoff against Jean Béliveau. "Great," said the defenceman. "The way I take faceoffs is illegal."

The puck was dropped and Stanley stepped into Béliveau and held his stick. The puck went to Kelly, who moved it up to Pulford. Pulford sent a perfect cross-ice pass to Armstrong, who was moving up the right boards. The Leafs captain, from long range, calmly drilled the puck into the empty Montreal net to guarantee the victory. Meanwhile, Béliveau was screaming "faceoff interference" at the referee. But the noise created by thousands of jubilant fans drowned out his words. Béliveau shrugged and conceded defeat. The Leafs had captured the Stanley Cup and spoiled the Habs' plans for a Centennial celebration of their own, with the Expo grounds the site of their grand soiree.

I worked the game that night with Bill Hewitt while my wife was in the crowd. Surely, we're not the oldest couple ever to see the Leafs win a Stanley Cup.

RED RETIRES

"I RETIRED after the '67 Cup win," Kelly said. "I accepted a coaching job in Los Angeles offered me by Jack Kent Cooke. His general manager was Larry Regan, who had been my teammate with the Leafs.

"Then I coached in Pittsburgh for three seasons and came back to the Leafs as head coach in 1973.

"We were in St. Louis one night and boy, it was noisy in there. I was trying to think of some sort of a gimmick to counteract all the noise, so I bought all these earmuffs for my players and I made them all wear earmuffs on the bench. Even I wore earmuffs, and wouldn't you know they scored a goal against us in the first minute we had them on.

"Then I came up with some other gimmicks, like the pyramid power. Boy, the guys really picked up on that. Some of the players put their sticks under the pyramids and swore it brought them more goals. Sittler scored five goals one night after placing his stick under a pyramid. Apparently, the pyramids produced positive and negative ions and I talked the Leafs into becoming believers. That was back when the Flyers brought in an aging singer named Kate Smith to their games—for good luck. Tiger Williams told the guys, 'I'd rather sit under Red's pyramid than sit under Kate Smith.'"

On *The Hockey News*'s 1997 list of hockey's top one hundred players, Red Kelly was listed at number twenty-two. He played in 1,316 regular-season games, almost 1,300 more than the mere twenty a scout had predicted for him. He scored 231 goals and 542 assists.

He was inducted into the Hockey Hall of Fame in 1969.

DOREY'S DEBUT WAS MEMORABLE

JIM DOREY made his NHL debut with the Toronto Maple Leafs on October 16, 1968, against the Pittsburgh Penguins. The twenty-one-year-old rookie defenceman would become an overnight celebrity for setting the NHL single-game record for penalty minutes, with forty-eight.

"It was the home opener for the Leafs," recalled Dorey. "In the second period, I got into fights with just about every Penguins player on the ice.

"I thought they'd never end," he said. "It was no way to start a career."

JOHN FERGUSON AND JIM DOREY

Dorey's debut included two fighting majors, two misconducts, a game misconduct and a high-sticking minor. Those were just six of a record nine total penalties. His mark has since been eclipsed by other NHL heavyweights, but remains a Toronto record.

Coach-GM Punch Imlach surprised Dorey after the game. "I thought he'd tell me I was an embarrassment and hand me a ticket to Rochester in the AHL. Instead, he patted me on the back and said, 'That's the kind of hockey I want from you.' Then he pulled out his wallet, handed me $100 and told me, 'Don't talk to the reporters. Get lost for the weekend.'"

Dorey patrolled the Toronto blue line for four seasons. "I have nothing but great memories. It was an honour to play for Toronto. I realize that today more than ever."

Dorey was traded to the New York Rangers late in 1971–72, then earned a huge salary when he jumped to the WHA. "When I jumped, I made some Rangers millionaires because they demanded as much or more than I got. My time in the WHA is special to me because I was a pioneer."

ORR GOES DOWN

IN THE 1969 playoffs, on April 2, the Leafs met the Boston bruisers in the first playoff round and it was no contest.

The Bruins humiliated the Leafs 10–0 in the opener.

Bill Hewitt and I were shoulder to shoulder in the Boston broadcast booth and were hard pressed to find anything complimentary to say about the Leafs. Then, with the score 6–0, defenceman Pat Quinn smashed into Bobby Orr as he skated out of his own zone with his head down. Orr crumpled to the ice, unconscious, and Quinn immediately became Public Enemy Number One.

It's not often that a burly Irishman is vilified in Boston, but Quinn was that night. The mob in the Boston Garden wanted to kill him. Quinn, with one thunderous check, became the most despised man in New England.

It was feared that Orr, then more popular in Boston than Bob

Cousy of the Celtics and Ted Williams of the Red Sox, had suffered a broken neck. And yes, it was scary.

Later, his injury would be diagnosed as whiplash and a concussion.

After the Bruins swept the Leafs, Punch Imlach was furious when told of my description of a second incident in the game involving a newcomer to the Leafs—Forbes Kennedy.

Punch wanted to have me turfed from the telecasts—and would have succeeded, but for a strange set of circumstances.

With his team hopelessly behind (10–0 the final score), Imlach ordered Kennedy, a player he'd picked up in a trade with the Philadelphia Flyers, to "get out there and start something." Kennedy leaped over the boards and ignited a brawl. In the midst of it, he deliberately punched linesman George Ashley in the face. The guy went down like water over Niagara.

"Oh boy," I said to Bill Hewitt. "Kennedy's in big trouble now. He'll be fined or suspended, maybe both."

Kennedy set a playoff record for penalties that night. When Imlach learned (his wife, Dodo, must have been listening) I'd said that Kennedy faced a possible fine and suspension, he told my bosses, "That bleepin' McFarlane has to go." His complaint went all the way to NHL president Clarence Campbell's office. Punch was still trying to figure out a way to have me canned when he was fired by Stafford Smythe.

As for Kennedy, as predicted, he was fined a thousand dollars and suspended for four games. He never played another game in the NHL. But he went out with a bang.

The Leafs went out with a whimper, swept by Boston by scores of 10–0, 7–0, 4–3 and 3–2.

WHY PUNCH WAS FIRED

WHAT WAS the real reason for Imlach's dismissal?

Stafford Smythe told the media, "I discovered that Punch had a financial interest in the Vancouver minor league team that served as one of our farm clubs. When I asked him about it, he assured me that he had no interest in the club. Well, everybody now knows that he did have."

Imlach was paid some $225,000 for his stake in the Vancouver Canucks when they came into the NHL from the Western Hockey League. Smythe said, "It's a matter of league record that Punch was selling some of our players to his Vancouver club when all the time I thought—and our board of directors thought—the players were still under control of the Toronto hockey club.

"When he left Toronto," Smythe concluded, "he left us with almost nothing because of his trades."

Imlach told the press, "And there I was, walking out of MLG after 11 seasons and four Stanley Cups, fired the way a foreman cans some casual labourer who's been leaning too much on his shovel."

When he left the Gardens, he and Dodo made a beeline for the parking lot. In the lot, all the cars had their keys in them and their engines running. Punch and Dodo jumped into their Lincoln Continental and drove off. They went about six blocks before Dodo noticed cigarettes in the ashtray.

"Punch, this isn't our car," she said. "We don't smoke."

Punch cursed his bad luck and returned to the lot.

With Punch Imlach's tenure as general manager finally ended, Jim Gregory, who had been an executive with the Junior A Toronto Marlboros, was named as his successor. The new coach was John McLellan, promoted from Toronto's farm team in Tulsa.

The 1969–70 NHL season was the longest in league history and was packed with changes. The Leafs, after qualifying for the playoffs the previous season, fell to last place in the NHL's East Division and did not qualify for the playoffs. It was the first time since 1958 that the club endured a last place finish.

When Norm Ullman signed a reported $58,000 contract, he became the highest-paid Leaf in history. Then Tim Horton was lured out of retirement with a bigger one—$84,000. Horton would be traded to the Rangers in March.

Johnny Bower, the oldest player in the NHL, began the season as an active player but soon accepted a position as a scout. He deserved but missed out on the huge salaries players began earning at that time.

But there wasn't much cheering in Toronto. A woeful defence and an impotent offence mired the Leafs in the East Division basement.

In December 1969, the NHL granted conditional franchises to Vancouver and Buffalo for an entrance fee of $6 million each. Both Punch Imlach and your author were offered positions with the Buffalo club, Imlach as GM and me as play-by-play announcer and public relations director. We both accepted, but suddenly my offer was retracted. Only later was I told that Imlach, still ticked off with me for the way I called the Forbes Kennedy incident the previous spring, insisted I not be part of the Buffalo organization. Ted Darling then became the play-by-play voice of the Sabres and soon endeared himself to Buffalo fans.

At the time, I thought: *Thanks for the favour, Punch. I wouldn't want to be in Buffalo, under your constant scrutiny.*

SITTLER, SALMING AND THE SEVENTIES

LEAFS MISSED TWO OF THE DECADE'S BRIGHTEST STARS

ON MAY 10, 1970, at the Boston Garden, the high-scoring Boston Bruins won the Stanley Cup with a dazzling display of bang-bang hockey. After forty seconds of extra time, Bobby Orr took a pass from Derek Sanderson to score the Cup-clinching goal against the St. Louis Blues' Glenn Hall. We've all seen footage and photos of Orr's spectacular goal a hundred times, scored as he was being hoisted high in the air by Blues defenceman Noel Picard's stick.

Orr's game winner, his ninth goal of the playoffs and his twentieth point—both records for a defenceman at the time—earned him the Conn Smythe Trophy as playoff MVP.

"This is the happiest day of my life," he said with a grin. "We have a hell of a team and let's hope we can do it all over again next year."

Orr's 1969–70 campaign, in which he became the first defenceman to win the scoring title, with 120 points, would one day be voted the most significant full season by an NHL player. Wayne Gretzky's ninety-two-goal, 212-point season in 1981–82 received just seven fewer votes in the balloting.

But why wasn't Orr a Toronto Maple Leaf? He grew up almost in their back yard. I asked long-time head scout Bob Davidson about it one day, and he mumbled something about "not going after kids who were not even in high school."

It didn't bother the Bruins to do precisely that.

Former Leaf star Darryl Sittler told blogger Howard Berger: "I faced Bobby near the beginning of my career and Wayne toward the end. Wayne established season records that will never be broken. But Bobby did things for the first time that will never be equalled. And, to me, that makes him the best. I don't believe I'm disrespecting Wayne by saying that. Both players were phenomenal...but someone has to be No. 1."

What about Wayne Gretzky as a Leaf, one might ask? He grew up in Toronto's backyard and somebody smarter than Harold Ballard stole him away to play in the WHA before he was even drafted. At seventeen, he signed a seven-year, $1.75 million personal-services contract with Nelson Skalbania, owner of the Indianapolis Racers. Even if Ballard (and others) were willing to pay such a sum for a rookie so skinny and frail—at one time, his nickname was Pencil—they'd have to wait for him to become eligible for the draft.

In 1979, when what was left of the WHA merged with the NHL, it raised the thorny issue of how to deal with players, like Gretzky, who were still too young to play in the NHL. Out of the merger talks came a rule change: the minimum draft age was lowered a year, from twenty to nineteen, and all underage players who had been in the WHA in 1978–79 were put into the draft pool—except for Gretzky, whose contract had been sold to the Edmonton Oilers just before the Racers folded, because he had never signed a standard player's contract, but was under that personal-services deal. The NHL ironed out this wrinkle by letting the Oilers name him as one of the two skaters they were allowed to carry over from their WHA roster. They were also bumped down to the twenty-first and final pick in each round of the upcoming NHL draft.

The Leafs weren't concerned about all the fuss over Gretzky. Toronto scouts—and those from other teams—had checked him out. Not a prospect, they judged. Too frail, for one thing, and not a great skater.

The Leafs got it wrong with both Orr and Gretzky. Between them, the pair would have brought some spectacular hockey to Maple Leaf Gardens for a couple of decades, and surely a few Stanley Cups. Did the Leafs management think they made two huge blunders at the time? Not really. They dismissed Gretzky and they knew Wren Blair of the Bruins had ingratiated himself so strongly with the Orr clan that signing him to a Boston contract was almost a *fait accompli*, although it did include stuccoing the Orr house, a new suit (ill-fitting, I was told) for Bobby and a car—a used one—for Doug Orr, Bobby's dad.

SAWCHUK'S PASSING WAS A MYSTERY

ON MAY 31, 1970, after a noisy Stanley Cup parade through the streets of Boston, there was shocking news. Goalie Terry Sawchuk, who had played a huge role in the Leafs' 1967 Stanley Cup triumph, had died in a Manhattan hospital.

The cause of Sawchuk's death remains a bit of a mystery. On April 29, Sawchuk and his New York Ranger teammate Ron Stewart—also a former Leaf—were living on Long Island.

Stewart was seen at the bar of a pub on that evening and was just about to leave when Sawchuk walked in. Soon after, there was a confrontation outside the bar that ended with Sawchuk being rushed to a hospital and in need of two major operations. A witness said that the two Rangers had scuffled and Sawchuk was badly injured when he fell on a drain pipe or a barbecue. Stewart declined to comment.

At the hospital, Sawchuk's gall bladder was removed. A few days later he required a second operation. Following the second procedure, he died of cardiac arrest.

NHL president Clarence Campbell stated, "It was a ghastly tragedy, which left seven children fatherless." Sawchuk was survived by his ex-wife Patricia (they had divorced a year earlier) and their children.

Rangers general manager Emile Francis said, "Sawchuk's passing was a shocking loss. He was one of the greatest goaltenders of all time. One year in eight playoff games, he had four shutouts and his goals against average was an unbelievable 0.62. He was rookie of the year in every league he played in."

Sawchuk often said his finest moment was leading the Leafs to their stunning Cup win over Montreal in 1967.

SPINNER SPENCER'S TRAGIC CAREER

BRIAN "SPINNER" Spencer, a native of Fort St. James, British Columbia, had always wanted to play for the Leafs. And he got his wish in 1970, just before Christmas.

His time in hockey would be short. So would his life.

"I wasn't really ready for the NHL,"' he admitted about his struggles to stay a Leaf. "Remember, I didn't get out of the British Columbia bush until I was eighteen."

His father, Roy Spencer, was killed on the night Brian was due to make his first appearance on *Hockey Night in Canada*. Roy was all set to watch when he discovered the nearest TV outlet in Prince George was carrying a Vancouver Canucks game. He grabbed his gun and drove to the station, where he brandished his weapon and demanded a switch to the Toronto game. When told it was impossible for them to switch the feed to the Toronto game, he herded the small staff into a studio. Minutes later, after Royal Canadian Mounted Police vehicles closed in, he was shot to death outside the station. While the bullets flew, Brian was being interviewed on *Hockey Night in Canada*.

Ironically, a few weeks later, Brian scored a hat trick for the Leafs and was named the first star.

The Leafs made Brian available in the 1972 expansion draft, and the New York Islanders snapped him up. Before he left Toronto, he told media members, "I will never forget how the Leafs treated me when my father was killed. I know a lot of people didn't like Stafford Smythe, but he and Jim Gregory, King Clancy and Punch Imlach did everything they could to ease the pain."

Brian's own life came to a sad and tragic end. In 1987, he stood trial on kidnapping and murder charges, facing the death penalty. Former teammates, including Dave Keon, testified as character witnesses, and the jury returned a not guilty verdict in October 1987. Seven months later, Spencer was dead, shot in a robbery attempt after the car his friend was driving was forced off the road.

A SURPRISING STREAK

JOHN MCLELLAN was named coach of the Leafs in 1969, and in his first season the team finished in the East Division basement with a record of 29–34–13. They were off to an even worse start (7–18–1) a third of the way into the 1970–71 schedule. Everyone agreed it would take a stunning turnaround to even consider a playoff run.

Then, as McLellan watched in wonder, there came a miraculous recovery that ushered them into the postseason. The remarkable run began on December 9, with a 4–0 shutout of Montreal at the Gardens. Over the next six weeks, they steamrollered their competition, with fifteen wins, three losses and two ties. Highlights included a 9–1 romp over the Philadelphia Flyers at the Gardens and a 13–0 destruction of Detroit a week later. The latter remains the second-largest shutout triumph in NHL history, exceeded only by a game in Detroit on January 23, 1944, when the Red Wings blanked the New York Rangers, 15–0.

Toronto finished the season in fourth place in the East Division, with a winning record of 37–33–8 and eighty-two points—nineteen more than Buffalo. But they were a playoff disappointment, losing in six games to the second-place Rangers in the opening round.

JACQUES PLANTE LOVED TORONTO

WHEN THE Leafs were winning Stanley Cups in the '60s, they had no interest in Jacques Plante. His days in the NHL seemed to be over. In 1964–65, Plante struggled through a final season split between the New York Rangers and Baltimore of the American League, and when it was suggested that he retire, he did. He was thirty-seven.

Three years later, after the NHL had expanded to twelve teams, the St. Louis Blues lured Plante back into uniform. He was joined by another oldtimer, Glenn Hall, soon to be thirty-seven. Many scoffed at the choices, but the two veteran puck stoppers stunned all the skeptics in 1968–69 with a combined goals against average of 2.07. They shared the Vézina Trophy—Plante's seventh.

On May 18, 1970, while Plante was recovering from a serious concussion in the postseason, Leafs GM Jim Gregory acquired him in a cash deal.

What was Gregory thinking? Plante was now forty-one, so this was a risky move.

But it worked.

"Hockey in St. Louis had become fun for me again," Plante said. "And Gregory said he needed me. My attitude was good and the Leafs made me feel welcome. The team went from last place to fourth and in 1970–71 to the playoffs.

"And I was amazed at what a nice place Toronto turned out to be. Everyone I met there was so friendly."

He stayed for three seasons and was able to pass along some useful goaltending lessons to young Bernie Parent while he was a Leaf.

MCKENNY'S MEMORIES

JIM MCKENNY was a colourful and often comical defenceman who played for the Leafs from 1965–66 to 1977–78. After retiring from the game, he became a popular television sportscaster in Toronto, as famous on the air as he was on the ice.

Fellow commentators could always count on McKenny to come through with a good quote and a funny story. Asked once about his views on violence in hockey, he quipped, "I always felt the violence made me play better. I never skated so fast in my life as I did when the game got violent—just staying away from it." He continued:

One night, we were playing against John Ferguson and the Montreal Canadiens. What a tough SOB Fergie was! Fergie was carrying the puck down the ice when a Leaf, Billy MacMillan, knocks him flat. When Fergie staggered to his feet, his nostrils flaring, the first Leaf he saw was me. He thought I'd flattened him. So, for two periods he's chasing me around and I know he's going to kill me in the next few seconds. So I screamed at him, "For God's sake, Fergie, get off my case. It was MacMillan who hit you, not me."

On the next shift, oh, it was brutal. Fergie grabbed MacMillan and beat the crap out of him. I felt badly about tattling on a teammate. But I took a moment to thank God it wasn't me that Fergie drilled.

I was a smoker back then—like Guy Lafleur was. And I sneaked out for a smoke one night during a game at the Forum. Who was in the hallway—Henri Richard. He saw the cigarette and gave me a frown. I said, "Hey, your guy Guy Lafleur does this all the time."

And he said, "Yeah, but you're no Guy Lafleur."

The funny thing was, I was making more money than Lafleur at the time. He'd signed with the Habs for seven years at $110,000. I should have told Henri, "I may not be Lafleur but he's sweating through twenty minutes a game at $110,000 and I'm sitting on the Leaf bench at $120,000."

[Harold] Ballard would shit on us from time to time but he paid us well—better than most clubs. If he hadn't let Bernie Parent jump to the WHA, and guys like Paul Henderson and Dave Keon and Jim Harrison get away, we might have won a couple of Stanley Cups.

BALLARD WAS A CONVICT, BUT STILL THE BOSS

IN 1969, Leafs president Stafford Smythe and vice president Harold Ballard were charged with fraud, theft and income tax evasion. The board of directors, led by chairman John Bassett, fired the two executives, but within a year they managed to regain their former positions. Defeated, Bassett sold his shares to Smythe and Ballard in 1971. Smythe died not long after, and Ballard bought his late partner's shares, giving him a controlling interest in the team.

Thus, with the prospect of a convicted fraudster in charge, the Leafs began the new decade.

Ballard was found guilty on forty-seven of forty-nine charges of theft and fraud in August 1972. (The tax evasion charges were eventually dropped.) A judge said Ballard showed "a clear pattern of fraud," including using $82,000 of the Gardens' money to remodel his home. The sixty-nine-year-old faced up to twenty years in prison. Before he could be sentenced, his friends pleaded with the judge. "Harold wants to fly to Moscow to see the 1972 series," they explained. "Sure, why not?" the judge said, and Ballard's sentencing was delayed a month.

In October, Ballard was sentenced to two concurrent sentences of three years each at the Millhaven Institution near Kingston. Eddie Shack, while paying a visit to the Leaf owner, told the convicts, "The only difference between me and you guys is you guys got caught."

In the summer of 1973, released from prison on a three-day pass, Ballard entertained the media (I was there) gathered in the Hot Stove Lounge at Maple Leaf Gardens, telling them that Millhaven was much like a country club, with steak dinners and colour TVs. Some of us rushed out to make reservations. His comments so angered Canadians that they were discussed in Parliament.

That October, Harold Ballard was released on parole. He had spent a day less than a year at Millhaven.

LEAFS LOSE PARENT

THERE ARE hockey trades that forever change the course of a franchise, and one of these took place on January 31, 1971, when the Philadelphia Flyers traded goalie Bernie Parent to the Leafs, then realized they'd made a huge mistake.

"I finalized the details with Flyers GM Keith Allen on a Sunday night and we had to wait until Monday morning for the NHL to officially register the trade," the Leafs' GM at the time, Jim Gregory, told sportswriter Bob Duff. "I remember thinking that Keith would call and back out of the deal.

"We'd been trying to get Parent ever since I was GM in Toronto [starting in April 1969]. Keith always said no. I figured he'd turn me down once again. But this time the trade went through."

It was a three-team transaction, with Toronto sending goaltender Bruce Gamble and a first-round draft pick to Philadelphia, while forward Mike Walton went to the Boston Bruins. The Flyers sent Parent and a second-round pick to the Leafs, and forwards Rick MacLeish and Danny Schock went from the Bruins to the Flyers. Bernie played his first game as a Leaf four days later.

"Who knows how the history of the Leafs may have changed if we'd been able to keep Bernie. It's something I have always regretted."

The Leafs should have kept Parent. But Gregory's boss, Harold Ballard, allowed the brilliant netminder to accept a proposal from the upstart World Hockey Association. When Ballard said, "Let him go," to the media, he was essentially handing Parent his outright release, daring his goalie to flee to the Miami Screaming Eagles for four times the money the Leafs were paying him—plus a yacht. That decision ranks as one of the biggest gaffes in Maple Leaf history.

When the Screaming Eagles folded without playing a single game, Parent surfaced with the Philadelphia Blazers.

"Really, I had no choice," Bernie told Duff. "I wasn't anxious to leave the NHL. In Toronto, Jacques Plante taught me things about goaltending I'd never noticed. He made me so much better. But how could I turn down a four hundred percent increase from my Toronto salary."

The like of Harold Ballard and NHL president Clarence Campbell scoffed at the upstart league, which was selling franchises for just $25,000, experimenting with blue pucks, and floating the idea of teams in oddball markets like Miami and Dayton, Ohio. But Parent wasn't the only player who was willing to give it a chance. The Leafs also lost defencemen Rick Ley and Brad Selwood and forward Jim Harrison. Bobby Hull fled the Chicago Black Hawks for the Winnipeg Jets. Boston's Derek Sanderson signed a deal that promised to make him the highest-paid athlete in team sports. And a year later, Gordie Howe came out of retirement to play with the Houston Aeros alongside sons Mark and Marty.

Weakened in goal, the Leafs stumbled through one of the worst seasons in franchise history in 1972–73, plummeting sixteen points in the standings and missing the playoffs.

Meanwhile, Parent lasted just one season with the Blazers. A dispute over money soured him on the WHA, and while he wanted to return to the NHL, he wanted nothing to do with Ballard or the Leafs. Gregory had no choice but to deal the netminder back to the Flyers.

Parent's goaltending became the key to Philadelphia's back-to-back Stanley Cups in 1974 and '75. He won the Conn Smythe and Vézina Trophies twice each. His popularity in southeastern Pennsylvania was matched only by that of team captain Bobby Clarke. In 1984, he was inducted into the Hockey Hall of Fame.

<line space>

One of the more bizarre moments in hockey history involved Bernie Parent. On April 8, 1971, in the midst of a brawl at Madison Square Garden, the Rangers' Vic Hadfield threw Parent's goal mask high into the crowd. Police searched for it, but Parent did not get his mask back—not for four decades.

It resurfaced forty-one years later, in a sports memorabilia auction. The purchaser contacted Parent to authenticate the mask. Plante nodded, "That's it, all right," and the owner promised to donate it to the Hockey Hall of Fame.

On the night it was lost, Leafs coach John McLellan pleaded with Parent to finish the game.

Parent said, "Are you crazy, Coach? I'm not going back in goal without my mask."

Jacques Plante, who must certainly have agreed with Parent, finished the game.

SALMING AND HAMMARSTRÖM SIGN

BY 1972, the NHL had swollen to sixteen teams, and the launch of the rival WHA added twelve more. The competition for talent had never been so fierce.

A total of twenty-six players skated for the '72–73 edition of the Toronto Maple Leafs—twenty-five Canadians and one American. But in the spring of 1973, the club added two Swedes and everything changed.

Leaf scout Gerry McNamara went to Moscow to watch the 1973 Ice Hockey World Championships, and when he saw Swedish defenceman Börje Salming and his teammate, left winger Inge Hammarström, perform, he said, "I've got to sign these two."

Salming dominated the blue line in the game McNamara witnessed, while Hammarström scored four or five goals. After the game, McNamara made his move, approaching Salming first.

"He wanted to know if I'd come and play for the Toronto Maple Leafs," Salming recalled. "I said, 'Yes, of course I will.' That was it. He said, 'Okay, fine! I'll be in touch,' and he left."

Former Leaf Billy Harris was coaching the Swedish national team at the time and encouraged the two to take McNamara seriously.

Hammarström said, "Billy told us, 'Guys, I think Toronto fans would love to see you both wearing Leaf uniforms.'"

Later, at the Hotel Ukraine in Moscow, the Swedish stars met with McNamara and Leaf scout Bob Davidson to iron out the details.

McNamara said, "It was a happy ending to a scouting mission that began with me thinking I'd bring home a goaltender. No other NHL scouts had yet discovered the potential gold mine that was European hockey.

"Salming and Hammarström were huge heroes in Sweden. I'll remember them for the rest of my life."

Of course, Leaf owner Harold Ballard had to chip in with an opinion. He mocked Hammarström's play one day, saying, "That kid could go into a corner with a dozen eggs in his pocket and not break any of them."

The comment stung.

"Of course it stung," Hammarström admitted. "Yes, it bothered me. But in the very next game I scored a hat trick and that made me feel better."

During a recent conversation with McNamara, I mentioned Ballard's insult to Hammerström. "That was so wrong," he said. "Talking about one of your own like that."

Hockey fans showed Salming how beloved he'd become in Toronto in 1976, when the Gardens hosted a few games of the Canada Cup tournament. Leaf heroes Darryl Sittler and Lanny McDonald, playing for Team Canada, received huge ovations when they were introduced. But so did Salming when he skated out, representing Team Sweden.

Salming would become the Leafs' all-time assists leader and ranks third on the all-time list of games played in blue and white. Early in 1977–78, Hammarström moved on to St. Louis, where he played for a couple of seasons before returning to Sweden.

TIM HORTON'S SUDDEN DEATH

THE SUDDEN death of former Leaf defenceman Tim Horton shocked us all in 1974. Bill Hewitt and I called Horton's last game. He was with Buffalo then, forty-four years old, and playing at the Gardens despite a painful jaw injury.

After the game, Horton was driving on the Queen Elizabeth Way from Toronto to his home in Buffalo in the early morning hours of February 21, 1974. After earning one of the three stars of the game, he was driving his Italian sports car at speeds in excess of one hundred miles an hour (160 km/h) and failed to negotiate a curve on the QEW where it crosses over Twelve Mile Creek in St. Catharines.

The car slid off the highway, slammed into a concrete drainage culvert at high speed, and flipped several times. Horton, who had failed to secure his seat belt, was ejected from the car. Police who had been pursuing him were on the scene in seconds and rendered aid, but all life was gone from the hockey superstar and budding business tycoon. He was reported dead on arrival at the local hospital.

I scanned the autopsy report when it was released in 2005, and it is gruesome. The documents show that Horton had a blood-alcohol level well beyond the legal limit for driving, as well as prescription drugs in his system at the time of death.

Horton left behind a wife, Lori, three children and a burgeoning doughnut shop franchise that became Canada's largest food service operator.

How large? Tim Hortons has more than 4,700 restaurants located in Canada, the United States and around the world.

One day, I was sitting across from Johnny Bower in a Tim Hortons in Cobourg (owned by Tim's daughter and her husband) and there was a large photo of Tim on the wall next to us. When a staff member walked by, I asked her if she knew the man in the photo. She said she did not. I pointed at Bower and said, "I guess you don't know who this man is?"

She smiled and said, "Sorry. Are you someone famous?"

HENDERSON MAKES A MAJOR DECISION

AS THE 1973–74 season drew to a close, Paul Henderson, the biggest hero on Team Canada '72, was deciding he no longer wanted to wear a Leaf uniform. It wasn't a choice he made lightly.

"I actually wanted to stay with the Leafs," he once confessed, "because I hadn't won the Stanley Cup. But John Bassett Jr. [who owned the Toronto Toros of the WHA] said he would double my salary and give me a no-trade contract. He had just signed Frank

Mahovlich from the Canadiens, and he'd decided to move the Toros into Maple Leaf Gardens.

"I told Mahovlich I wanted to stay in the NHL to win a Cup and he said, 'Paul, if that's your goal, then sign with them. But they will never win anything with Harold Ballard running the team. You'll never win a Cup.'

"So, I phoned Bassett and accepted his offer. It was the best move I ever made."

No, Paul, it was your second-best move. Beating Tretiak was your best. And I'll bet you were surprised to discover that Mahovlich was a clairvoyant.

Throughout the '70s, Harold Ballard was the face of the Leaf franchise. He was brash, bold, boorish and belligerent. He rented the Gardens to Johnny Bassett and the Toros for $15,000 per game. But on the night of their home opener in 1974, the arena was in gloomy darkness. "The TV lights will cost you extra," he told an enraged Bassett. He demanded another $3,500 per game. Ballard also chuckled about ordering the cushions removed from the team benches. "Let the Toros buy their own cushions," he told the media.

Ballard showed similar contempt for his own players, and many of them besides Henderson elected to jump to the WHA.

TIGER THREATENS KEON

DRAFTED THIRTY-FIRST overall in 1974, Saskatchewan-born Dave "Tiger" Williams was called up from the Oklahoma City Blazers in January of '75 and immediately gained a reputation as a colourful and quotable player.

Dave Stubbs once wrote of Tiger: "He wasn't popular with everyone in the dressing room, not that he tried to be. His resolute goal was to win hockey games, and he did that with a steely-eyed focus and uncompromising sense of purpose that could intimidate both opponents and teammates."

It may surprise fans to know that one teammate Williams didn't much care for is the one who was named the greatest Leaf of all time.

"Most fans loved Keon, the Leaf captain," Williams once said. "Not me. He never did what a captain should do. He wore me down with his criticism. When I'd heard enough, I grabbed him by the shirt one day in an elevator. 'Listen, Davey,' I warned him. 'I don't need any more of your shit. Now get off my back or I'll break your neck.'"

Keon was famous for avoiding the sin bin. In 1962 and '63, he won the Lady Byng Trophy as the NHL's most gentlemanly player, and in an NHL career that lasted 1,296 games, he drew only one fighting major. He'd have been no match for Tiger if he and his tormentor had come to blows.

"Had I been given a few more inches and another twenty pounds," Keon said with a smile, "I might have become quite a different player. I never thought my size [he was five foot nine and 165 pounds in his playing days] was a problem."

SITTLER ARRIVES, KEON DEPARTS

DARRYL SITTLER, selected eighth overall by the Maple Leafs in the 1970 amateur draft, was named team captain in the fall of 1975. He would become the team's dominant personality throughout the rest of the 1970s and become the second-highest scorer in the team's history.

With Sittler at emerging as the team's number one centre, Harold Ballard had no further use for captain Dave Keon, who had been with the team since 1960. When Keon's contract expired in 1975, Ballard showed little interest in renewing it. But when other teams were keen to grab the veteran centre, Ballard set a steep price for his services, so steep that suitors stopped calling. "Forget it, Harold," they said. "Your price is ridiculous."

Keon was lured to a WHA club, the Minnesota Fighting Saints. And when that club folded, Keon received an attractive offer from Bill Torrey, the GM of the New York Islanders. But Ballard insisted that the Leafs still owned Keon's NHL rights, again forcing Keon to return to

DARRYL SITTLER

the WHA. After stints with Indianapolis and a revived Fighting Saints franchise, Keon landed with the New England Whalers, with whom he would return to the NHL in 1979. Keon never forgave Ballard for how he'd been treated, and it was more than forty years before he was reconciled with the Leafs.

SITTLER'S TEN-POINT EXPLOSION

DARRYL SITTLER was at the centre of one of the greatest moments in the history of the Toronto Maple Leafs, the NHL—and hockey in general. And I was fortunate to be as close as anyone to what transpired.

When Toronto hosted Boston in a game at Maple Leaf Gardens on February 7, 1976, there was a lot to be excited about. The Bruins, coached by colourful Don Cherry, were looking for their eighth straight win, and veteran centre Jean Ratelle was looking for his 350th career goal. There was even a chance that goalie Gerry Cheevers, lured back to Boston from the WHA a day or two earlier, would be the Bruins' starting goaltender.

What the fans were treated to was a record-smashing performance from the Leafs' captain, a scoring rampage unequalled in the more than 13,000 games played in the NHL up to that night.

Sittler was in a sour mood. His pregnant wife, Wendy, had not been well and not able to prepare his pre-game meal. And Ian Turnbull, who was to pick Sittler up to drive to the Gardens, was late. The captain was unusually grumpy as he wolfed down a meal of takeout barbecue chicken from Swiss Chalet in the car.

Moments before our telecast that night, we learned that Cheevers would not be the Bruins' starter. Cherry handed that assignment to a kid out of college, rookie Dave Reece. We also knew that Leaf owner Harold Ballard was not happy with Sittler. The cantankerous Ballard had blasted his captain for not being a better centre. "We'd set off a time bomb if we had a hell of a centre in there," he told the *Toronto Star*.

But coach Red Kelly had formed a new line that placed Sittler between two skilled wingers, Lanny McDonald and Errol Thompson.

Ratelle did score his milestone goal early in the first period, but his feat would be totally overshadowed by Darryl Sittler's astonishing performance. The Leaf captain demolished Reece and the Bruins, collecting six goals and ten points in Toronto's 11–4 romp. He broke by two points the previous NHL record for points in a game, held by a pair of Canadiens, Rocket Richard and Bert Olmstead.

I recall trying to watch the action on the ice while scrambling through the NHL record book, but it was almost impossible to keep up as Sittler kept on scoring.

Entering the second period with a pair of assists, Sittler scored three goals against Reece, and then three more in the third, making him the first NHLer to score hat tricks in consecutive periods, and only the eighth to score six times in a game. His goal output fell one short of the all-time record of seven, held by Joe Malone of Quebec, a mark set in 1920. It all added up to the greatest individual scoring performance in NHL history.

Sittler not only shattered records, but the hockey future of young Reece. The Boston goalie was dispatched to the minors the following day and never played another NHL game.

Sittler said, "The thing I'll always remember about that game was the ovation I received when I broke the record with my ninth point. It was unbelievable."

That was nearly fifty years ago. Since then, Wayne Gretzky, Mario Lemieux and other great scorers have zeroed in on Sittler's mark, but all failed to equal, much less surpass it. In fact, nobody has ever racked up *nine* points in a game!

Poor Reece often took a ribbing from Sittler at sports banquets. Sittler would quip, "The guy was so despondent over the ten points he gave up that he decided to end it all. He went down in the Toronto subway and threw himself in front of a train. But the train went right through his legs."

Another memorable game for Sittler—one that he later called his career highlight—came on September 15, 1976, in the Canada Cup final at the Montreal Forum. That night, he scored the tournament-winning goal in overtime against Czech goalie Vladimír

DARRYL SITTLER

Dzurilla, giving Team Canada a 5–4 win.

"That was the only championship team I was on," he said later. "When you represent your country, there's something pretty exciting about that."

LEAFS COULDN'T TOPPLE THE FLYERS

GENERAL MANAGER Jim Gregory was busy rebuilding the Leafs in 1973, drafting prospects Lanny McDonald, Bob Neely and Ian Turnbull in the first round and signing the brilliant Swede, Börje Salming. These additions brought new life to the team. However, the Leafs had the back luck of drawing the same opponent—the marauding Philadelphia Flyers, aka the Broad Street Bullies—in the quarter-finals three years in a row.

The Flyers would win all three, beginning with a sweep in '75, en route to a second Stanley Cup championship in as many years. But in the next two meetings, they won very narrowly. In 1976, Darryl Sittler scored five goals in Game 6, tying the record held by Rocket Richard for most goals in a playoff game and forcing a seventh game. The Flyers' Reggie Leach went on to duplicate the feat in Game 5 of the semifinals against Boston. In '77, the series lasted six games, four of them decided by just one goal,

SALMING AND TURNBULL SET TEAM MARKS

IN THE late '70s, defenceman Ian Turnbull was a cornerstone of what may be considered the Leafs' greatest-ever starting five. Turnbull and his amazing partner Börje Salming formed a superb defence pair, backing up what was arguably the top offensive threesome in the NHL—Darryl Sittler, Lanny McDonald and Errol Thompson.

Salming and Turnbull established a team record in 1976–77, when they combined for 157 points: Turnbull with seventy-nine (still a franchise high for a Toronto blueliner) and Salming, seventy-eight (second most).

LANNY MCDONALD

BÖRJE SALMING

Turnbull's popularity never matched Salming's, and some teammates thought his passion for the game was a bit too casual. But he gets full credit for a game he played against Detroit at the Gardens on February 2, 1977, one that ended 9–1 in favour of the Leafs.

Turnbull had a total of five shots on goal in the rout and he scored on every one of them, establishing an NHL record that still stands, despite the scoring skills of defencemen like Bobby Orr, Paul Coffey, Nicklas Lidström and others. Soon a half century will have passed since he set the mark.

Tiger Williams was no fan of the high-scoring defenceman. "Ian Turnbull was quick and smart, but he was a rebel—yeah, a pure rebel," Williams once said. "Ballard loved the guy. But Turnbull didn't look after his body and it disgusted me that so much talent was being wasted. Just thrown away. And that a good coach like Roger Neilson could be wrecked by such an attitude. I had the urge to just clobber him, to really work him over. I told Roger, 'If you don't get rid of Turnbull, he'll get rid of you.'"

Turnbull was traded to the Los Angeles Kings in 1982, as the Toronto Maple Leafs were sliding downhill in their darkest decade following the departures of captain Darryl Sittler and Lanny McDonald. Turnbull enjoyed the laid-back life style of Californians and seldom—if ever—returned to his roots. He played two more years before retiring in 1984.

Dave Hodge told me of Turnbull's questionable attitude one day.

"I was talking to Ian off camera and I asked him how much winning the Stanley Cup would mean to him. He said, 'Oh, it would mean everything, Davey. Then, on the other hand, I'm having a good life in hockey and I've got lots of friends, so really, who gives a shit.'"

BLOWN LEADS WERE A PLAYOFF PATTERN IN '77

THE 1976–77 Leafs were led by Darryl Sittler and Lanny McDonald, each of whom ended the year with ninety points. In the playoffs, they

ROGER NEILSON

ousted Pittsburgh in a best-of-three preliminary round series (Darryl Sittler figured in nine of Toronto's thirteen goals), but were given no chance of upsetting the rough-and-ready Philadelphia Flyers, a team they'd never matched up well against.

Surprise! Toronto shocked Flyers fans with two wins in Philly and were leading Game 3 at the Gardens by a 3–2 score with thirty-eight seconds to play. Just thirty-eight seconds! Incredibly, Rick MacLeish dealt them a crushing blow with a goal to tie the score, followed by the game-winner in overtime.

Toronto fans were absolutely stunned. How could their beloved Leafs have coughed up such an opportunity?

History repeated itself two nights later. With the Leafs in front 5–2 midway through the third period, Mel Bridgman scored, followed by Tom Bladon. Then Bobby Clarke tied the score a mere minute and a half from the final buzzer. Reggie Leach potted the series-tying goal with less than a minute left in overtime.

The Leafs could not recover from such a calamity and lost the next two games. The Flyers were swept four straight by the Boston Bruins in the semifinals, who in turn were beaten four straight in the final by the Montreal Canadiens team that had lost just eight times in the regular season while winning a then-record sixty games.

NEILSON REPLACES KELLY

AFTER THE 1976–77 season, Red Kelly was relieved of his coaching duties and replaced by Roger Neilson. And like his predecessors, he would have to learn to deal with the obstinacy and oddball decisions of the team owner.

Neilson, who had been recommended for the position by Jim Gregory, found out he'd been hired while reading an old newspaper in Austria—in a library—in the summer of 1977.

In their first year under the popular young coach, the Leafs tied a team record for wins (forty-one) and reached their highest point total (ninety-two) since 1950–51. The Leafs beat the LA Kings in two games in the preliminary round, before upsetting the New York Islanders in seven games in the quarter-finals, putting them in the Stanley Cup semifinals for the first time since 1967. But the Leafs were no match for the Montreal Canadiens, who swept them en route to their third straight Stanley Cup championship.

In his second year, Neilson and his Leafs struggled, ending the schedule with eighty-one points. Ballard was not convinced that Neilson was the right man for the job—his innovative use of game videos and his defensive focus particularly rankled the owner.

"But the players love him, Harold."

"The players? What the hell do they know?"

Neilson was fired by Ballard after a 2–1 loss to the Canadiens at the Forum with eighteen games left to play. His dismissal was met with outrage from players and most Leaf fans. Behind the scenes, there was another story.

I was there with Bill Hewitt and Dick Beddoes at the Forum when the story broke and was saddened to see Neilson cut loose. When I bumped into him quite by accident in a downtown Toronto restaurant the following day, I offered my sympathies and assured him he'd be back coaching soon because he was—in my opinion—an outstanding mentor.

What a surprise, then, when Ballard reinstated Roger the very next day, just before a Saturday night game with Philadelphia, because he couldn't find a replacement. In a bizarre move, Ballard demanded that Neilson appear behind the Leaf bench wearing a paper bag over his head. "It'll be a big surprise to our fans when you remove it," he chuckled.

Neilson wisely declined, unwilling to make a mockery of the game.

When I approached Leaf scout Gerry McNamara prior to the game and asked him, "Gerry, please tell me who's going to be coaching tonight," he replied, "Sure. They've asked me to coach." At the beginning of our *Hockey Night in Canada* telecast, I echoed McNamara's words: "Look for Gerry McNamara to be coaching tonight."

Seconds later, Neilson stepped behind the Leaf bench while I wiped some egg from my face.

I accosted McNamara later and accused him of lying to me. He smiled and said, "I didn't lie. I told you they asked me to coach. I didn't say I *would* be the coach."

"Gosh, that's a thin line, Gerry," I told him. "Very thin."

McNamara, like others, was cowed by Ballard. In 1986, when McNamara was GM, Ballard said he wanted John Brophy to be the new coach. McNamara was not a Brophy fan and said so. Ballard hired him anyway.

Here's a story about Brophy from a recent conversation with McNamara: "The Leafs were on the road, and after a game there was some partying and misbehaviour. Someone called Brophy and asked if there was some way to get things under control. 'Yeah,' Brophy said. 'Call the police.'"

Several of the Leafs hated Brophy, but Ballard and the media enjoyed the white-haired warrior's stories about his battles in the minor leagues. And his sometimes salty quotes: in one postgame rant, Brophy dropped the f-bomb more than fifty times.

McNamara left the Leafs and the game in 1988. Ballard made a phone call to tell him he was toast.

And Brophy? In the middle of the '88–89 season, Ballard assigned McNamara's replacement, Gord Stellick, to notify Brophy *he* was fired. Stellick himself left after a few months to take a position in the New York Rangers front office.

Neilson's Leafs won the "paper bag" game, 4–3, and went 10–6–2 down the stretch, putting them just above .500 for the season. After defeating the Atlanta Flames in the preliminary round, they thought they were ready to take on the Montreal Canadiens in the quarter-finals, a team that had finished the regular season with 115 points and was seeking its fourth consecutive Stanley Cup.

In Game 4, the Canadiens defeated the Leafs 5–4 in overtime, sweeping the series. After the game, Lanny McDonald said, "Obviously we weren't as close as we thought. It hurt because it's against a team you desperately want to beat."

When Ballard didn't make Neilson an offer to return for a third season, he joined the Buffalo Sabres, assisting Scotty Bowman. He would also spend time behind the benches in Vancouver, Los Angeles, New York, Florida, Philadelphia and Ottawa (with whom he coached the 999th and 1,000th games of his career).

In 1982, Neilson and the Vancouver Canucks surprised everyone by reaching the Stanley Cup final against the New York Islanders. In the conference final, he felt the referee was favouring the Chicago Blackhawks, so he grabbed a trainer's white towel, put it on top of a player's stick and waved it like a flag of surrender. It cost him a $1,000 fine, but when the Canucks returned to Vancouver, they were greeted by fans waving towels. To this day, fans in Vancouver cheer their team with a display of "towel power."

TIGER HAD MURDER IN MIND

IN THE spring of 1978, the Leafs and the powerful New York Islanders met in a quarter-final playoff series. The Isles had soared to 111 regular-season points, and rookie Mike Bossy had scored fifty-three goals. I worked with the late Dan Kelly on the seventh game on Long Island—a match that was tied 1–1 after sixty minutes. And then, at 4:13 of overtime, Lanny McDonald snared a loose puck and floated it—yes, floated it—past Chico Resch for an unexpected Toronto win.

The Leafs were then humbled by the Montreal Canadiens in the semifinals. Tiger Williams took a high-sticking penalty late in the deciding game, and when the Habs scored on the power play, he bounded out of the box, intending to pounce on referee Bob Myers.

"When I came out of the box, I went straight for the son of a bitch. I wanted to kill him. But Larry Robinson, the big Montreal defenceman, intercepted me and saved my ass. He wrapped his big arms around me and wouldn't let go. He may have saved Myers' ass, too, because I was determined to do him serious harm. In the dressing room I broke down and cried. I'd never done that before and I never did it again."

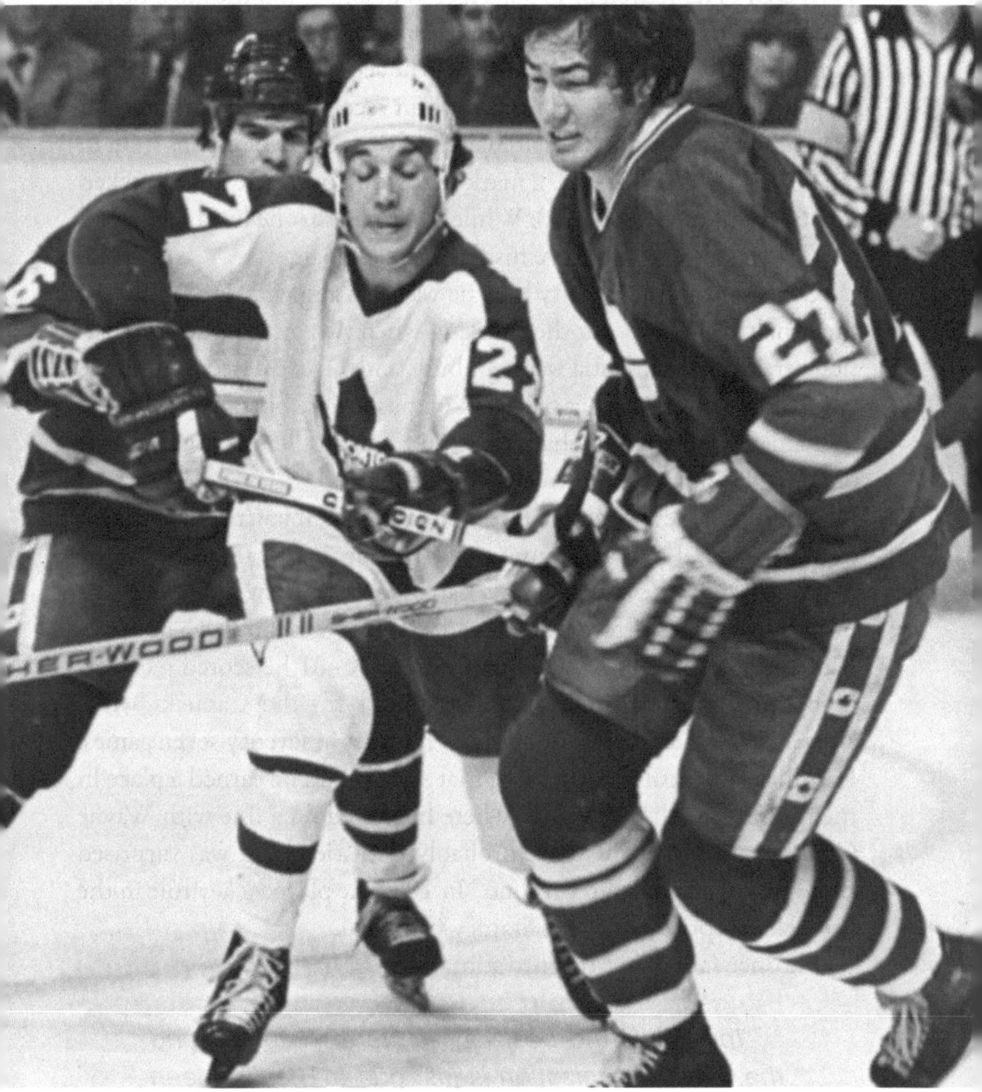

TIGER WILLIAMS AND HAROLD SNEPSTS

TIGER WAS A POPULAR, AND OPINIONATED, LEAF

THOUGH HE retired in 1988, Tiger Williams is still the most penalized player in NHL history, with 3,971 minutes in 962 regular-season games. And that doesn't include the 455 he accumulated in eighty-three playoff games. In 1975–76, he set a team record with 299 minutes in the sin bin, and outdid himself in each of the next two seasons (338 in '76–77 and 351 in '77–78, a mark that stood until Tie Domi racked up 365 minutes in 1997–98). While it seemed that he lived in the "sin bin," he was also able to score his fair share of goals.

One night in the penalty box, he was chatting with Joe Lamantia, the penalty timekeeper at the Gardens, when two or three more penalties were called. Lamantia was kept busy, and Tiger offered a hand. He reached out and said, "Let me help you push those buttons, Joe."

Lamantia slapped his hand and said harshly, "Don't touch those buttons, Tiger. Just sit down and shut up."

Tiger gave Joe a wounded look and said, "Joe, if you're going to talk to me like that, I'm never coming back here again."

In 1979–80, he was having a career year with twenty-two goals in fifty-five games before he was traded to the Vancouver Canucks in February (he ended up with thirty). In 1980–81 he scored a career-high thirty-five goals and sixty-two points for the Canucks while amassing a league leading 343 penalty minutes in seventy-seven games. His thirty-five goals led the team that season, and he earned a place in the midseason All-Star Game, where he played on a line with Wayne Gretzky and Mike Bossy. He probably told friends, "I was surprised those two could keep up with me." In 1982, he played a key role in the Canucks' surprise run to the Stanley Cup final.

He once said of his Toronto stint:

> *Toronto is the best city in North America, and the Leafs organization is just great. They've been wonderful to me and stuck by me. There's the tradition that you can't match. They can say what they want about other teams, but this is the place to be.*

It's the place where the great ones played, and I'm just proud to be a part of it, to wear that Leaf sweater. This organization treats you better than any other. Look, I may not be the greatest player, but they gave me the chance and helped me and now I'm a lot better than I was.

Tiger gave me some memorable quotes in interviews, like when he said, "Them Penguins are done like dinner" on a playoff game telecast. And when Greg Hubick joined the Leafs, his wife and Tiger's wife delivered baby boys a few days apart. When I asked Tiger (off camera) how baby Ben was doing, he said, "Just great. I know this: he can beat the shit out of Hubick's kid."

JIM GREGORY DESERVED BETTER

JIM GREGORY'S role as general manager of the Toronto Maple Leafs has never been given the attention it deserves.

Gregory joined the Leafs as a scout in 1968 and became the GM following the 1969 playoffs, inheriting an unenviable task. The draft brought future Hall of Famers Darryl Sittler and Lanny McDonald. The goaltending void was addressed by trading for Jacques Plante and Bernie Parent. The blue line needed a seasoned veteran, so Bob Baun was brought back.

When Smythe died in in October 1971, and Harold Ballard took over as Leafs president, Gregory's job became immensely more difficult. Ballard nixed many of Gregory's proposals, and he had to become an expert stickhandler to earn approval for many of his decisions.

Then the WHA came along and lured away a number of Leafs. Forced into rebuilding mode again, Gregory was among the first NHL general managers to sign players from Europe, including Hall of Fame defenceman Börje Salming. The next few drafts yielded several Leaf regulars, including Ian Turnbull, Tiger Williams and Mike Palmateer.

KEN MCKENZIE, RALPH MELLANBY,
PUNCH IMLACH, BILL HEWITT, JOHN ANDERSON

Over Gregory's decade, the Leafs won more games than they lost, but playoff success proved elusive. Then, in the summer of 1979, Jim Gregory was at his cottage when the phone rang. It was NHL executive Brian O'Neill, calling from Montreal.

"Jim, I'm offering you the position of director of Central Scouting for the NHL. It'll mean a pay raise and lots of benefits. You interested?"

"Brian, why're you calling me? I've got a job I love—general manager of the Leafs."

"Jim, you don't know yet? I talked to Ballard yesterday and he told me he'd fired you."

That's how Gregory found out his days with the Leafs were over.

He served the NHL well for several years as director of Central Scouting and later became senior vice president, hockey operations and supervision.

He died in Toronto in October 2019 at age eighty-three.

"The NHL family adored Jim Gregory." NHL commissioner Gary Bettman said. "Jim was one of the first to welcome me to the NHL and I have relied upon his wisdom every day since. Nobody loved the game more. Nobody ever served it better. We will miss him terribly."

"Jim was the GM back in 1970 when I was drafted," Darryl Sittler said. "He put a really good team together, with players like Lanny McDonald, Tiger Williams, Börje Salming, Mike Palmateer and Errol Thompson. We all grew up under his guidance. He was just a wonderful man."

"Jim was one of the great gentlemen of hockey. He was a friend to so many within the game," Maple Leafs president Brendan Shanahan said. "His contributions to hockey were so deeply rooted. He was a living, breathing piece of hockey history. He will be greatly missed."

OH NO, NOT YESTERDAY'S MAN

ON JULY 4, 1979, Leaf owner Harold Ballard had another dumb idea, possibly at the suggestion of his pal King Clancy: he rehired

Punch Imlach to manage the franchise.

Imlach, put out to pasture by the Buffalo Sabres, had won four Stanley Cups for Toronto in the '60s, and starting from scratch in Buffalo had built a team that reached the Stanley Cup final in five years. But his return to Toronto would begin and end in controversy—and without a single Cup. Not even a sniff at one.

There would be no repeat of the success of the 1960s. Imlach was yesterday's man.

"That team you've got isn't good enough," Imlach told Ballard. "It needs my old-fashioned approach to make it better."

"Sounds good to me, Punch. Pitch right in."

But the team was good. It didn't need an old-fashioned approach. It needed better management.

When the 1979–80 season got underway, Imlach immediately began finding fault with several of the Leafs and was soon at odds with captain Darryl Sittler. Sittler enjoyed the total respect of his mates. He also had an agent Imlach detested: Alan Eagleson. Eagleson was executive director of the NHL Players Association, which Imlach had opposed since the late '60s. The NHLPA was involved in a skills competition called "Showdown," which aired between periods on *Hockey Night in Canada*. Imlach tried to block Sittler from appearing, despite contracts that obligated NHL teams to let their players participate. Relations between GM and captain went from there, and because Sittler had a no-trade clause in his contract, Imlach decided to swap the talented individuals who were close to him.

It was nonsensical and it was nasty. And it was all so unnecessary.

The trade purge began with feisty Pat Boutette, dealt to the Hartford Whalers, where he skated alongside Gordie Howe, Dave Keon and Bobby Hull. Pat was a lucky guy. In 1980–81 he scored a career high in points—eighty points in eighty contests. Did he send Punch a thank you note? I wonder.

On December 29, 1979, Imlach spoiled every Leaf fan's New Year's party by trading Lanny McDonald, Sittler's best friend and linemate, to the lowly Colorado Rockies. Defenceman Joel Quenneville joined McDonald in return for wingers Wilf Paiement and Pat Hickey.

How dare Imlach do such a thing? No GM should be allowed to trade a heart-and-soul player like Lanny McDonald—and at the peak of his career.

Leaf fans were livid and noisily protested the trade outside of Maple Leafs Gardens before a Saturday night game against the Winnipeg Jets.

"I believe I was traded out of spite," a teary-eyed Lanny would say. "I think Punch really wanted to show who was boss. It didn't matter how much he hurt the club or tore it apart, he only wanted to make sure everyone knew who was running the team. When Punch stuck out his right hand and wished me good luck, I refused to accept it. I was tempted to smack him right in the face. In Denver, I told people I felt so sorry for the guys staying behind, who had to play on a disappointed, disorganized, disgruntled hockey team,"

He might have added another "D" word: dysfunctional.

The Leafs, sitting in their dressing room when Lanny's departure was announced, were stunned. Most slumped back as if hit in the gut by a slapshot. Others cried or cursed or did both. They became so agitated, so angry, that they began to tear their room apart.

Before the team's next game, Sittler stripped the *C* from his jersey. "They couldn't get me so they traded my best friend," he explained "The war between Mr. Eagleson and Mr. Imlach should not overshadow the most important matter—the Toronto Maple Leafs."

One Leaf fan growled, "It has become a madhouse. I guess Imlach is succeeding in doing what he set out to do from the start—tear the team to pieces."

As the calendar rolled over into 1980, Imlach kept dumping Sittler's buddies. On January 10, he shuffled defenceman Dave Hutchison off to Chicago. Hutchison recalled that a "victory party" was held for him at a local pub to celebrate his good fortune at being traded away—his escape. He said, "I don't like the idea of leaving the guys, but God, anything to get away from this situation." Pinned to the pub's dartboard was a picture of Punch Imlach, riddled with pinholes.

February 18 brought another trade. Tiger Williams was packaged with Jerry Butler and sent to Vancouver for Rick Vaive and Bill

Derlago. That deal was Imlach's best. Vaive and Derlago blossomed in Leaf uniforms.

And Punch wasn't done yet. On March 3, Walt McKechnie was shipped to Colorado for a draft pick. McKechnie believed that the trade was prompted by comments he made about coach Floyd Smith, a long-time Imlach crony. "I said Smitty's practices were a joke, and I wasn't the only player on the Leafs who said that. As for Sittler, he was a pal. How does anyone treat a player and a man the calibre of Darryl Sittler the way the Leafs and Imlach treated him?"

The *Toronto Star* added an opinion: "Somehow, Sittler has managed to maintain his dignity and class while being strung out to dry for all to see."

Sittler said, "I had a lot of respect for Punch Imlach for bringing Toronto the four Stanley Cups, but when he came back in 1979, I said, 'Oh, oh, things are never going to be the same.'"

True enough. In the '80s, free agents, as well as potential top draft choices such as like Craig Simpson would tell their agents, "I want to play in the NHL, but not in Toronto."

Despite all the upheaval in the dressing room, Toronto managed to make the playoffs in 1979–80. But in the first round, they were swept by Minnesota in three games, outscored 17–8. More significantly, their record of 35–40–5 made this the first of ten consecutive losing seasons.

As writer Brian Westland summed it up: "The Toronto Maple Leafs finished the 1979–1980 season with a record of thirty-five wins and forty losses. It's far from being their worst showing. However, the vindictive actions of GM Imlach that season set the stage for years of suffering—the worst decade in the history of the Toronto Maple Leafs."

While Imlach ran a pretty good hockey club into the ground, Ballard never grimaced or growled. Or waved his arms, shouting, "Stop this travesty." If only he'd done that.

Some hockey people—managers and coaches, especially—who were around when the NHL expanded from six teams to twelve had to adjust quickly or be sent packing. The game was changing, and so were the players' attitudes. One change that players welcomed was the ability to negotiate contracts with the help of agents.

Punch Imlach hated agents, and he was one of those aging hockey men who couldn't adjust. Like Napoleon, like Vladimir Putin, he was accustomed to having full control—as he did in the good old six-team days. But in an era of expansion, player agents and soaring salaries—fuelled by the arrival of the WHA—Punch had trouble coping with the new-look NHL. He was elected to the Hockey Hall of Fame in 1984 for his past triumphs—remembered as a tough hombre who brought Toronto their last four Stanley Cups, and not the greybeard who dismantled a promising lineup over a decade later.

The dismissals of Lanny McDonald, Tiger Williams and others at the onset of the 1980s were a gloomy precursor of what was to come—the worst decade in the history of the Toronto Maple Leafs. It would be ten long years, during which the team posted losing records season after season.

BREWER REJECTED IN COMEBACK BID

ALL-STAR DEFENCEMAN Carl Brewer had feuded with Punch Imlach in the early 1960s—the team's golden years. He found the coach's practices demoralizing and exhausting, both physically and emotionally. "We're just puppets," he once declared, telling the coach, "You expect us to dance when you holler." During training camp in 1965, Brewer walked out, never to play for the Maple Leafs again. "My damaged psyche—destroyed by Imlach—would no longer allow me to accommodate playing hockey and being a hockey player," he later said.

In time, Brewer was able to regain his amateur status, and he later played for the Canadian National Team, winning a bronze medal at the 1967 World Championships.

After NHL stints with St. Louis and Detroit, as well as the Toronto Toros of the WHA, he became a popular addition to our NHL Oldtimers' club and fit right in. One day in 1979, his old nemesis Punch Imlach called, and the two decided that Brewer should rejoin the Leafs. He hadn't played pro since 1973–74, but began playing himself back into shape. After a few games with the farm club in Moncton, he was called up.

When the forty-one-year-old Brewer showed up to his first workout with the Leafs, there were a few chuckles, but those quickly subsided once he showed that he had no trouble skating with them, even though he was twelve years older than team captain Darryl Sittler.

But his comeback was short-lived. The team was in chaos, and coach Floyd Smith didn't want to play him. "Carl," he said, "the guys won't even talk to you, let alone pass you the puck. It's a big problem."

The players were suspicious of Brewer. A few thought he was acting as a spy for Imlach, even though anybody who knew about the history between the two men would've known that was hogwash.

Carl Brewer's fourth and final comeback lasted twenty games, and he assisted on five goals. He did not star, nor did he stumble. Once the postseason arrived, he was not on the roster.

I always liked Carl Brewer. He came to visit me just hours before he died (in bed of sleep apnea). He supported me. How could I not like the man?

Brewer felt that retired players were not getting their due, and he discovered that the league's owners had been diverting portions of the NHL pension fund into their own pockets for decades. He launched a lawsuit against the league that eventually led to a Supreme Court ruling ordering the reimbursement of over $40 million to players, coaches, trainers, referees, general managers and executives. This lawsuit also led to the conviction of Alan Eagleson, executive director of the NHL Players Association, on charges of fraud and embezzlement. Eagleson served time in jail, and under new leadership the players association became more responsive to the players.

THE AGONIZING EIGHTIES

A DARK, DEPRESSING DECADE

THE 1980S have often been described as the darkest, gloomiest years in Maple Leafs history, remembered more for the bizarre antics of owner Harold Ballard than the team's few accomplishments on the ice. Throughout the decade, the Leafs sputtered, with Ballard the cause of much of the sputtering. Front-office chaos was a recurring theme, as the crusty octogenarian replaced three general managers and seven coaches.

In the early '80s, Harold Ballard promised Leaf fans a Stanley Cup "in a year or two." His teams never finished above .500 and missed the playoffs four times in the decade—in an era when all but five of twenty-one teams qualified. And when NHL president John Ziegler announced that more new clubs would be joining the NHL by the year 2000, Toronto's chances for a Cup win seemed more remote than finding a Tim Hortons on Pluto.

The 1980s were miserable for everyone connected to the franchise. Following Imlach's dismissal after a heart attack in 1981 (the second he had suffered during his term), Gerry McNamara spent six losing seasons in the GM's chair. With the franchise facing a bleak future, some prospects made it known they would prefer to play elsewhere if possible. But not all: promising players like Wendel Clark, Russ

Courtnall, Vincent Damphousse, Al Iafrate, and Gary Nylund were proud to don the blue and white jersey.

LOWLIGHTS OF THE SECOND IMLACH ERA

PUNCH IMLACH'S heart issues early in the decade should have served as a warning: All this feuding is not healthy, Punch. Why not step aside? What more have you got to prove? A Leaf icon. Four Stanley Cups. Then you started with a blank page in Buffalo and went to the Stanley Cup final in five years. A berth in the Hall of Fame is waiting for you. You've done it all, pal. Time to bow out. Over time, people will forget about the mess you made of things in your second go-round.

Punch didn't listen, and after suffering an attack of chest pain he dismissed it as a bump in the road, took some time off and returned to run the Leafs in 1980–81.

As he kept dumping Sittler's buddies, discontent grew into open hostility. After a flight home from a game in Montreal, Imlach found that his car, which he'd parked at the airport, wouldn't start. He barked at some players walking by, "Got any battery cables?"

None appeared to hear. But moments later, one car drove past Imlach with booster cables trailing from the trunk.

The trade on February 18, 1980, that sent Tiger Williams and Jerry Butler to Vancouver for Rick Vaive and Bill Derlago took place after a game on Long Island—a game we telecast. Williams went face to face with Imlach and called him a lot of nasty names. He and Butler then flew back to Toronto and jumped on a connecting flight to Vancouver. As their flight took them over Winnipeg, Butler turned to Williams and said, "I sure hope you heard right, Tiger. Nobody yet has told me I've been traded!"

On March 3, 1980, Walt McKechnie was shipped to Colorado for a draft pick. McKechnie, who played with nine NHL clubs during a seventeen-year pro career, believed the trade was prompted by negative comments he made about coach Floyd Smith—whom Imlach had appointed—as well as his friendship with Sittler. "Smitty's practices were a joke," he commented. "Everybody said so."

McKechnie added a question: "How does anyone treat a man the calibre of Darryl Sittler the way the Leafs have treated him this season?"

Smith served as coach of the Maple Leafs for the first sixty-eight games of the 1979–80 season. In March 1980, he was charged with criminal negligence and impaired driving stemming from a fatal automobile accident near St. Catharines, Ontario. He was acquitted and remained with the Leafs as a scout until 1989, when he was promoted to general manager, a position he held for two seasons.

Smith is remembered for one quote in particular: "I have nothing to say and I'll only say it once."

In 1980–81, Joe Crozier, another long-time Imlach buddy, was named head coach at the start of the season. However, the Leafs wobbled out of the starting blocks with a record of 13–22–5 through the first half, and Crozier was replaced by Mike Nykoluk.

Nykoluk, a career minor leaguer, had a bit of NHL coaching experience—he'd assisted Fred Shero with the Philadelphia Flyers and New York Rangers in the 1970s. But when he got the call from the Leafs, he was working as a colour commentator on the team's radio broadcasts. Ironically, he soon found himself spending as much time battling with the Toronto media as he did changing lines, but in the second half of 1980–81 he managed to steer the team to a 15–15–10 record and a spot in the playoffs. Their first-round opponents were the New York Islanders, but this was no longer the Toronto team that had eliminated Bossy, Trottier, Potvin and company just a few years earlier. The Leafs were swept in three games by a combined score of 20–4.

Nykoluk coached the team for three more seasons, but they missed the playoffs in 1982 and '84, and lost to Minnesota in the first round in 1983. In his 280 games behind the bench, the Leafs won eighty-nine, lost 144 and tied forty-seven.

BALLARD SIDELINES IMLACH—BUT DOESN'T TELL HIM

IN SEPTEMBER of 1981, Punch Imlach suffered his second heart attack in as many years. Harold Ballard made a decision to keep him on the sidelines and assign the title of "acting" GM to a man with the same initials as his job—Gerry McNamara. Ballard made noises about Imlach being finished as GM, but he was never comfortable delivering bad news in person. Imlach learned he was through when he showed up at the Gardens one November day to find his parking space no longer had his name on it. And McNamara's vehicle was parked there. Imlach, figuring McNamara was more than an acting GM, drove away.

After being elected to the Hockey Hall of Fame in 1984, Punch Imlach suffered a suspected heart attack in November of 1985. He died on December 1, 1987, after a final attack.

I've been hard on Imlach in this tome. But he's responsible for the course he took, one that altered his legacy. On the one hand, he's a deserving Hall of Famer for his four well-won Stanley Cups in the '60s. On the other, he's the guy who—with Harold Ballard's blessing—ripped a Stanley Cup contender apart with vindictive, personal decisions that left a proud franchise in tatters. What more need be said?

BILL HEWITT'S FINAL BROADCAST

BILL HEWITT, Bob Goldham and your author were in the gondola at the Gardens for the first telecast of the Leafs' 1981–82 season. It was a meaningless game, a pre-season match between the Canadiens and the Leafs.

Bill had been a solid play-caller for *Hockey Night in Canada* on a regular basis since 1958, but almost from the outset, it seemed something was amiss. He began misidentifying players on the ice, which set off alarm bells in the production truck. Producer Don Wallace rushed up to the gondola, took me aside and asked if Bill had been drinking.

I said, "No, there's no sign of that. Perhaps Goldham and I should take over?"

Wallace said he'd talk to Hewitt first—and he did, during the intermission. He decided to let Bill finish the game—a poor choice because Bill continued to be disoriented and his call of the game was the worst of his long career.

Sadly, it also turned out to be his last broadcast. He went home and never came back. His career ended that night. And a fifty-year tradition of Hewitts on *HNiC* ended abruptly.

HNiC head Ted Hough followed up, having a long discussion with Bill, but Hough went to his grave without revealing exactly what Bill suffered from that night.

Danny Gallivan from Montreal joined our Toronto crew for midweek games, while long-time CBC broadcaster Bob Cole took over the national broadcasts from Toronto.

In 1984, Don Wallace, the eventual successor to Ralph Mellanby as *HNiC*'s executive producer, hired former NHL coach Harry Neale as a colour commentator and paired Neale with Cole in the booth. They became the top duo on *Hockey Night* for over twenty years.

Another change in our telecast crew occurred in March of 1987. Popular host Dave Hodge, perturbed that the CBC did not switch to coverage of an out of town game still in progress in overtime, protested on air by simply flipping a pencil. That was enough to get him tossed from the show. That's when young Ron MacLean, a former weatherman from Alberta, got his big break as a replacement.

SITTLER JOINS THE FLYERS

IN NOVEMBER of 1981, Darryl Sittler told Ballard and acting general manager Gerry McNamara that he would waive his no-trade clause in order to be dealt to another team, a team of his choosing. By January of '82, Sittler, under stress and mentally depressed, walked out on the team prior to a road game in Minnesota on advice from his physician. When I showed empathy for Sittler on the hockey telecast that night, Ballard was furious and banned me from the broadcast booth—forever. It was harsh punishment for simply presenting the facts, although suggesting that the Leafs treat Sittler "like the Flyers treat Bobby Clarke" was bound to antagonize the Leaf boss.

On January 20, Sittler was traded to the Philadelphia Flyers in a deal that left few people happy. "I would have been pleased to have retired a Maple Leaf," he said. "I am not proud of having to leave the team like this."

At the time, Sittler was the club's all-time leader in goals (389) and points (916). Only Mats Sundin, with 420 goals and 987 points, has surpassed him.

What Toronto got in return was not nearly enough. Rich Costello played twelve career games in Toronto, while Ken Strong appeared in fifteen. Each managed just two goals and two assists. A draft pick yielded Peter Ihnačák, the only player who could be described as a regular. He scored twenty-eight goals and sixty-six points in eighty games in his first year as a Leaf, but never again cracked fifty points.

In 1984, Bobby Clarke retired and was appointed as the Flyers' general manager. Heading into the '84–85 season, Sittler was led to believe he'd inherit the captaincy from Clarke. Instead, the team reneged and traded him to Detroit. He retired at the end of the year.

Was jersey number twenty-seven a jinx? Both Sittler and Frank Mahovlich wore it with distinction, yet both were discarded in the midst of their Hall of Fame careers.

As one writer observed: "The thing that makes the Sittler trade one of the worst deals in Maple Leafs history is the fact it didn't need to happen. The players Toronto got back for Sittler didn't matter as much as the entire story of how he was treated by the organization. Having such little regard for one of the greatest players in franchise history is a major black eye and a black page in the Leafs history book. But such uncommon disasters were rather common throughout the bleak Ballard era."

NOT A SINGLE WINNING SEASON

IN THE decade of the 1980s, the Leafs lost forty or more games in eight consecutive seasons (1981–82 to 1988–89), with an all-time low of fifty-two defeats in 1984–85. Eight times they failed to win even thirty games, and they broke even just once (38–38–4 in 1989–90). Somehow, they managed to get some playoff action on six occasions between 1980–81 and 1989-90—twice when their season's point total was in the fifties.

Their goaltending was porous and their defence was pitiful, the worst in the league, with Börje Salming the lone standout game after game.

Under head coach Dan Maloney, the 1985–86 edition of the team, despite posting the fourth-worst record in the league (25–48–7), qualified for the last playoff spot in a very weak Norris Division.

Surprise! They were still alive after the first round.

The Leafs swept the Chicago Black Hawks in three games in the Norris semifinals before being eliminated by the St. Louis Blues in a seven-game division final.

Maloney resigned as coach after he was offered a contract renewal for one year rather than two. He was quickly hired to coach the Winnipeg Jets, with whom he signed a three-year contract paying much more than the approximately $80,000 the Leafs were paying him. His assistant, John Brophy, took over, and the Leafs improved to seventy points, but again finished fourth in the Norris, clinching their playoff spot on the final night of the regular season.

This time, Toronto and St. Louis met in the first round, with the Leafs prevailing in six games. In the division final, Toronto won the first two games at Joe Louis Arena before falling to the Detroit Red Wings in seven.

"That's still a long way from the Stanley Cup," a few doubters reminded Leaf management.

CLARK WAS A KEEPER

A SIDE effect of the Leafs' nosedive in the standings is that they were frequently in a position to select early in the NHL draft. And the decade brought a number of fresh faces, including Jim Benning (sixth overall in 1981), Gary Nylund (third overall in '82), Russ Courtnall (seventh in '83) and Al Iafrate (fourth in '84). All oozed potential. They had size and smarts. But Harold Ballard was reluctant to pay the salaries their agents demanded and by the time their talent blossomed, they were performing with other teams.

That pattern was about to break, at least for one year.

In 1984–85, the Leafs lost fifty-two games (still a team record forty years later) and finished last in the twenty-one-team NHL, earning them the first-overall pick in the '85 draft. The player they chose was an average-sized defenceman who made an oversized, and lasting, impression on Leaf Nation, becoming an idol of the fan base almost overnight.

When general manager Gerry McNamara called out Wendel Clark's name at the 1985 NHL Entry Draft, he may not have known he was getting a hockey gem. McNamara was on the receiving end of hints and suggestions that he should pick someone else. After all, Craig Simpson, a high-scoring left wing at Michigan State University, was the number-one prospect according to the NHL's Central Scouting bureau. Another defenceman from the Western Hockey League, Dana Murzyn, had a bit more size. But McNamara kept saying, "No, Clark's the kid I want for the Leafs."

For once, Harold Ballard, intrigued with Clark's feistiness, allowed his GM to make the sensible choice.

The Leafs switched Clark from defence to left wing, and the rugged eighteen-year-old from Kelvington, Saskatchewan, embarked on a career that would put him among the Leaf elites, mentioned in the same breath as names like Conacher, Clancy, Apps, Kennedy, Sittler and Sundin. He became a rock star, the kind of guy you'd want next to you in any hockey scuffle.

WENDEL CLARK

Six months before turning pro and donning a blue and white jersey, Clark helped Canada win a gold medal at the 1985 World Junior Championships. In his rookie season, Clark scored thirty-four goals and forty-five points, and racked up 227 penalty minutes, in sixty-six games. He could body check with the best of them, and when the gloves were dropped, he was a George Chuvalo on skates.

However, while Clark was an important contributor and a crowd pleaser, his physical style took its toll. Over his time with the Leafs, Wendel lost 260 games to injury, and 437 overall in his fifteen-year career.

"Wendel, at 185 pounds, played like a 210-pounder, and in most of his games he was held together by the training staff," said Leafs GM Cliff Fletcher, who succeeded McNamara.

Doug Gilmour said of Clark: "He was on the trainer's table all the time in the '90s. Getting acupuncture back then when it wasn't as common as it later became. He had more needles in him than you can imagine."

Clark spent as much time in therapy as he did on skates, as much as three hours per day. "From 1990 on, trainer Chris Broadhurst was the guy that kept me together—taped together," he said.

Clark said it would have been folly to change his playing style. He told writer Mark Zwolinski, "I was hoping when I played that I would always be known as someone who battled every game—whether it was getting a goal, or doing something physical."

The captain's leadership and aggressive play helped the team make it through to the second round of playoffs in both 1986 and 1987, tallying eleven goals and seventeen points in twenty-three games. In 1986–87, he played in all eighty matches, racking up thirty-seven goals and sixty points. But, battered and bruised, he was able to skate in a mere eighty-one games over the next three seasons, and would never again take to the ice more than sixty-six times in a regular season.

It's too bad he was often out of the lineup, because he was a fearless, productive player who inspired his mates. In 1993 and '94, when the Leafs reached back-to-back conference finals, he skated in all thirty-nine playoff games, with nineteen goals and thirty-six points.

Wendel Clark retired in 2000. He was only thirty-three years old. In 793 regular-season games of nose-to-the-grindstone hockey, he scored 330 goals and 563 points with 1,690 minutes in penalties. No Leaf would ever again wear his number seventeen sweater, and it was officially retired in 2016.

MIRO THE ZERO MEETS MESSIER

IT WAS like the sequel to a thrilling spy novel. Three years after the Toronto Maple Leafs spirited Peter Ihnačák out of Czechoslovakia, they played a role in the defection of his brother, Miroslav.

Early one morning in December 1985, GM Gerry McNamara got a phone call, notifying him that Miro and his girlfriend, Eva Olach, had been smuggled from behind the Iron Curtain and were in Vienna, Austria. No baggage with them—not even a pair of skates.

Harold Ballard reportedly spent over $100,000 to get the young couple to the West. And though Czechoslovak secret police were searching for Ihnačák to bring him back home, where he faced three years' imprisonment, Ihnačák and his girlfriend arrived in Vancouver on January 4, 1985.

Ballard was quoted as saying, "Any communist that I could get out of there who wanted to be a Canadian and a Leaf, I'm very happy about it."

The Leafs had faltered badly at the beginning of the 1985–86 NHL season, and held a woeful record of 10–21–5 on the day of Ihnačák's arrival. Less than a week after touching down, he suited up for the Leafs in Darryl Sittler's old number twenty-seven and scored a goal. Over the Leafs' next forty-one games, he was in the lineup for just twenty, scoring one more goal and adding four assists. His lack of production earned the nickname "Miro the Zero."

Leaf announcers Joe Bowen and Bill Watters recall a game in Edmonton in which young Miro hoped to make an early impression.

Bowen said, "Oh, yeah, the kid was in his second or third game when he raced up the ice and runs into Mark Messier with his big elbow sticking out. What a smack! The kid falls down and Watters and I start to laugh. The poor kid is lying there quivering, there's blood flying, he's got CCM tattooed on his bugle and we're hysterical. Now they're scraping Miro off the ice and we can't control ourselves, so I call for a commercial—right in the middle of the play. I'd never done that before."

Bill Watters added, "We come back on and everything's good. Then we see Miro jump back on the ice."

"That's when we lost it again," said Bowen. "We had that image of Miro going down like a sack of wheat. We were cackling so hard, I can't believe we got through the rest of that period."

Miro scored eight goals in fifty-five games with the Leafs and was released. After a one-game stint with the Red Wings, he returned to Europe, where he played fifteen more seasons as a pro.

THE BROPHY-FRYČER FEUD

AFTER SERVING as an assistant to Dan Maloney, John Brophy became head coach of the Leafs for the 1986–87 season. GM Gerry McNamara strongly opposed the signing, but owner Harold Ballard said, "Too bad. Brophy's my guy. You don't like it, get lost."

The Canadian Press published a report on a Leaf practice on November 26, 1986, before a big game in Detroit, noting that Brophy literally laid the lumber on his defencemen, hacking and slashing them with a stick to demonstrate how he wanted them to play against the Wings.

The talkative Maritimer guided Toronto into the second round of the playoffs that season. But in 1987–88, it was a much different story. The team was agonizing to watch and difficult to broadcast. Except for the performance of new arrival Ed Olczyk (forty-two goals and seventy-five points), there were no "feel-good" stories. In early February, with the team in a 1–15–6 tailspin, McNamara was fired. The Leafs finished the schedule with twenty-one wins, forty-nine losses and ten ties, for fifty-two points—the second-worst record in the league.

As it happened, the worst record belonged to their Norris Division mates, the Minnesota North Stars, who ended up with fifty-one points, so the Leafs qualified for the playoffs with the lowest winning percentage (.325) in the NHL's long history. Their first-round opponents, the Detroit Red Wings, who finished forty-one points ahead of Toronto in the standings, polished the Leafs off in six games—how they managed to win two games is anybody's guess.

Once the series was over, the verbal fireworks erupted. Winger Mirko Fryčer snarled, "Brophy's completely nuts and everybody hates him." The coach shot back, "Every time Fryčer took to the ice, he fell down and injured himself. There's not enough plaster cast in Toronto to keep him together."

Neither man would be around for long. Fryčer was traded to Detroit on June 10. Brophy was fired a few days before Christmas of 1988, after the Leafs skated off to a disappointing 11–20–2 start.

George Armstrong reluctantly took over as coach, and got them within striking distance of a playoff berth, but an overtime goal by Chicago's Troy Murray in the final game of the regular season ended Toronto's postseason hopes.

FRYČER'S CONFESSIONS

FRYČER TALKED freely with journalist Dave Feschuk after leaving Toronto, a city he loved.

"It was a smooth transition to Canada [from the Czech Republic]. I remember booze was everywhere," he said. "It was the wild '80s. The parties were everywhere. In the Leafs dressing room, there were two cases of beer after every single game. That part of my life was the same as back home."

Pulled over a few times while driving drunk, Fryčer's fame as a Maple Leaf usually saved him. But not every time. He served about a week in jail for one impaired-driving conviction, which endeared him to Ballard, who'd spent a lot more time than Fryčer behind bars.

He recalled a lot of women, booze and even cocaine.

"There was tons and tons of women," Fryčer said. "They just wanted to be with us. Now they see a lot of money behind a hockey player. They've got cellphones. It's a lot different from our day."

Question: Who wants women when they come by the ton?

"Cocaine, it was there, but not as much as these days. I saw it. I was there. Back then it was alcohol, alcohol, alcohol. Girls and alcohol."

In his memoir, Fryčer wrote of having his hand around Brophy's throat in the midst of a confrontation. And how, as a Red Wing, he gave Brophy the finger after a two-goal game against the Leafs.

"I'm still bitter. I loved Toronto," said Fryčer. "We had great young kids but they needed a teacher. Under Brophy, they got nothing."

After battling a series of health problems, in part brought on by alcohol abuse early in his NHL days, and surviving liver and kidney transplants, Mirko Fryčer died in the Czech Republic in 2021 at age sixty-one.

VAIVE TO CHICAGO, OLCZYK BECOMES A LEAF

IN SEVEN and a half years with Toronto, Rick Vaive averaged over a point per game and scored 299 goals, thirty-one of them game winners. That's impressive. Were the Canucks blind to all this potential when they traded him to the Leafs?

He was the team's best forward in the '80s, and was often looked on as a superstar. In three consecutive seasons, Vaive scored over fifty goals (including fifty-four in 1981–82, a team record that stood for forty years) and he had over thirty, four other times. He scored at least sixty points in each of his seven full seasons, with a high of 93 in '83–84.

A healthy 10.4 percent of the goals he scored for Toronto were game-winners, a dazzling feat considering the team had such little success in the win column (190 wins) during Vaive's time in Leafland. He was popular and served as captain from 1981 until 1986, until he overslept one morning, missed practice and was stripped of the *C*.

For whatever reason, he never earned the respect and adulation showered on other Leaf greats. But give the Maritimer credit: he was the go-to guy on the team during a very frustrating, tumultuous decade.

ED OLCZYK

In 1987, Vaive was sent to Chicago in the deal that made Ed Olczyk a Maple Leaf. This trade has been one of the most highly criticized deals made by Leaf management. Vaive scored forty-three goals with the Blackhawks in 1987–88.

"I requested the trade," said Vaive, "A lot of things happened behind the scenes that people don't know about. I had a lot of ups and downs—a heckuva lot of downs."

Olczyk was about fifteen when he approached me in a corridor of the Chicago Stadium one day and said politely, "Mr. McFarlane, I'm going to play in the NHL someday. Perhaps you should remember my name. Who knows? I may even be a Leaf one day."

I did remember his name, and in time, I could even spell it. Olczyk had been selected by his hometown Chicago Blackhawks third overall in the 1984 NHL Entry Draft. He scored his first NHL goal in his first NHL game on October 11, 1984, and was traded to the Leafs with Al Secord for Vaive, Steve Thomas and Bob McGill.

Over three full in Toronto he scored between thirty-two and forty-two goals and earned between seventy-five and ninety points. He should be remembered, but he's not. Mention his name, and people ask, "Did he play for Toronto? I did not know that."

He is known today as an Emmy Award–winning broadcaster of hockey games and major horse-racing events like the Kentucky Derby—and, fortunately, as a survivor of colon cancer.

GORD "KID" STELLICK GETS A SHOT

THE TORONTO Maple Leafs surprised everybody in April of 1988, when owner Harold Ballard named thirty-year-old Gord Stellick as the new general manager, making him the youngest GM in league history.

Stellick had first started working at Maple Leaf Gardens at age seventeen, when he was still in high school. He was a "gofer," an eager young fellow who helped out in the team's press box.

Ballard said Stellick would have "lots of authority. The guy he's responsible to is me and I don't know what I'm doing so he can do what he wants. Yes, he can hire or fire the coach or he can hire and fire me—but only if he's got enough money to buy the place."

Stellick lasted sixteen months in the job before resigning.

On November 7, 1988, in his first important move, Stellick traded forward Russ Courtnall to Montreal for winger John Kordic; the Habs clearly got the best of that deal. Courtnall was one-third of the Leafs' productive Hound Line, which also featured Gary Leeman and Wendel Clark. (All three had played for the Notre Dame Hounds in Wilcox, Saskatchewan.) Kordic was known more for what he could do with his fists than his stick. Between 1988 and 1990, he played 104 games, with ten goals, six assists and 446 penalty minutes. Courtnall, meanwhile, went on to play in the 1989 Stanley Cup Final, in which the Habs lost to the Calgary Flames, and would score a career-high thirty-six goals in 1992–93.

In time, it would emerge that Kordic was addicted to alcohol and cocaine. These substances, combined with his steroid use, altered his personality—he was known to fly into a violent rage. Such was the case in August of 1992, when police in L'Ancienne-Lorette, Quebec were called to a motel where an intoxicated Kordic was trashing his room. It took eight officers to overpower him, and two pairs of handcuffs to restrain him. Police also tied his feet together. An ambulance was called, and he was strapped to a stretcher. En route to the hospital, his heart and lungs gave out. He was pronounced dead at the hospital.

BROPHY ENDED UP BACK WHERE HE BELONGED

AFTER THE Leafs let him go, John Brophy went back to the minors and became coach of the Hampton Roads Admirals of the East Coast Hockey League for the 1989–90 season. His luck would be better in the minors: he led the Admirals to three league titles over eleven seasons.

As a minor-league player, Brophy was famous for his take-no-prisoners style, racking up nearly four thousand career penalty minutes from 1955 to '73.

He was suspended and fined several times, for transgressions including: "attempts to assault referee," "physically abusing referee," "deliberately shooting puck at referee," "jabbing stick at fan after fan bit him," "pushing referee to the ice," "throwing stick at referee" and "throwing object at referee." Needless to say, he had anger issues.

When Brophy died on May 23, 2016, at the age of eighty-three, many glowing tributes were paid him. Some named him as the coach who won more games than anyone not named Scotty Bowman.

One night after a Leaf loss, Brophy delivered seventy-two F-bombs in a two-minute rant to reporters covering the game. It's an NHL record—albeit an obscure one.

He was a colourful character, one who could be as funny as he was infuriating. His feud with Mirko Fryčer was like no other. He left his mark—good or bad—on the game and the franchise.

LEAFS GET KURVERS, LOSE NIEDERMAYER

IN OCTOBER of 1989, Leafs GM Floyd Smith traded away his team's 1991 first-round pick to the New Jersey Devils for defenceman Tom Kurvers. But Kurvers didn't stay. After eighty-nine games with Toronto, he was traded to the Vancouver Canucks.

New Jersey wound up with a stunning reward two years after the deal, when they took Scott Niedermayer with the third-overall pick. He developed into an All-Star defenceman who won a Norris Trophy in 2004 and a Conn Smythe Trophy in 2007. He played on four Stanley Cup-winning teams, and with Team Canada won two Olympic gold medals and a World Championship. He might have out-Salming-ed Salming had he been a Leaf. He's in Canada's Sports Hall of Fame, the Hockey Hall of Fame and the IIHF Hall of Fame.

BULLISH ON BELLEVILLE

"YES," GORD Stellick says, "the Toronto Maple Leafs are the only team in NHL draft history to select three players from the same team in the first round."

How is that even possible?

Stellick was the Leafs' general manager at the time, so let's have him explain.

"That season, Ken Wregget, our No. 1 goaltender for about five years and one of my all-time favourites, required a change of scenery. I made it clear that we were only interested in prospects and/or draft picks in exchange for Wregget.

"The Flyers' GM, Bob Clarke, offered the most. He said, 'I know my scouts are going to kill me, but we have Calgary's first-rounder as well as our own, and I will give you those picks for Wregget.'"

The Leafs consummated the trade on March 6, a day before the NHL trade deadline. A little over two months later, the draft was held at the Met Center in Minnesota, with Toronto scheduled to select third, twelfth and twenty-first.

The Quebec Nordiques picked Mats Sundin first overall. Next up were the New York Islanders, who selected Dave Chyzowski, a winger from the Kamloops Blazers. "We really liked Chyzowski," Stellick says, "but now he was gone." So, with the third pick, the Leafs chose Scott Thornton, a forward with the Belleville Bulls of the Ontario Hockey League.

Stellick was also high on Thornton's linemate, Rob Pearson, although his durability was in doubt—he had played just twenty-six games in his first year of major junior. The Leafs were thrilled to get him with the twelfth pick.

With the final pick of the first round, Stellick chose defenceman Steve Bancroft, also of the Bulls. Jokes made the rounds that George Armstrong, then the team's head scout, had a budget that only allowed his scouts to travel as far as Belleville, which is 190 kilometres east of Toronto.

"Just before we announced the pick, we realized we were about to select a third Belleville player in the first round," said Stellick. "One of our scouts was a huge Bancroft booster, and that was a big factor in our decision."

None of the three Bulls wound up sticking with the Leafs. Thornton, who ended up playing seventeen seasons in the NHL, was traded after just thirty-three games in blue and white. Pearson made it into the lineup 192 games over three seasons before he was dealt. Bancroft was a career minor leaguer who played in six NHL games, none with Toronto.

SALMING THE SUPER SWEDE

IN JUNE of 1989, long-time Leaf defenceman Börje Salming became an unrestricted free agent. After sixteen seasons, the thirty-eight-year-old—who had recently become the NHL's oldest active player—decided it was time to move on. The offer he chose came from a Norris Division rival, the Detroit Red Wings.

At the time, Salming said he'd had enough of playing for a losing team. (Ironically, Toronto would have a .500 record in 1988–89, while Detroit finished nineteenth overall.) After forty-nine games as a Wing, he returned to Sweden.

The Leafs were blessed to have Salming on the roster. He longed for a chance to win a Stanley Cup, but accepted that it was unlikely to happen. He watched in dismay as the promising team of the late '70s was dismantled and restructured poorly.

A two-time runner-up for the Norris Trophy, Salming performed brilliantly on the Leaf blue line. He was a classy player known for his clean style and his courage. He never backed down when a game got overly physical—even when the Broad Street Bullies tried to intimidate him with hacks and whacks. There's never been another like him.

In 1996, Börje Salming was the first Swedish player inducted into the Hockey Hall of Fame. The Toronto Maple Leafs retired his number, twenty-one, in 2016, and a year later the NHL named him one of the league's one hundred greatest players of all time. Across Canada, Börje Salming is revered as one of the greatest NHL players ever.

A TOO-BRIEF MOMENT OF BRIGHTNESS

THE LEAFS closed out a dismal and forgettable decade on a bit of a high.

In 1989–90, under new coach Doug Carpenter, the Leafs enjoyed their first non-losing season since 1978–79. They broke even at 38–38–4, a giant leap forward from their 28–46–6 finish the year before and good enough for third place in the Norris Division—their highest ranking since 1983.

Newcomer Rob Ramage, a former first-overall pick obtained from the Stanley Cup champion Calgary Flames, was named team captain, a position that had been left vacant for three seasons.

With 337 goals, Toronto had the third-best offence in the NHL. Gary Leeman became the second Leaf to score fifty in one season, while three other shooters—Daniel Marois, Vincent Damphousse and Ed Olczyk—had thirty-plus. But four goalies—Allan Bester, Jeff Reese, Mark LaForest and Peter Ing—combined for a goals-against average of 4.36, third-worst in the league. Not good.

The Leafs met St. Louis in the playoffs and were eliminated in five games. A year later, after a 1–9–1 start, Carpenter was fired, replaced by Tom Watt. The team reverted to form, posting a winning percentage of .388 over the next two years and missing the playoffs both times.

NEW HEIGHTS IN THE NINETIES

BALLARD'S REIGN ENDS

ON APRIL 11, 1990, four months into the new decade, the flamboyant eighty-six-year-old owner of the Toronto Maple Leafs, died peacefully in his sleep. His body succumbed to kidney failure, a weak heart and a long-standing issue with diabetes. As team owner, he battled with his players, his own family, and members of the media, including me—although, to be honest, initially we got along. I worked for him for several months in public relations. But he sensed I did not like Punch Imlach's return and that I had great respect for Darryl Sittler as captain. Not a good combination. King Clancy was his only close friend.

Conn Smythe assumed his fabled franchise would be passed down to his son Stafford, and then to his grandson Tommy. Stafford bought the franchise from his father in 1961, but it was Ballard who drove the deal, finding a bank that delivered the money and, in 1971, establishing himself as head of the Leafs organization.

Winning hockey games was never Ballard's chief focus; increasing profits was. When the Beatles played the Gardens, he scheduled two shows instead of the agreed-upon one. And before each performance, he cut off the flow of water to the drinking fountains and charged double (some say triple) prices for soft drinks. He tossed a large portrait of Queen Elizabeth into a dumpster and replaced her special place with more seats. And at one point, he picked up an axe and threatened to cut a TV conduit line unless *Hockey Night in Canada* agreed to his demands. Many of these shenanigans were overlooked while Toronto was winning four Stanley Cups between 1962 and 1967.

Ballard's hockey teams were often dreadful, finishing at .500 or better in only six of the eighteen seasons he was the boss. They never finished higher than third in any division of the NHL. Ballard was inducted into the Hockey Hall of Fame as a builder of hockey in 1977, but he was more a spoiler of hockey, and his actions tarnished the great tradition of excellence on the ice at Maple Leaf Gardens. When someone asks why he's in the Hall of Fame as a builder of the game, nobody can explain it.

TOM WATT'S BOYHOOD DREAM

ON OCTOBER 20, 1990, Tom Watt, for years a hugely successful college coach at the University of Toronto, was hired as an assistant coach with the Toronto Maple Leafs. He took over as their thirtieth head coach just eleven games into the 1990–91 NHL season, replacing Doug Carpenter after the team got off to an abysmal 1–9–1 start.

In a previous NHL coaching stint, Watt had won the Jack Adams Award when he prodded the Winnipeg Jets to a forty-eight-point improvement—in one season! Such a surge sounds impossible, but it's true—an NHL "first."

He wouldn't have that kind of impact on the Maple Leafs, who went 52–80–17 on his watch and missed the playoffs twice.

Watt told author Kevin Shea: "My boyhood dream was to *play* for the Leafs, but I was never good enough for that. I was a coach with the University of Toronto for fourteen years, so I was considered to be old by the time I got my first job in the NHL.

"With Toronto, I had to get to the Gardens early, so I would take the subway. You know you're the coach of the Leafs when you walk onto the subway and every head turns. I would get off at Carlton

Street and people would say, 'Go get 'em, Tom!' Those were 'feel-good' moments. The fans were very positive, never negative."

ENTER FLETCHER AND GILMOUR

JUST BEFORE Harold Ballard died, businessman Donald Giffin stepped in as president of Maple Leaf Gardens. Giffin had known Ballard for decades and been a Gardens director for twenty years. And in the summer of 1991, he made a move that would change the Leafs' fortunes immensely, when he hired Cliff Fletcher.

Fletcher had led the Calgary Flames to hockey's pinnacle, a Stanley Cup title, in 1989. Could he find similar success in Toronto?

The man they called the Silver Fox served as president and general manager of the Toronto Maple Leafs. When he arrived, he inherited a team coached by Tom Watt that had gone 23–46–11 and was consigned to the basement in the Norris Division. Fletcher opted to keep Watt on as coach for the 1991–92 season.

On January 2, 1992, Fletcher made a blockbuster trade with Calgary. The Maple Leafs acquired Doug Gilmour, along with Jamie Macoun, Ric Nattress, Kent Manderville and Rick Wamsley, in exchange for Gary Leeman, Alexander Godynyuk, Jeff Reese, Michel Petit and Craig Berube. The ten-player deal was the largest in NHL history, and in time would be considered one of the most lopsided. Then, in the off-season, Fletcher hired Pat Burns to replace Tom Watt as head coach. These decisions paid off immediately as team morale soared.

In 1992–93, the Leafs set team records in wins (forty-four) and points (ninety-nine), while the awesome Gilmour emerged as a superstar, the gem of the deal, scoring a franchise-high 127 points. Gilmour finished as runner-up for the Hart Trophy and was awarded the Frank Selke Trophy as best defensive forward, while Burns won the Adams Award as coach of the year. These were the first major NHL individual awards that any Leaf player or coach had won since 1967. Fletcher was honoured as well, named Man of the Year and Executive of the Year by

The Hockey News in 1993. The word *honours* replaced a more familiar "H-word," *horrors*, in Leafland.

In 281 games behind the bench, Burns went 133–107–41, and his teams made the playoffs in each of his three full seasons. In his first two years, the Leafs reached the conference finals, falling to the LA Kings in 1993 and the Vancouver Canucks a year later. When he was let go, only Punch Imlach, Pat Quinn, Hap Day, and Dick Irvin had won more games.

Doug Gilmour, proud to wear the blue and white, entertained us with the best hockey of his career, topping one hundred points in consecutive seasons. In 1993, he followed up his record-setting regular season with thirty-five points in the playoffs. When Gilmour missed a press conference one day, Burns quipped, "Dougie's gone back to his planet to rest."

LEAFS SHOCK THE WINGS IN '93

ON MAY 1, 1993, the Maple Leafs capped a thrilling playoff upset of the 103-point Detroit Red Wings by scoring in overtime of Game 7 in the Norris Division semifinals. It was a hockey shocker.

The Leafs were led by Doug Gilmour and Nikolai Borschevsky, a previously little-known Russian rookie who finished a remarkable first season with thirty-four goals and seventy-four points. Twenty-one-year-old Félix Potvin was a revelation in goal, leading the NHL with a 2.50 goals-against average. Daren Puppa, picked up from Buffalo before the trade deadline, was a steady backup, winning six of eight games.

Dave Andreychuk, acquired from the Sabres in the same trade as Puppa, was an offensive force. In just thirty-one games, he scored twenty-five goals and thirty-eight points. But Gilmour and Wendel Clark were the players Detroit feared the most.

The series began in Detroit's Joe Louis Arena, with the Leafs losing a pair, outscored 12–5. "Looks like four straight" was the gloomy verdict of Leafs Nation.

FELIX POTVIN

But a much different team showed up on home ice. Toronto allowed only four goals in the next two tilts, and the series was tied 2–2 heading back to Detroit.

Toronto veteran Mike Foligno's overtime winner gave the Leafs a 5–4 comeback win and a 3–2 series lead. Then Detroit dominated Game 6 in Toronto, with Dino Ciccarelli's hat trick the highlight.

Late in Game 7, the Leafs were trailing, 3–2. Clark chased down a loose puck and thew it to Gilmour, who scored! Tie game, 3–3, with 2:43 left on the clock.

Then, at 2:35 of extra time, young Borschevsky tipped a pass from Bob Rouse into the Detroit net, ending the game and the series.

The Maple Leafs had done what everyone thought was impossible.

A lasting image of the series: Gilmour's play inspired Don Cherry to give him a kiss on *Hockey Night in Canada*.

A MISSED HIGH-STICK

THE 1992–93 season was a triumphant one for the Maple Leafs—until the final two playoff games, that is. The team made it to the final four, the furthest they had advanced since 1978. Their playoff run ended in a loss to Wayne Gretzky's LA Kings in Game 7, but it's what happened in Game 6 that makes Leaf fans shudder to this day.

Late in the game, Gretzky high-sticked Doug Gilmour, drawing blood. "Penalty! Penalty!" screamed the Leafs. But there was no call! Then the Leafs' Glenn Anderson took—let's call it what it was—a dumbass penalty with thirteen seconds left in the third period, and the Kings came out for the overtime with a man advantage and an unpunished opponent—the Great Gretzky—ever greedy for a goal, which he promptly scored. Of course he did. That's what he always did when he put his hockey pants on. The Kings won Game 7 by a score of 5–4, and went on to meet Montreal in the Stanley Cup Final.

"That had to be the worst-officiated game ever," Gilmour said years later in discussion with writer Dave Feschuk of the *Toronto Star*. "Not only the high stick, but all the other penalties [Kerry Fraser] missed. I can't wait to see him one day and tell him, 'Okay, you missed the high stick. That's fine. But what a bad game you reffed.'"

How come, he might have added, all four officials on the ice missed Gretzky's high stick?

Fraser admitted he didn't see it.

"I skated to my linesmen and said, 'Guys, help me out.' Rob Finn had the balls of an elephant. He said, 'Kerry, I didn't see it. I was looking through their backs.' Kevin Collins said, 'Well...I dunno.' I had to make a decision. In referee school, they hammer it into you: Call what you see. Don't guess. The honest-to-God truth is, I didn't see it. I had to eat it. I said, 'No penalty.'"

His non-call would be monumental.

Feschuk writes:

> *Gretzky was great, sure, sending L.A. to its first Stanley Cup final by playing what he has often described as the best game of his incomparable career....*
>
> *Gilmour said he still regularly meets fans who feel a need to vent their frustrations about a result that's nearly thirty years in the rear-view.*
>
> *"When I go places or do banquets, people just want to talk about 1993," Gilmour said... .*
>
> *What if Glenn Anderson hadn't been called for boarding Rob Blake with thirteen seconds remaining in regulation?...Anderson has since claimed he was used as a scapegoat by teammates in the dressing room in the wake of Game 6.*
>
> *"I know they were blaming me. They were looking for an excuse," he was quoted as saying in Damien Cox's book, The Last Good Year.*
>
> *All these years later, both Gilmour and Clark shake their heads at the memory of that call.*
>
> *"If I'm reffing, I let the teams decide it in overtime," Clark said.*

Clark played a magnificent game that night, scoring three goals, two of them late in the contest. Mike Foligno was amazed. "Wendel took over and gave us a chance to win," he said. "Yeah, it was a career game for the captain."

This Leaf club was so popular, so beloved by Leaf fans that it was feted by the City of Toronto on June 1.

"But we didn't win anything," coach Pat Burns protested.

"You won our hearts," he was told. "Be there."

He and his players were astonished when ten thousand fans showered them with affection. It was the largest gathering at City Hall since the pope's visit ten years earlier.

"I've been fortunate to be a part of two great traditions," Burns would say. "In Montreal and Toronto. You guys are the greatest."

Another strong bid for the Cup followed a year later. But Nik Borschevsky had injuries and potted only fourteen goals. He never scored again as he did in his rookie season.

A LONG WEEK IN VANCOUVER

IN 1993–94, the Leafs opened the schedule with an NHL-record ten consecutive wins, and finished in second place in the Central Division with a record of forty-three wins, twenty-nine losses and twelve ties for ninety-eight points. They ousted the Chicago Blackhawks in six games in the conference quarter-finals, then eliminated the San Jose Sharks in a seven-game conference semifinal. Then came a stumble. They opened the conference final against Vancouver with a 3–2 overtime win at the Gardens, followed by a 4–3 loss. On the West Coast, they were shut out twice before falling in double overtime in Game 5.

"We were in Vancouver for a week and lost all three games," GM Cliff Fletcher moaned. "It was the longest week of my hockey life."

But it put smiles on the faces of the New York Rangers, who captured their first Stanley Cup since 1940. Brian Leetch (thirty-four playoff points) and Mark Messier (thirty playoff points) were the dominant Rangers in their seven-game triumph over the Canucks in the finals.

Hockey Night in Canada's telecast of the deciding game attracted an average audience of 4.957 million viewers, making it the most watched program in CBC Sports history to that time.

CLARK FOR SUNDIN

DURING THOSE gloomy seasons of the Ballard era, the Leafs seldom soared. One beat writer called them "putrid." Another said they would "roll over and let you kick them in the ass, literally." The Leafs would routinely get beaten up on the ice by the quick-tempered goons who were added to rosters in the '80s.

But Wendel Clark, drafted number one by the Leafs in 1985, brought the club some muscle and much-needed backbone. Challenge him by dropping your gloves, and you might find yourself flat on your back. Clark must have been a John Ferguson fan when he was growing up in Kelvington, Saskatchewan.

With the addition of Clark, the Leafs began to look respectable again. There were even playoff games to watch. Clark's rough-and-tumble style of play endeared him to Leafs fans during the thirteen seasons he spent with the club. He captained the Leafs from 1991 to 1994, and in 1993–94 he set career highs in goals (forty-six), assists (thirty) and points (seventy-six).

But nine years of dishing out—and more important, absorbing—punishment had caught up with him. He was an old twenty-seven in the summer of 1994, when Cliff Fletcher orchestrated a deal that astonished fans of the Leafs in general and Clark in particular. He sent Clark, Sylvain Lefebvre, Landon Wilson and a first-round pick in the 1994 draft (which yielded Jeff Keatley) to Quebec, in exchange for Mats Sundin, Garth Butcher, Todd Warriner and the Nordiques' first-round pick in 1994 (the Leafs selected Nolan Baumgartner).

Basically, it was Wendel Clark for Mats Sundin. The husky, pink-cheeked kid from Sweden arrived from Quebec City wondering if

MATS SUNDIN

he could ever replace a Leaf icon like Clark. But he was coming off a monster season—114 points—and over the next thirteen seasons in Toronto, he would prove himself to be among the greatest Leaf players in history, wearing the *C* for eleven years and becoming the franchise leader in goals (420) and points (987). He led the team to the conference finals twice, and appeared in eight NHL All-Star games.

Sadly, like Clark, Sundin never got to wear a Stanley Cup ring.

Writer Mark Pare says: "You can't breathe the name Mats Sundin without thinking of something amazing he has done for this team. He didn't bring a Cup to Toronto, but his offensive skill, size and leadership qualities make him the most iconic Leaf ever."

FÉLIX THE CAT

IN 1993 Félix Potvin became the Leafs' number one goaltender after Grant Fuhr was traded to Buffalo. He backstopped the Maple Leafs to the conference finals in 1993, only to lose to the Los Angeles Kings in that bitterly fought and well-remembered seven-game series. His brilliant play made him a finalist for the Calder Trophy. And by then, he had a new nickname: "The Cat."

He was a playoff standout the following year, recording three shutouts in the first round, all by a 1–0 margin, including the final NHL game ever played at the ancient Chicago Stadium. Potvin again brought his team to the conference finals in a losing effort against the Vancouver Canucks. When the Leafs began a downhill slide, Potvin could not save them. No longer brilliant—and with knee problems—he was traded to the Islanders in January 1999.

EVERYONE LOVED BURNSIE

WELL, MAYBE that title isn't accurate. Not *everyone* loved him. Perhaps John Kordic didn't love Pat Burns after the angry coach threw an ashtray at the Habs bad boy's head and chased him from his office.

That was during Pat Burns first NHL coaching stint, in Montreal.

Kordic is alleged to have said, "The guy is crazy," as he fled the Forum.

But most everyone else in hockey who knew the former Gatineau policeman thought he was perfectly sane. Wayne Gretzky hired him to coach the junior team he owned in Gatineau. Gretzky was the first to tell him, "Pat, you'll be an NHL coach one day."

Gretzky's prediction came true in 1988–89, when Serge Savard hired Burns to coach the famous Canadiens, even though he was relatively unknown and had no NHL experience. In his first season, he took the club to the Stanley Cup Final, losing to the Calgary Flames. If he'd won the Cup, he might have dunked Kordic's head in it.

Stéphane Richer became a fifty-goal scorer under Burns in the NHL, but also played for him in junior. Richer uttered these words in praise of Burns: "Pat may have saved my life. I came from a little town in Quebec with four hundred people. If Pat hadn't got me out of my village, I don't know where I would have ended up."

Wendel Clark, a former Leafs captain, said, "Pat was a tough father figure to all the players he coached. Away from the rink, he was a totally different person. Pat was a friend to the players. Pat loved the game, loved life and all the players he coached."

In 1995–96, however, the Leafs faltered under Burns, and sixty-five games into the year, he was let go. He left amid an eight-game losing streak that dropped the Leafs to a 25–30–10 record.

Burns soon found himself coaching the Boston Bruins, and with his third team, the New Jersey Devils, he won the Stanley Cup in 2003. Three times in his career, with Montreal, Toronto and Boston, Burns would win the Jack Adams Award as the NHL's top coach.

Then came a battle with cancer.

Burns's last public appearance came in October 2010, when he attended the groundbreaking ceremony of a hockey arena to be named for him in Stanstead, Quebec.

He died on November 19, 2010, in Sherbrooke, Quebec, after the cancer spread to his lungs. He was fifty-eight.

Shortly after his funeral, thieves broke into Burns's widow's car, stealing credit cards and hockey memorabilia. Some of the items were recovered.

Pat had said, "I know my life is nearing its end and I accept that. As for my career, I always said to my kids, 'You don't cry because it's over, you're happy because it happened.' That's the main thing. I'm happy it happened."

BURNS WASN'T FIRED

AFTER THE Leafs lost in the first round of the 1995 playoffs, and followed up with a midseason slump, Coach Burns was fired. Or did he quit? It makes a difference, because there was big money at stake.

After a 4–0 defeat to the Avalanche in Denver, the team's eighth loss in a row, Burns was called to GM Cliff Fletcher's hotel room. "I didn't plan to fire him," Fletcher said later, "but he felt he'd lost the team. He looked so miserable and frustrated."

Both men became teary-eyed during their chat. They deeply respected each other. But their team had lost sixteen of their last twenty-two games. By letting Burns quit, Fletcher was granting him a full season's salary—$850,000.

"I loved Pat Burns," Fletcher said.

The coach's departure was a well-kept secret—at least for a few hours. Back in Toronto, Burns drove to the Gardens and stood behind the Leaf bench for a few moments. Then packed a few belongings and drove to Kingston, where he phoned Fletcher.

"You can tell the media guys I'm gone, Cliff."

His leaving drew a nod of approval, if not a cheer, from a few of the players. Most others, like Gilmour, were saddened.

Fletcher named Nick Beverley as interim coach, and somehow the club slipped into a playoff spot on the final day of the season. The Leafs played their last playoff series at Maple Leaf Gardens against St. Louis, losing four games to two in the conference quarter-finals.

For a last few words about Pat Burns, we bring in Gare Joyce, author of *Young Leafs* and a young beat writer for the *Globe and Mail* at the time.

"With the possible exception of Doug Gilmour and Wendel Clark, Burns was Joe Toronto's favourite Leaf. Everyone recognized his glower, his menace enough to make house plants wilt. Everyone knew his backstory, the ex-cop who made good in the game. He was an iron fist in a mitten knitted with razor wire, cruel but fair. Doubtless, he was a despot. But he was our despot."

MURPHY WAS A SHORT-TERM COACH

PRIOR TO the 1996–97 season, assistant coach Mike Murphy was promoted, replacing Nick Beverley as head coach. Despite a lineup that boasted stars like Doug Gilmour, Mats Sundin, Larry Murphy, Kirk Muller and the reacquired Wendel Clark, his team was impotent, finishing in the Central Division cellar and missing the playoffs for the first time since 1992. General manager Cliff Fletcher was let go at the end of the season, bringing to a close the most successful Leaf era since the late 1970s.

Ken Dryden took over as GM in 1997–98, but the Leafs' on-ice fortunes were no better, and Murphy's coaching stint came to an end. He went on to better things; in the summer of 1999 he accepted the position of the NHL's senior vice-president and director of hockey operations, a job he held for twenty-three years.

THE GARDENS SEX ABUSE SCANDAL

JOHN MCCARTHY shudders at some of his teenage memories from the 1980s.

In 1979, at age fourteen, McCarthy helped his single mother as she struggled to raise a large family. When he needed time to play, there was a rink in downtown Toronto where he played shinny with his pals. That's where he met a man named Gordon Stuckless, who claimed he worked at Maple Leaf Gardens. Stuckless took McCarthy on a tour of the Gardens and handed him tickets to hockey games.

McCarthy says, "Stuckless and two other Gardens employees would often lure me into locker rooms where they'd have sex with me. It happened a lot. And people at the Gardens knew all about it."

Other young boys suffered the same fate, but the victims kept the Gardens' secret. Finally, Martin Kruze, at thirty-four, became the first victim to tell his story. His account led to the arrests in 1997 of Stuckless, forty-seven, and John Paul Roby, fifty-four, a part-time usher. Both were charged with gross indecency and indecent assault.

I knew Roby by sight, and George Hannah from coffee-shop sessions. Hannah was a former equipment manager with the junior Marlboros who died in 1984. I was shocked to learn he was involved in the scandal.

One of the victims testified: "Owner Harold Ballard would often walk by as Hannah and a group of kids were coming out of the team sauna naked—even though the teens had no good reason for being there."

McCarthy and Kruze blamed their drug addiction and alcohol consumption on guilt and depression that they suggest were caused by their abusers—Stuckless, Hannah and Roby.

Stuckless was convicted on twenty-two counts of indecent assault and two of sexual assault. When a judge handed him a sentence of two years less a day, the sense of injustice was too much for Kruze. On October 30, 1997, he jumped from the Prince Edward Viaduct, the bridge that spans Toronto's Don Valley, ending his life.

GOODBYE MLG, HELLO ACC

THE 1997–98 season was Toronto's last full season playing at Maple Leaf Gardens. In February 1999, the club would move a mile down Yonge Street to their new digs at the Air Canada Centre.

Air Canada purchased the naming rights to the arena for US$30 million over a twenty-year term. While a number of nicknames for the building were coined, most notably "The Hangar," it became best known by its initials, ACC.

The ACC had a seating capacity of 18,800 for hockey—over three thousand more than the Gardens held—and standing room for several hundred more. Remarkably, the ACC wasn't originally designed with the Leafs in mind; it was conceived as the home of the NBA's Toronto Raptors. The Raptors invited the Leafs to come onboard with them, but owner Steve Stavro had his heart set on a hockey palace all his own. Then, in 1998, Stavro and his backers ended up buying the Raptors, and decided the ACC was just the home his Leafs were looking for after all. Plans were modified to accommodate a rink.

In 2018, the building got a new name, the Scotiabank Arena, after the Bank of Nova Scotia signed a twenty-year sponsorship deal worth $800 million—more than twenty times what Air Canada had paid. Neither Conn Smythe nor Harold Ballard—nor anybody else—could ever have envisioned such mind-boggling revenues.

Your author takes some pride in convincing Scotiabank of hockey's importance to Canadians when he sold them on the concept of the Scotiabank Hockey College in 1971. With this program, kids who opened a bank account could pick up a monthly hockey-themed magazine when they stopped by their local branch. They learned about the game and about the importance of saving money. The Hockey College lasted almost twenty years. I served as dean and founder, and a number of luminaries got involved, including Jean Béliveau, Gordie Howe, Howie Meeker, Darryl Sittler and the immortal Peter Puck.

Before I met with Scotiabank, I was told by a businessman whose advice I respected, "Why take it to Scotiabank? They have no money. And they don't have the least interest in hockey."

And in time, they did show enough interest—and coughed up enough money—to make Air Canada's deal look like chicken feed when it came to arena naming rights!

ANNE MURRAY SINGS

IN A postgame ceremony at the closing of the Gardens, Canadian singer Anne Murray performed "The Maple Leaf Forever" while wearing a Toronto jersey. If Anne wasn't the team's biggest fan, she might have been the most famous. She told me on *Hockey Night in Canada* that she tried to purchase the Leafs in the early 1980s with an offer of $64 million. Harold Ballard scoffed at her proposal.

Both Harold and Anne would be amazed at what the club is worth today.

In 2022, the Sportico website valued the Maple Leafs at US$2.12 billion—$110 million more than the second-place New York Rangers.

When Anne Murray was on tour, she had the Leafs' playoff games taped and air-mailed to her so she could view them the next day. Her band members were sworn to silence when it came to discussing the scores.

When I asked her who the anthem singer might be if she ever acquired the Leafs, she replied, "Why, I'll sing it myself."

MIKE MYERS LOVED THE LEAFS

LET'S END the decade—and century—with a few words from a staunch Leafs fan, actor and comedian Mike Myers.

Myers performed with his Second City pals on a *Hockey Night in Canada* intermission segment I produced, and he was hilarious. He did spot-on impressions of Howie Meeker and Danny Gallivan, and introduced Canadians to one of his signature characters, Wayne Campbell, years before "Wayne's World" became a recurring sketch on *Saturday Night Live*.

In one of his chats, he talked of his love for the Leafs. "Some of my earliest memories are of my love for the name 'Leafs.' I loved that name and that the Leafs wear blue. I loved the little maple leaf the players wore on the shoulders of their sweaters. I loved Maple Leaf Gardens, the Gardens marquee and Doug Laurie Sporting Goods off the lobby.

I loved *Hockey Night in Canada*'s broadcast booth—the gondola—which was suspended from the Gardens ceiling, fifty-six feet above the ice. I loved the *HNiC* theme and 'Coach's Corner' with Don Cherry."

That love of the team was evident in his 1997 comedy movie *Austin Powers: International Man of Mystery*, which included three characters—Commander Gilmour, General Borschevsky and General Clark—named after stars on the Leaf teams of the early 1990s.

I was proud of the feature with Myers and suggested we have him back one day. But my boss, Ted Hough, said, "Don't bother. He's not funny."

FROM FIRST NIGHT TO FINAL WHISTLE

THE CLOSING of Maple Leaf Gardens brought tears to the eyes of devoted fan Tom Gaston, then eighty-four, the Leafs' longest-tenured season ticket holder. Gaston was at the very first game played in Maple Leaf Gardens in 1931, and had been to every one of the Maple Leafs' opening nights since. He watched the Toronto franchise play in nine different decades, in three arenas—he'd even seen them play at the Mutual Street Arena as a boy. He followed them through eleven Stanley Cup victories.

Tom passed away in January 2002.

Leafs historian Mike Wilson recalled his first game, and walking through the turnstiles. "All you'd hear was 'popcorn, programs, cold drinks.' Then you'd walk through a small tunnel and stop and say, 'Wow!' There was all that space and colour. It overwhelmed you. As a kid, you're thinking, 'Is this real?' And you could hear pucks hitting the sticks, the grinding skates, shots off the boards."

Celeste D'Agostino began as an usherette in the '70s.

"I went down expecting a formal interview. The woman said, 'Girl, here's a uniform. If it fits, the job's yours.' Well, it fit. When I started it was a dress with a jacket, a pillbox hat and white gloves.

"Walt McKechnie, one of the Leafs, asked me why all the girls were wearing white gloves. I said, 'It means they're all virgins.'

"I cried most of that final day—February 13, 1999. I'd been here such a long time. But I got to escort Mush March out on the ice. The ninety-one-year-old scored the first goal in Gardens history—for Chicago."

An usher said, "There was a couple doing the wild thing up in a private box the other night. I guess they wanted to say they were the last to do it at the Gardens."

Former Leaf GM Gord Stellick said, "Every night was magic. I had a key that opened the building door and one that opened the dressing room door. I was the youngest GM at thirty, and it wasn't long before I became the youngest ex-GM at thirty-one."

Here are some others who shared their Gardens memories.

Mike Murphy: Former Player and Coach

What a thrill to be there at any time. My dad had season's tickets and at least once was able to squeeze me and my sister into one seat. It made you appreciate what the team meant to everyone.

Bob Haggert: Team Trainer in the 1950s and '60s

For years, my mother made cakes and coffee for the media in a room next to the Leafs' dressing room. All the great names in sports journalism and broadcasting gathered there at intermissions. But you'd seldom see Foster Hewitt there. Or Bill Hewitt. They stayed in the background. Foster would climb to the gondola and say, "Hello, hockey fans in Canada and the United States," give the lineup changes and go to the national anthems. After the game, he'd go home. The Leaf players never saw the Hewitts.

Paul Patskou: Film Archivist

In the beginning, player Hap Day had a drugstore in a corner of the Gardens. And there was a coffee shop where so many hockey deals were done. Punch Imlach couldn't get in the building on his first day because nobody knew who he was. I like the story about King Clancy coming over from the old Mutual Street Arena to see the Gardens under construction. He'd shake his head and say, "Where they gonna find enough people to fill this place?"

Casey Kelly: Red Kelly's Daughter

Mr. Ballard used to give me ice time once a week to practice my figure skating. And he let my mom put on a charity ice show. That was after my dad was no longer coaching, so Mr. Ballard did have his good side.

Jimmy Holmstrom: Organist

When Wendel Clark came back after his trade to Quebec, I played a cassette of the *Welcome Back Kotter* theme. There were tears in everyone's eyes, even Wendel's. It was the best moment of my life, even though I'm paid to make people stomp and clap.

Harry Sinden: Long-time Boston Bruins Coach and GM

Leaf fans booed Bobby from the start, but I knew how good he was. We eliminated the Leafs four straight in the '69 playoffs, and I was walking to our room with Punch Imlach just ahead of me. I saw Stafford Smythe rush up and say, "Punch, you're through." I was elated we'd won, but stunned that a guy like Punch was suddenly fired. Fired for all to see. Right in the corridor. "Punch, you're through," he was told.

Wayne Gillespie: Building Superintendent

For games and concerts, we trusted everyone, but we put tamperproof screws in the back of those old hockey photos in the lobby. Just in case. I must say, we could have the raunchiest rock and roll shows there, but young people treated those pictures with reverence.

Leaf fan Mike Shea shared an odd memory: "In the '70s, we had golds behind the Leafs bench. They were great, but who could forget taking a leak in that big trough in the men's washroom? Whatever happened to that trough? And where did all that piss go?"

Mike, the trough was bought by a farmer who used it to water and feed his pigs. Like you, I was standing at that trough once as an inquisitive ten-year-old, probably wondering where all that piss went.

The Leafs played their last game at Maple Leaf Gardens on February 13, 1999, a 6–2 loss to Chicago. The Hawks' Bob Probert scored the final goal in Gardens history. A week later, on February 21, the first game at the new Air Canada Centre was played. It was against the Canadiens, won by the Leafs, 3–2, on an overtime goal by Steve Thomas.

Three memorable on-ice events come to mind when I think of the hundreds of nights I spent covering Leaf games at the Gardens. All three held the element of complete surprise: the last Stanley Cup championship in 1967, Pete Mahovlich's spectacular goal against the Soviets in Game 2 of the Summit Series in 1972 and Darryl Sittler's remarkable ten-point night against Boston in 1976.

There are many bigger, fancier, more glamorous hockey arenas around, but there was no place quite like Maple Leaf Gardens.

SKATING INTO A NEW CENTURY

A SIZZLING START

AS THE 1990s drew to a close, the Toronto Maple Leafs not only had a sparkling new home in the Air Canada Centre, but a new coach, Pat Quinn, and a new goaltender, Curtis Joseph. Quinn's career as a hard-hitting NHL defenceman had begun in Toronto in 1968–69, and as a coach he had taken the Philadelphia Flyers and Vancouver Canucks to the Stanley Cup Final. Joseph was a finalist for the Vézina Trophy in 1992–93.

The moves paid off right away, as the Leafs jumped from sixty-nine points to ninety-seven in 1998–99, setting a franchise record with forty-five wins. They eliminated Philadelphia and Pittsburgh in the playoffs before falling to Buffalo in the Eastern Conference final.

The 1999–2000 edition of the team got off to a fast start, en route to another forty-five-win season. This time, they racked up one hundred points for the first time ever, and finished atop the Northeast Division, which was akin to them landing on the moon. First place had eluded them since the 1962–63 season. In the playoffs, they defeated Ottawa in the first round, but the New Jersey Devils eliminated them in six games in the conference semifinals.

Just after the season's midpoint, the Leafs brought back a familiar face. Former team captain Wendel Clark had been released by the

CURTIS JOSEPH

Chicago Blackhawks, and Toronto signed him as a free agent.

It was Clark's third stint in the blue and white. After nine seasons of stability with the Leafs, the left winger's career had taken some twists and turns, to Quebec, Long Island, Toronto again, Tampa Bay, Detroit, and finally Chicago.

After appearing in twenty regular-season games and six of the team's twelve playoff matches, he said, "I'm done, guys," and shook hands with his mates.

DOMI'S DUMB PENALTY

FOR THE second time in as many years, the Leafs' 2000–01 season ended with a second-round defeat to the well-coached, well-balanced New Jersey Devils. This year, a bonehead decision by Tie Domi played a role.

Trailing the Devils two games to one in the Eastern Conference semifinals, the Leafs found themselves in a must-win situation heading into Game 4 on home ice. They took a 3–1 lead into the third period, and as the clock ticked down, a series-tying victory was within their grasp. Then, in a few agonizing moments, tough little Tie Domi suffered the worst brain cramp of his career. He was enjoying one of his best games—and he knew it. In less than twenty seconds, he knew he was going to be named the game's first star. He'd bask in a thunderous ovation.

Bu suddenly, he became unfocused.

With eight seconds to play, Domi saw the Devils' Scott Niedermayer skating close by. Sticks were raised and Domi was bloodied. There was no penalty, and Niedermayer laughed at him. So, Domi raced after Niedermayer and threw an elbow. When Niedermayer's head hit the boards, the Devils' star defenceman collapsed and lay unconscious. Domi fans were silenced. Their hero had crossed a line, and everybody saw it. Niedermayer was out for the remainder of the series. Within hours, Colin Campbell, the NHL's police chief, suspended Domi for the rest of the playoffs.

The Devils regrouped and outscored the Leafs 9–3 over the next three games. Toronto was eliminated in Game 7 in a 5–1 Devils romp.

The Devils reached the Stanley Cup Final in 2001, but lost in seven games to the Colorado Avalanche. Niedermayer's absence left a huge void—he was always a difference maker, a leader. With him in the mix, the Devils might have won their third Stanley Cup in seven years.

Domi held a news conference in an effort to explain his rash attack. He said he tried to apologize to Niedermayer, who was not overly impressed. The Devils' star shrugged and turned away. It was really difficult for him to forgive a blatant attack that robbed him of a chance to lift another Stanley Cup.

Domi would say, "That was the stupidest thing that I did. It's my biggest ever regret. I wish I'd stayed cool, stayed in that series. I could have made the difference. Instead, I let my team down."

QUINN GETS MOGILNY

PRIOR TO the 2001–02 regular season, the Leafs signed pure scorer Alex Mogilny, who was coming off a forty-three-goal season with the New Jersey Devils, to a four-year deal worth a reported $22 million. Mogilny had once enjoyed a seventy-six-goal season with Buffalo, his first club. For coach Pat Quinn, he would tally fifty-seven points in sixty-six games as a Leaf newcomer. The following season, Mogilny led the team with seventy-nine points, while Mats Sundin settled for seventy-two.

It baffles me that Mogilny has been overlooked for years by the Hockey Hall of Fame. Look at his career stats compared to recently enshrined forwards.

PLAYER	GP	G	A	P
Alex Mogilny	990	473	559	1032
Daniel Alfredsson	1246	444	713	1157
Guy Carbonneau	1318	260	403	663
Martin St. Louis	989	402	587	989

Mogilny has often been called the first player from the Soviet Union to play in the NHL. In 1989, he risked his life to join the Sabres as a twenty-year-old, setting the stage for others to follow.

But he was not the first. On the day that Wayne Gretzky joined the Kings, in Los Angeles, I met a forgotten Russian player—Viktor Nechayev—who was married to an American. Nechayev was with a film crew, helping capture Gretzky's debut in LA.

In 1982, at age twenty-seven, Nechayev played three games with the Kings and scored one goal, which means *he* was the first Russian in the NHL. Or, to be more specific, the first Russian-*trained* player. Dave "Sweeney" Schriner, whose family emigrated from the Russian Empire to Canada when he was still a baby, played six seasons for the Leafs in the 1940s and lifted the Stanley Cup twice. There was also Johannes (Johnny) Gottselig, a two-time Cup winner with Chicago in the '30s, who emigrated to Canada from Ukraine (then part of the Russian Empire) as a lad. Both of these players learned their hockey in Canada, however.

CUJO WAS A SURVIVOR

IN 1997–98, goaltender Curtis Joseph put in a solid season with the Edmonton Oilers, then signed with the Toronto Maple Leafs in the off-season. Joseph, nicknamed "Cujo," would be a force for Toronto over the next few seasons and deserves Hall of Fame consideration for his brilliant nineteen-year career.

In 2001–02, despite setting a career-best 2.23 goals-against average, Joseph's time in Toronto was ending. He and Leafs coach/general manager Pat Quinn couldn't agree on the terms of a new contract. Cujo would sign with the Detroit Red Wings that summer.

He would return to the Toronto Maple Leafs in a backup role in 2008–09, before retiring at the age of forty-one.

He was one of the best goaltenders in the NHL in an era when many of the greatest goaltenders of all time played (Martin Brodeur, Patrick Roy, Dominik Hašek, Ed Belfour and others).

Joseph was the first goalie in NHL history to win thirty games in a season for five different teams. Though he never got his teams to a Stanley Cup Final, he finished his NHL career with 454 wins. At the time, he trailed only Brodeur, Roy and Belfour, and through 2023–24, still ranks seventh in NHL history.

He was adored by Leafs fans, and he beat long odds to make it to the NHL. He was never drafted, and didn't play major junior hockey. But those facts are not what truly set him apart.

"I had a weird life," he writes in his autobiography. "Two moms, three dads and I grew up in a home full of mentally ill patients run by a crazy person. The last thing anybody expected was that I would someday make a living from hockey." Cujo's home was a "rehab centre" north of Toronto. His adoptive mother ran the place. An addict, she was unstable and left him to fend for himself. His surname was Munro for the first twenty years of his life.

He was always hungry, and his bed was a mattress on the floor. His mother's cats used it as a litter box. "Mom treated her animals better than she treated her kids," he writes.

SIX SHOTS IN A GAME

ON MAY 8, 2000, the Toronto Maple Leafs set an NHL record, but not one that anybody would point to with pride.

Coming off their first-ever hundred-point season, the Leafs were viewed as a contender for the Stanley Cup. After dispatching the Ottawa Senators in six games in the first round, they met the New Jersey Devils in the conference semifinals. Facing elimination in Game 6, the Leafs—one of the highest-scoring teams in the NHL that season—could muster only six shots on goalie Martin Brodeur.

The Elias Sports Bureau reported that no team had taken fewer shots in a game since the start of the expansion era in 1967–68.

The Leafs had had better luck on March 4, 1999, when they travelled to St. Louis to play the Blues. On that night, they won 4–0, even though they took only nine shots on goal—the fewest ever by a winning team. Steve Sullivan, Mats Sundin, Lonny Bohonos and Gary Valk were the scorers. The Blues fired twenty-eight shots at Curtis Joseph, who earned the shutout.

JFJ BECOMES GM

ON AUGUST 29, 2003, with training camp looming, the Leafs introduced John Ferguson Jr. as the team's twelfth general manager. The thirty-six-year-old had been an agent and a scout before joining the St. Louis Blues' front office in 1997. His selection was immediately questioned by members of the media, who suggested that Ferguson's lack of management experience made his hiring a gamble.

Ferguson's subsequent decisions involving signings, trades and draft choices—and the dismissal of popular Pat Quinn as coach—would make his own future rather tenuous.

Ferguson's first season at the helm seemed promising. In 2003–04, the Leafs accumulated a franchise-record 103 points and finished second in the Northeast Division with a record of forty-five wins, twenty-four losses, ten ties and three overtime losses. This was a top offensive team, sniping the fourth most goals in the NHL. Stable goaltending was provided by veteran netminder Eddie Belfour, but it soon became obvious the team needed a steadier backup than either of Trevor Kidd or Mikael Tellqvist.

"JFJ" made a couple of decent trades, sending some prospects to New York for future Hall of Fame defenceman Brian Leetch, and six days later, picking up another Hall of Famer in waiting, centreman Ron Francis, from the Carolina Hurricanes for a fourth-round pick.

Leetch scored fifteen points in fifteen games, while Francis managed ten in twelve. But Francis retired at the season's end, while Leetch became a free agent and signed a one-year contract with Bruins before retiring.

Belfour's strong season carried the Leafs to a playoff position, and their opponents in the first round were the Ottawa Senators. The series went the full seven games, meaning that the "Battle of Ontario"—being waged for the fourth time in five seasons—lived up to its name.

Belfour delivered three shutouts as the Leafs advanced to the conference semifinals. The Leafs and Philadelphia Flyers each won two of the first four games, but the Flyers waltzed to a 7–2 victory in Game 5. In Game 6, Toronto forced overtime with a pair of third-period goals, but Darcy Tucker was penalized in extra time for a nasty hit on Sami Kapanen, and moments later Jeremy Roenick buried the winner.

The Leafs missed the playoffs in the next two seasons, which ultimately cost Ferguson his job in January 2008. In fact, they did not qualify for the playoffs again until 2012–13, and would not make it past the first round of the playoffs until 2022–23.

A SEASON CANCELLED

IN SEPTEMBER of 2004, the agreement between the NHL and its players association expired, and because attempts to negotiate a new deal had not succeeded, the owners locked out the players. The impasse ultimately meant an entire season's worth of NHL games were cancelled. And, for the first time since 1919, the Stanley Cup was not awarded.

Never before had a major North American professional sports league erased a full season because of labour squabbles.

A new agreement was finally signed in July of 2005, and with it came a salary cap, which would pose a huge problem for many teams, especially the Leafs. Previously, there had been no limit on how much a club could pay its players; now, they were allowed to spend $39 million in 2005–06, which required the Leafs to shed more than a third of their $62.5 million payroll. As a result, seventeen players left the team over the next two seasons, including five of their top ten scorers during the 2004 playoffs.

RASK WAS A GEM, BUT WHO COULD'VE KNOWN?

AT THE 2005 NHL Entry Draft in Ottawa, the Leafs used the twenty-first-overall pick to draft a promising Finnish goaltender, Tuukka

Rask. Rask would go on to enjoy a career that will probably earn him a Hall of Fame berth one day. But not as a Leaf. In no time, general manager John Ferguson Jr. shunted Rask off to Boston, where he became a huge star, in return for goalie Andrew Raycroft, a Calder Trophy winner who flopped in the blue and white—as did Justin Pogge, another Leaf netminding hopeful. The trade for Raycroft rates high on my list of worst Leaf trades ever.

LEAFS SIGN LINDROS, THEN MISS THE PLAYOFFS

WHEN PLAY resumed in 2005–06, there was a new face in the lineup. Eric Lindros, by now a thirty-two-year-old veteran, signed a one-year deal with the Leafs. He got off to a solid start, scoring seven goals in his first eight games, but wrist injuries limited him to thirty-three games, and he finished with eleven goals and eleven assists. In the off-season, he signed with Dallas.

Mats Sundin was struck in the eye by a puck on opening night and was sidelined for a month. Even so, he finished with thirty-one goals and forty-seven assists for seventy-eight points, three more than in 2003–04 and ten more than any other Maple Leaf that season.

The Leafs finished the regular season with a 41–33–8 record for ninety points, two points behind the Tampa Bay Lightning, who captured the eighth spot in the Eastern Conference. Because of their ninth-place finish, the Leafs missed the playoffs for the first time since 1998. There was a big "if only"—as in, if only they hadn't been traumatized by their divisional rivals, the Ottawa Senators, against whom they went 1–5–2 in eight meetings.

KEON WAS FINALLY COAXED

IN FEBRUARY 1999, former Leafs began reaching out to the team's seldom-seen one-time captain, Dave Keon. The final game at Maple Leaf Gardens would soon be played and all living alumni were invited.

George Armstrong begged Keon to put aside old grievances and fly up from his Florida home to be honoured. But the number one Leaf of all time could not be persuaded and turned down all entreaties. The memorable night carried on without him.

Keon has good reasons for his estrangement—or at least, he thinks he has.

From all appearances, Harold Ballard treated him abysmally, so snubbing the team during those years was understandable.

Keon would have a change of heart, but not for years—not until he was invited to take part in a ceremony for the fortieth anniversary of the 1967 Stanley Cup team. That was at the Air Canada Centre on February 17, 2007.

Keon received an extended standing ovation. He said he was "very happy. I was very appreciative of the people—they've always been very good to me."

Bob Pulford said, "Seeing him come back and get the recognition he deserves is a wonderful thing."

"It's nice that he's dropped the resentment," Pete Stemkowski, a former Maple Leaf centre, said. "I told him that all the people he was fighting with are dead, so let's get back to Toronto and get on with it. Now he's back and he's happy to be one of the boys, and he doesn't want to be the centre of attention. It's great to see him."

LEAFS MISS BY A SINGLE POINT

ON JANUARY 4, 2007, the Maple Leafs walloped the Boston Bruins 10–2, with Alex Steen scoring a hat trick. It was the first time in nearly a year that an NHL team had scored ten goals in a regular-season game—since January 14, 2006, when the Buffalo Sabres defeated the Los Angeles Kings 10–1.

In a bid to keep their opponents from running up the score, Toronto signed thirty-two-year-old Mike Peca, a two-time winner of the Frank Selke Trophy as the NHL's top defensive forward. Like Eric Lindros the year before, Peca's tenure as a Leaf was cut short by injury—Peca broke his leg in a December game and missed the rest of the season.

The Leafs finished in third place in the Northeast Division, but failed to qualify for the playoffs. On the last day of the regular season, the New York Islanders defeated the New Jersey Devils 3–2 in a shootout, clinching the eighth and final playoff spot. Toronto missed out on the postseason by a single point.

KABERLE'S ALL-STAR SHOTS WERE A HIGHLIGHT

WHEN ONE of the high points of a hockey season is a player hitting all four targets in a shooting contest at the All-Star skills competition, perhaps it's an indicator that the club is not enjoying a banner season.

Leaf defenceman Tomáš Kaberle was a perfect four-for-four in the first round of the shooting accuracy contest in Atlanta in January 2008. In the final round, he beat out the Nashville Predators' Jason Arnott. Ironically, Kaberle wasn't known for his shot. Fans at the ACC were known to chant, "Shoot! Shoot!" whenever the blueliner had the puck in the offensive zone.

In a bid to get back into playoff contention in 2007–08, the Leafs acquired goaltender Vesa Toskala from the San Jose Sharks. He quickly supplanted Andrew Raycroft as the team's number one netminder. Winger Mark Bell was also part of that deal, but his debut in the blue and white would be delayed, because a drunk-driving charge prompted the NHL to suspend him for fifteen games. He ended up playing just thirty-five games, scoring four goals.

Free agent Jason Blake was signed to a five-year, $20 million contract. He was coming off a forty-goal season with the Islanders, and had averaged twenty-five in the three seasons before that, so hopes were high. But on the eve of the season, the winger announced that doctors had diagnosed him with chronic myelogenous leukemia, a treatable form of cancer. While undergoing treatment, he played in all eighty-two games. But although he shot the puck a career-high 332 times, he beat opposing goalies only fifteen times. His performance earned him the Bill Masterton Memorial Trophy. And a year later, his scoring touch returned: he scored twenty-five goals.

In mid-November, Leaf rookie Jiří Tlustý was caught in a scandal when nude photos of him appeared on the internet. The nineteen-year-old apologized and admitted that he had used poor judgment. He scored ten goals in that season, but never scored another in two stints amounting to sixteen games while wearing blue and white. Traded to Carolina, he scored eighty-nine career goals in a nine year career. All of them, we assume, while fully clothed in his hockey gear.

With the Leafs struggling to avoid last place in the Northeast Division, club president Richard Peddie admitted that hiring John Ferguson Jr. had been "a mistake." So, management asked former GM Cliff Fletcher to take over on an interim basis. On January 22, Ferguson's time with the club ended and Fletcher earned some office space—and a whole lot of money.

The Leafs missed the playoffs again, meaning there was little to look back on but Kaberle's straight shooting at the All-Star break. Tlustý's internet photos were long forgotten.

BURKE BUILDS A CASE

WHEN THE Leafs gathered for training camp in 2008, it was without Bryan McCabe, Darcy Tucker, Kyle Wellwood, Andrew Raycroft and long-time captain Mats Sundin. There was a new coach, in Ron Wilson, and a new/old backup goalie in forty-one-year-old Curtis Joseph. Besides Cujo, much of Toronto's roster was short on experience and talent, and expectations were low. Those expectations would be met.

In November, Brian Burke turned down the Anaheim Ducks' offer of a contract extension, and they concluded that if he wasn't going to stay beyond the end of the 2008–09 season, they might as well cut him loose immediately. A couple of weeks later, he joined the Maple Leafs as president and general manager. "Burkie" didn't make sweeping changes to the front office, but he did bring in Dave Poulin (an excellent hire), Dave Nonis (who travelled with him) and Claude Loiselle (a smart, talented guy).

"I kept Ron Wilson as coach," he says. "My college teammate at Providence, even though I knew he wasn't the right fit. He'd been beaten up so badly by the media, he'd become sour, jaded and sarcastic."

On the final day of March 2009, the Leafs were mathematically eliminated from the playoffs with six games yet to be played. They ended the season with thirty-four wins in eighty-two games.

In the last three seasons of the "aughts," the Leafs needed a revolving door in their locker room. They employed thirty-five players in 2007–08, thirty-nine in '08–09, and thirty-eight in '09–10. By comparison, in the NHL's first season, 1917–18, Toronto used fourteen players. In one game, the Blueshirts and Ottawa Senators iced exactly six players—every man on the ice performed for the full sixty minutes. I couldn't find anyone who saw that game, but I'm guessing all the players were sliding around on their knees at the finish.

A BAFFLING LACK OF PLAYOFF SUCCESS

BURKE LANDS KESSEL AND PHANEUF

AFTER THE John Ferguson Jr. era proved to be a flop, there was plenty of pressure on Leafs brass to hire a replacement who oozed hockey smarts, a puck professor who could take the team back to the heights it had scaled in its glory days of the 1960s.

Glory days? Was that even conceivable?

In November 2008, the club believed it had secured just such a leader when it hired Brian Burke, who had won the Cup with Anaheim in 2007.

The Leafs brass wanted to know how long it would take Burke to put together a contending team.

"Five years," he told them. "It will take me two years to shovel out the stable so I can bring in some fresh horses."

Then Burke asked *them* a question. "I want to know if you plan to sell the team and that Richard Peddie will still be involved [as CEO of Maple Leaf Sports & Entertainment]. He's a real force."

"Brian, we make $80 million a season. Why would we sell? There's no chance we'll do that."

So, Burke signed on. By the middle of his fourth year as GM, Peddie was gone and the Leafs' parent company was up for sale.

In September 2009, Brian Burke made a splash by trading away two first-round draft picks, plus a second-rounder, to the Boston Bruins for winger Phil Kessel. The twenty-one-year-old had just enjoyed a breakout season, scoring thirty-six goals. It was a bold move, at what many considered to be a massive cost.

Kessel gave the Leafs plenty of offence, slamming in thirty goals to justify his new five-year, $27 million contract. But when the draft choices the Leafs gave up to get him yielded high-scoring forward Tyler Seguin and defenceman Doug Hamilton, both VIPs (very important players), Leafs Nation wondered if the deal should have been consummated in the first place.

On January 31, 2010, Burke made two more daring deals. From the Flames, he acquired defenceman Dion Phaneuf, who blossomed in blue and white and became hugely popular. Then Burke sent two players who had lost their way—goalie Vesa Toskala and forward Jason Blake—to the Anaheim Ducks for goalie Jean-Sébastien Giguère.

Giguère posted shutouts in his first two starts, and the Leafs played .500 hockey for the rest of the season, but the damage had already been done. This edition of the team won just thirty games, finishing dead last in the East—twenty-ninth of thirty teams overall. Their power-play and penalty-killing units were both the worst in the league.

In June, Dion Phaneuf, then twenty-five, was named Leafs captain—filling a void that had existed for two years, since Mats Sundin's departure—and wore the *C* through a tumultuous six-year stretch that brought just one postseason berth.

Brian Burke says, "I loved Dion as a player. I thought he was fabulous. But I did not like the team I inherited here. I couldn't stand watching Toskala play anymore."

Burke said he truly believed he'd put together a promising squad. And there was improvement in 2010–11, as the team put up thirty-seven wins. The Leafs burst out of the gate in 2011–12, winning seven of their first ten games, and they were a few games over .500 as late as February 6. But they went into a tailspin, losing ten of their next eleven, and on March 2, Burke fired coach Ron Wilson. A few months earlier, the GM had generously given his college pal a questionable contract extension. Wilson must have been happy with the extension and the additional salary it brought, but we may never know.

He decided to cut off all contact with Burke after his dismissal. On his watch, the Leafs won just forty-two percent of their games.

Wilson was replaced by another Leaf from the 1970s, Randy Carlyle, who also had a history with Burke: together, they had guided the Ducks to their 2007 Stanley Cup championship. Toronto was five points out of a playoff spot at the time of the coaching change; they went 6–9–3 the rest of the way and ended up twelve points back of Washington.

In 2012, the NHL locked out its players for the third time in Gary Bettman's nineteen-year tenure as commissioner. A settlement was reached in January, with teams playing a forty-eight-game regular-season schedule, as they had in 1994–95. Days after the new collective bargaining agreement was signed, the Leafs—the only team that had not made the playoffs even once since the 2004–05 lockout—fired Brian Burke. Assistant GM Dave Nonis took his place.

Burke stayed around as senior advisor to MLSE president Tom Anselmi, but he no longer had anything to do with hockey matters. And in September, he joined the Calgary Flames as president of hockey operations.

Under Nonis and Carlyle, the Leafs had a winning record (26–17–5) and finally made it to the playoffs. Brace yourself as we look back on their first-round series against the Bruins.

A MIND-BOGGLING BREAKDOWN

IN THE 2013 playoffs, the Leafs drew the fifth seed, which paired them with Northeast Division rivals the Boston Bruins in the first round. Boston had won three of the four regular-season meetings, but had only outscored Toronto 10–7.

The Bruins took Game 1 at TD Garden by a 4–1 score, but Toronto came back to tie the series at one. At the Air Canada Centre, the Leafs fired forty-seven shots at Tuukka Rask, but came out on the wrong end of a 5–2 decision. Two nights later, the Bruins pulled ahead three games to one on David Krejčí's overtime goal.

But the Leafs weren't done yet. They pulled off back-to-back 2–1 victories to tie the series and force a deciding game in Boston.

Little-used defenceman Matt Bartkowski opened the scoring, but a pair of goals by Cody Franson put the Leafs ahead 2–1 after forty minutes.

Phil Kessel chipped in his fourth of the series at 2:09, then assisted on Nazem Kadri's first at 5:29. With less than fifteen minutes to play in the third period, it seemed everyone could loosen up just a bit, breathe a bit easier. Gotta be a win, right? Get ready for the post-game handshake line, right?

But then the seemingly impossible happened. A senseless series of Leaf flubs and miscues allowed the Bruins to tie the score with fifty-one seconds to play, and then win the game on a Patrice Bergeron goal scored at 6:05 of OT. It was an ending that defied belief, one that left the astonished Leafs stumbling and mumbling as they headed for the showers.

Glum and *gloomy* are words that might reflect the reaction of Leafs Nation.

Gut-wrenching and *dumbfounded* would also apply.

Even more unbelievably, Toronto would not qualify for the playoffs again until 2017.

Writer Lance Hornby later observed:

"How different today's Leafs world might look if not for frittering away a late 4–1 lead on May 13, 2013, at TD Garden. Would they have gone another round or two, lionizing Kessel, Phaneuf, Jake Gardiner and James Reimer? Would Dave Nonis have remained GM and Carlyle coach, negating the need for a Shanaplan, Mike Babcock and Lou Lamoriello?"

CARLYLE GONE AFTER TWIN TAILSPINS

IN 2013–14, the Leafs got off to another quick start, winning ten of fourteen games in October. And as late as mid-March, with fourteen games to play, they were second in their division and seemed to have a firm grasp on a playoff spot. However, they went on a dreadful 2–12 run the rest of the way and missed the fun and frolic of the postseason.

Their most memorable game was on New Year's Day, when they played in the NHL Winter Classic against the Detroit Red Wings at Michigan Stadium in Ann Arbor, home of the University of Michigan's football team. The Leafs won 3–2. The game was seen by an NHL-record crowd of 105,491, beating the previous standard of 71,217 set by the 2008 Winter Classic in Buffalo's Ralph Wilson Stadium.

The Leafs' troubles continued to perplex management in 2014–15. The team stumbled through October and November, before seeming to put it together after American Thanksgiving, when they won eight of nine. But their fortunes quickly made a U-turn: they lost seven of their next nine.

On January 6, 2015, Coach Carlyle was fired and assistant coach Peter Horachek was named as the interim bench boss. That didn't work. Horachek watched in horror as the Leafs set a franchise record futility: an eleven-game losing streak. The last time the team had lost ten games in a row was in the 1966–67 season—a Stanley Cup year. This was far from a Cup contender.

The Leafs finished the season with only sixty-eight points, matching their lowest total since the NHL began playing an eighty-two-game schedule in 1995 (they also had sixty-eight points in 1996–97).

THE "SHANA-PLAN" ERA DAWNS

THE OWNERSHIP of the Toronto Maple Leafs didn't even wait for the 2013–14 season to end before they unveiled the team's latest would-be saviour. Brendan Shanahan, who had been heading up the NHL's player safety department, became the team's president on April 11, 2014—one day before the Leafs played their final regular-season game.

The forty-five-year-old Shanahan had signed his first NHL player contract with New Jersey general manager Lou Lamoriello in the late 1980s. Over a career that spanned twenty-one seasons and 1,524 games, Shanny had scored 656 goals, played on three Stanley Cup winners, won a gold medal at the 1994 World Championships and another at the 2002 Winter Olympics, and was a key part of the team that won the 1991 Canada Cup. He was in the Hall of Fame and in 2017 was named one of the NHL's one hundred greatest players. The epitome of a power forward, he is the only player in NHL history with over six hundred goals and two thousand penalty minutes.

After watching the team go through its paces for close to a year, Shanahan went to ownership with his plan to rebuild the Toronto Maple Leafs, and on April 12, 2015, the day after the season ended, he sprang into action. GM Dave Nonis and interim coach Peter Horachek were let go. As were most of the team's scouts. Over the summer of 2015, Shanahan appointed Lou Lamoriello as the club's 16th general manager. Lamoriello had served the New Jersey Devils well for almost thirty years, bringing them three Stanley Cup–winning teams.

BABCOCK IS SHANNY'S CHOICE

ON MAY 20, 2015, Shanahan announced that Mike Babcock would be the team's new head coach, signing him to an astonishing eight-year, $50 million contract. That's a far cry from Punch Imlach's remuneration when I first became a Leaf broadcaster—said to be $25,000 a year and a company car.

Babcock had guided the Detroit Red Wings to a Stanley Cup victory in 2008. On the world scene, he had led Canada to gold medal wins at the 2010 and 2014 Olympics. His eight-year contract made him the highest paid coach in NHL history.

Goaltender Frederik Andersen was acquired from the Anaheim Ducks and happily signed a five-year, $25 million contract. The Leafs selected Mitch Marner of the London Knights fourth overall on draft day, and picked defenceman Travis Dermott in the second round.

On July 1, 2015, the Maple Leafs parted ways with Phil Kessel, as part of a multi-player deal that saw Phil Kessel moving to the Pittsburgh Penguins. Later, captain Dion Phaneuf and four other players were traded to Ottawa in exchange for four players plus a second-round draft pick in 2017.

How sad were the Maple Leafs of 2015–16? They broke the franchise record for losses in a season, with fifty-three (forty-four in regulation time, eight in overtime or via shootouts). Even though they ended up with sixty-nine points, one more than in 2014–15, the Leafs finished last overall in the NHL standings for the first time since 1984–85. But the news wasn't all bad. On April 30, 2016, the Leafs won the draft lottery, a stroke of good luck that would net them an elite player in Auston Matthews.

AUSTON MATTHEWS AND THE CENTENNIAL SEASON

ON JUNE 24, when director of player personnel Mark Hunter stepped up to a microphone at Buffalo's First Niagara Center and announced who Toronto was selecting with its lucky pick, it's difficult to imagine that anyone was surprised.

Auston Matthews, who had just finished his first season of pro hockey in Switzerland, was the clear choice of all the scouts to be the number one pick. Born in Northern California, raised in metropolitan Phoenix, and based in Michigan when he played junior hockey, the young centre was already well-travelled. And he was about to make his new home in Canada.

"It's a dream come true and such a big honour, especially to be with a storied franchise like the Toronto Maple Leafs," Matthews said.

Matthews stepped right into the Leafs' lineup, and on opening night he became the first player in modern NHL history to score four goals in his NHL debut (against Ottawa). Hockey history buffs will note that Harry Hyland of the Montreal Wanderers and Joe Malone of the Canadiens each scored five goals on the NHL's first night, in December 1917. Of course, neither of them were fresh-faced rookies when they did it. Hyland had played seven years in the old National Hockey Association before it gave way to the NHL, while Malone had six seasons under his belt.

Matthews went on to score forty goals in his first season, setting the Maple Leafs rookie record and becoming just the fourth teenager in league history to accomplish the feat. He won the Calder Trophy as the NHL's top rookie, something no Leaf had done since Brit Selby in 1966.

Matthews was joined by a raft of young talent—the Leafs were the first team in NHL history to have six different rookies play at least seventy games—the others were Connor Brown, Zach Hyman, Mitch Marner, William Nylander and Nikita Zaitsev. The blue line was anchored by twenty-six-year-old Jake Gardiner and twenty-two-year-old Morgan Rielly—already in his fourth NHL season. Behind them all, Frederik Andersen played sixty-six games in goal, and his thirty-three wins were the most by a Toronto goalie in nine years.

The Leafs ended their centennial season on a high. Their point total of ninety-five was the highest since 2003–04, and proved to be just enough to put them back in the playoffs for the first time since 2013, as they squeaked in ahead of the ninety-four-point Tampa Bay Lightning and New York Islanders.

At first blush, they seemed mismatched against Alex Ovechkin and the first-place Washington Capitals, but all six games were decided by one goal, and this was only the third playoff series in NHL history in which five game were went into overtime—the first was the 1951 Stanley Cup Final, in which Toronto defeated Montreal, four games to one. Marcus Johansson scored at 6:31 of extra time in Game 6 to give Washington a 2–1 victory and a 4–2 series win.

"They're young, but they're strong," Alex Ovechkin said of the Leafs after his Caps survived a scare. "They have a very good future."

"This is just the start for us," said Nazem Kadri. But there were playoff problems ahead for the young centreman.

MARVELLOUS MARNER

AS A junior, Mitch Marner of the London Knights was a teenage marvel and a gem. He led the Ontario Hockey League in scoring for most of the 2014–15 season until Dylan Strome recorded six points for the Erie Otters in the final game, bumping Marner down to second. In sixty-three games, he had 126 points. A year later he came in third, with 116 points in fifty-seven games, and skated off with the Red Tilson Trophy as the OHL's most outstanding player.

As a kid, I saw Red Tilson play for the Oshawa Generals, and he was a dandy. But I never saw him again. After helping his team win the Memorial Cup in 1943, he went off to war and never returned, killed in action on October 21, 1944. That news made a young fan very sad.

Marner has millions of fans, and he makes most of them happy. He led the 2015 OHL playoffs in scoring with forty-four points in eighteen games, and racked up another fourteen in four games in the Memorial Cup tournament, which London won. Marner was awarded the Wayne Gretzky 99 Award as playoff MVP. Drafted fourth overall by the Leafs in 2015, he joined the club in 2016–17 and set off on an astonishing pro career.

PRIDE AND CONFIDENCE

THE TORONTO Maple Leafs began their second century during the 2017–18 season, and built on the gains they had made the year before. The team set new franchise records with forty-nine wins and 105 points, and scored twenty-six more goals while cutting goals against by ten.

On the afternoon of December 19, 2017, the franchise marked the hundredth anniversary of its first game—and the first game in NHL history—by hosting the Carolina Hurricanes in what was branded as the Next Century Game. The Leafs wore sweaters that were replicas of those used by the 1918–19 Toronto Arenas in the game, which was an 8–1 laugher for the home team.

Mitch Marner scored one of the Leaf goals, just his third in thirty-four games. His first came on opening night, but he went seventeen games without finding the back of the net. His second goal of the year was followed by a fifteen-game drought. Coach Mike Babcock shifted him to the fourth line for a while to try to relieve the pressure, and the young star's offensive touch returned in time. On February 10, he had two goals and three assists—the first five-point game by a Leaf since 2009. He ended up leading the team with sixty-nine points, including twenty-two goals.

Toronto finished third in the Atlantic Division, meaning they made the playoffs for the second consecutive year. These young Leafs had pride and confidence. Surely there would be a Stanley Cup in their future.

In the third period of Game 1 against Boston, Nazem Kadri was suspended for three games for a vicious hit on Tommy Wingels. It was a costly, ill-advised foul that strongly influenced the outcome of the series. The Leafs lost two of the next three games. Had Kadri—a thirty-two-goal scorer in the regular season—been in the lineup, there might have been no need for a seventh game and a crushing first-round loss.

The Leafs led Game 7 by a score of 4–3 after two periods, but then imploded, allowing four Boston goals and leaving Coach Babcock and his boys speechless after the debacle.

TAVARES COMES HOME

ON JULY 1, 2018, New York Islanders captain John Tavares made the decision of a hockey lifetime—to join the Toronto Maple Leafs, the team he rooted for as a child. He was headed home—leaving behind several thousand teary-eyed fans—and with a seven-year contract valued at $11 million per season in his pocket.

Tavares posted a note on Twitter. In part, it read:

> *To All Islanders fans,*
>
> *The island has been home, it's what I know, it's part of me—it always will be. I can't thank you all enough for the dedication you have all showed. I'm sorry if this decision pains you, as you can tell it wasn't easy, but have trust in the future because it is bright. The Islanders are in great hands. I am thankful that I had the opportunity to be an Islander*

for as long as I did. The island, the fans, the organization, my teammates will always be special to me and my family but it's time to live my childhood dream here in Toronto.

On becoming a Leaf at age twenty-seven, Tavares said, "I just felt this opportunity was just so rare, the timing of where the organization's at and obviously the connection [of] being from here. I really believe there's a big window here to win, to be part of something special. It just felt right."

Tavares spoke of his new teammates, Auston Matthews and Mitch Marner, as reasons to be optimistic about the future.

"They've accomplished so much in so little time. That's what gets me excited," Tavares said. Tavares gave up the opportunity to sign an eight-year extension with the Islanders and passed on dazzling offers from five other NHL clubs.

Tavares was a five-time All-Star as an Islander. He had been the face of the franchise since he was the first-overall pick in the 2009 draft and made his NHL debut as a nineteen-year-old.

He admitted that the decision to change teams was heart-wrenching. In Toronto on June 29, he told the media, "My gut was just tearing apart. And my heart was tearing apart trying to figure out what I wanted to do."

Drew Doughty, a star defenceman with the LA Kings who avoided his own free-agency deliberations by signing an eight-year, $88 million extension, told the media, "I texted Tavares right after he signed. 'Congrats man, you got big cojones. That's huge.'"

KADRI'S PLAYOFF PROBLEMS

THE 2018–19 season had a lot in common with the year before: another hundred points, another third-place finish in the Atlantic Division, and another first-round matchup with the Bruins. And, unfortunately, another Nazem Kadri brain cramp that resulted in a suspension. In the third period of Game 2, with the Buds trailing 3–1,

Kadri cross-checked Jake DeBrusk in the head. Prior to Game 3, the league ruled he was done for the series.

In his absence, the Leafs managed to pull ahead 3–2 in the series, setting up a glorious opportunity to eliminate the Bruins on home ice. But they fell behind in the first period and were never able to dig their way out of the hole, losing 4–2. Toronto's season ended two nights later when they lost 5–1.

That was curtains for Kadri, who was traded to the Colorado Avalanche for Tyson Barrie, Alexander Kerfoot and a sixth-round pick in 2020.

"When I hit DeBrusk, I never thought that would be the last time I'd wear a Leafs jersey," Kadri said. "But I crossed a line—again—and I let our guys down. Getting the call from [general manager] Kyle Dubas, that was tough."

THE FUTURE OF THE FABLED FRANCHISE

AYRES TO THE RESCUE—FOR THE VISITORS

THE CAROLINA Hurricanes found themselves out of options at a key position during their game against the Leafs at the Scotiabank Arena on February 22, 2020. Who provided the help they needed? A forty-two-year-old emergency backup goalie named David Ayres.

Every hockey fan is sure to know the story of how Ayres threw on his pads and a 'Canes jersey and filled in for the visitors after both of their goalies, Petr Mrázek and James Reimer, got injured. Then he went out and beat the Leafs, stopping eight of the ten shots he faced.

It was a stunning individual accomplishment for the kidney transplant survivor from Whitby, Ontario.

Ayres was the building operations manager at the Mattamy Athletic Centre—which you may remember as Maple Leaf Gardens—at Toronto Metropolitan University. Before that, he worked in maintenance at the Ricoh Coliseum, home of the Leafs farm club the Toronto Marlies, doing everything from driving the Zamboni to pitching in as the team's practice goalie. And he was the designated backup for both teams on that Saturday night.

As he had done many times before, he was biding his time in the media room under the stands when he got a text message. "Get ready," it said. This was at 6:10 of the first period, when Reimer left the game.

So, he got halfway into his goalie gear and waited for a call that might not come.

Midway through the second period, with the Hurricanes up 3–1, he was pressed into action. Mrázek had collided with Leaf winger Kyle Clifford and was unable to continue.

Teuvo Teräväinen scored to give Carolina some breathing room, but then the untested Ayres was beaten on the first two shots he faced. After forty minutes, the lead was down to 4–3.

During the intermission, his new teammates urged him to relax, while the equipment manager urged him to replace the blue shell of his Marlies hockey pants with a Carolina red one.

In the third period, Ayres stopped all seven shots thrown at him, and for the first time in NHL history, an "EBUG" had recorded a win. Leaf superfan Steve Dangle's YouTube video, titled "THEY LOST TO A ZAMBONI DRIVER," went viral.

As one fan wrote: "When Toronto wants to play well, they are as good as any team. When they don't give a crap, they couldn't even beat a forty-two-year-old over-the-hill beer leaguer. No disrespect to David Ayers who is awesome! He was named the game's first star. North Carolina Governor Roy Cooper is going to name him with an Honorary North Carolina citizen. How is this even possible?"

Jacob Di Girolamo, twenty, an amateur goalie and coach said, "It was outstanding. You think, 'Wow, that could maybe be me.' I don't know if there are any other sports that have a rule like that where someone that's not really in the league can just jump in."

The CBC's Dan Séguin had a different take.

"It was really Carolina who did such an incredible job of stopping the Leafs from having a chance to shoot at the guy," he said. "I think it looks poorly on the NHL that you can allow anybody to come in and win an NHL hockey game. I don't like that it happened, but I think it's a great story for him personally."

Ayres embraced his fifteen minutes of fame, then left the Leafs organization. He even managed to get himself a couple of coaching jobs. But his personal life has been turbulent. His wife, Sarah, reportedly left him after experiencing what she calls "emotional abuse."

She posted on Twitter that "I chose to leave, my mental health and my ability to parent are most important."

PLAYING THROUGH A PANDEMIC

THE STANLEY Cup playoffs have treated fans to some bizarre moments over the years, but never has the postseason been as strange as in 2020. Play began in midsummer, on August 1. Games were staged in only two cities, Toronto and Edmonton, meaning that for the first time since 1925, the Stanley Cup playoffs would be contested entirely within Canada. There were no fans in the stands. And on September 28, when general managers and coaches usually ponder their last few roster cuts before opening night, the Tampa Bay Lightning skated off with their second Stanley Cup championship, defeating the Dallas Stars four games to two.

All because of a worldwide pandemic that claimed millions of lives and was viewed as a threat even to the toughest of hockey players.

In March of 2020, soon after COVID-19 was declared to be a pandemic, the regular season had been suspended indefinitely. The remaining games would be scrapped, as the NHL went to work on a "Return to Play Plan" that would see the Cup awarded.

The Leafs drew the Columbus Blue Jackets as their opponent in the best-of-five opening round, called a "qualifying round" this year. But the Leafs' prolific snipers managed only ten goals in the five games, which were bookended by Joonas Korpisalo shutouts, and their post-season came to another early end.

After this defeat, and the playoff losses to Boston in 2018 and '19, it was becoming apparent that playoff hockey was not where Toronto teams excelled.

The outcome was a disappointment for the Leafs' latest bench boss. On November 20, 2019, Mike Babcock, the NHL's highest-paid coach, was fired a quarter of the way into his fifth season, with the team off to a so-so 9–10–4 start. The fact he'd steered his teams into the playoffs in each of the previous three seasons meant little.

Sheldon Keefe, head coach of the Toronto Marlies, was named as the Leafs' next bench boss. This choice came as no surprise, because he and general manager Kyle Dubas had been friends going back to their junior hockey days in the Soo. His resumé included a Calder Cup championship with the Marlies, back-to-back division titles with the Soo Greyhounds and five consecutive championships with the Junior A Pembroke Lumber Kings. Over the rest of the season, the team went 27–15–5 and finished third in the Atlantic Division before falling to Columbus in the playoffs.

A CLASH WITH THE HABS, AND AN UPSET

ANYONE EXPECTING an immediate return to normal after the topsy-turvy 2019–20 season would be disappointed, as COVID-related precautions continued to affect the NHL's operations. In particular, cross-border travel remained restricted, and local public health measures limited the sizes of crowds, if fans were allowed in at all.

On January 13, 2021, teams kicked off a fifty-six-game regular season. The league was also temporarily realigned, with the seven Canadian teams grouped into the North Division, playing each other exclusively. In fact, no Canadian team would play an American one until the third round of the playoffs.

The Leafs clinched the North Division title, their first since 2000, with seventy-seven points. Auston Matthews scored a league-high forty-one goals, becoming the first player in team history to win the Maurice "Rocket" Richard Trophy—and the first Leaf to lead the league in goals since Gaye Stewart in 1945–46. Matthews was also a finalist for the Ted Lindsay Award, given to the Most Valuable Player as chosen by players. Mitch Marner collected sixty-seven points, one more than Matthews.

Goalie Jack Campbell, acquired in February 2020 from Los Angeles to back up Frederik Andersen, took over as the starter late in the season, posting a 17–3–2 record and a 2.15 goals-against average.

In the playoffs, the Leafs were paired with the fourth-place Montreal

Canadiens, who had clawed their way to fifty-nine points. Toronto was the prohibitive favourite, seeing as they had won seven of the teams' ten regular-season meetings.

In Game 1, John Tavares got bowled over by Habs defenceman Ben Chiarot. Montreal winger Corey Perry tried to leap over Tavares, but his knee smacked Tavares in the head. Tavares was rushed to a hospital. "I know John well and I just hope he's OK," Perry told media members. The Canadiens won the game 2–1.

Two nights later, Auston Matthews scored a goal and two assists in a 5–1 Leafs victory. Can you believe this was the first time Toronto won a playoff game over the Habs since their Stanley Cup–clinching game in 1967? In Game 3, goalie Jack Campbell sparkled in a 2–1 Leaf victory, and followed up that performance with a 4–0 shutout, giving the Leafs a 3–1 series lead. Series over, right? On to the second round, right?

Well, hold on.

In Game 5, the Canadiens held a 3–0 lead in the second period, but the Leafs scored three unanswered goals to tie it and force overtime. Cornballers might say the Leafs had Moe Mentum in uniform.

But a hockey disaster was about to follow.

Less than a minute into extra time, Toronto forward Alex Galchenyuk gave the puck away and Nick Suzuki scored to spoil the comeback.

Game 6 remained scoreless until the third period. Corey Perry and Tyler Toffoli put the Habs up 2–0, but the Leafs again came back to tie the score. But at 15:15 of overtime, Jesperi Kotkaniemi (Jesperi Who?) scored the game-winner and the series was tied, 3–3. When the Habs cruised to a 3–1 victory in game seven, sending the men in blue reeling off to the summer doldrums, they tied the NHL record for most series victories after being down three games to one.

Again, the Leafs and their fans were stunned, disbelieving. Like passengers on the *Titanic*, it was a sinking, stinking feeling. How could this have happened?

After sweeping Winnipeg in the second round, Montreal would again play the role of giant-killers in the semifinals. There, they needed six games to eliminate the Vegas Golden Knights, who with eighty-two points had tied Colorado for first place overall in the regular season. The Canadiens' Cinderella run ended in the final, where they fell to the defending champions from Tampa Bay in five games.

THE BEST REGULAR SEASONS EVER

IN 2021–22, the NHL resumed its usual October-to-April schedule for the regular season. There were still a few COVID-related hiccups, with many games having to be rescheduled on the fly, but all teams played a full eighty-two games for the first time since 2018–19.

The Maple Leafs stumbled out of the gate, dropping five of their first seven games before hitting their stride. On April 17, their 4–2 victory over the New York Islanders was their fiftieth of the season, the first time they'd ever hit that milestone. They went on to finish second in their division, and fourth overall, with a record of 54–21–7 and an all-time-high 106 points. Toronto's prolific offence (315 goals, the club's most since 1989–90) was led by Auston Matthews, who scored a career-high sixty goals and won the Rocket Richard Trophy for the second year in a row.

Kudos also to captain John Tavares (twenty-seven goals and seventy-six points) and Morgan Rielly (the top blueliner, with sixty-eight points). And thanks to Jack Campbell for his standout goaltending—thirty-one wins and five shutouts.

The Leafs' first-round matchup, with the Tampa Bay Lightning, was daunting. The Lightning had won the Stanley Cup in each of the past two seasons. The Leafs took three of the first five games, and after forty minutes in Game 6 they were up 3–2. But Nikita Kucherov tied the score midway through the third period, and Brayden Point won it in overtime. In Game 7, Toronto outshot Tampa, 31–25, but lost 2–1. Another first-round defeat. It's not easy, going up against the two-time defending champs, but hockey playoffs have seldom been easy. The top teams find a way to pick it up a notch.

The Lightning certainly did. They advanced to the Stanley Cup final, hoping to claim the trophy for a third straight season. (Has it really been nearly forty-five years since the Islanders dynasty won four straight?) No three-peat this year, though. The Colorado Avalanche prevailed in a six-game final.

In 2022–23, the Leafs had another strong regular season, with fifty wins and 111 points. Matthews and William Nylander each potted forty goals, and Mitch Marner had a ninety-nine-point season—his sixty-nine assists the most by a Leaf since Doug Gilmour racked up ninety-five in 1992–93.

On December 3, Marner scored two goals, which gave him points in nineteen consecutive games—overtaking Darryl Sittler (1977–78) and Eddie Olczyk (1989–90), who had eighteen-game point streaks. Magic Mitch's run ended at twenty-three games (eleven goals and twenty-one assists for thirty-two points) in a 3–1 loss to the New York Rangers on December 15.

General manager Kyle Dubas overhauled the team's goaltending, trading with Ottawa for Matt Murray, who'd backstopped the Pittsburgh Penguins to Stanley Cup wins in 2016 and '17, and signing Ilya Samsonov, formerly of the Washington Capitals.

Murray was frequently injured, and Samsonov became the starter. Despite missing a month to a major injury of his own, Samsonov played forty-two games with a career-high twenty-seven wins.

The Leafs clinched a playoff spot with nine games to play, and drew a first-round rematch with the Tampa Bay Lightning. Fans could hardly be blamed for anticipating a re-*run*, in the form of yet another first-round exit.

But at last, the Leafs delivered. It wasn't easy. They dropped Game 1, 7–3, before emerging on the winning end of a 7–2 blowout. In Games 3 and 4, they came from behind, gutting their way to overtime wins to take a 3–2 lead. And on April 29, once again in overtime, John Tavares ended Tampa Bay's season. For the first time in nineteen years, the Leafs had won a playoff series—an achievement that seemed as likely as putting astronauts on Mars.

Then came the inevitable letdown.

Toronto's opponent in round two was another Florida club, the Panthers. Perhaps taking a giant step closer to the Cup left the Leafs unnerved or even paralyzed. But what is certain is that they ran up against a hot goalie. The cerebral stopper Sergei Bobrovsky dazzled the Leaf shooters, and the series was over in five games.

With a new GM—Brad Trevliving, who'd been fired by the Flames after a nine-season run that included just five playoff appearances—the Maple Leafs clinched a playoff spot for the eighth consecutive season. Matthews scored with the ease of a Gretzky or a Bossy, sniping a league-leading sixty-nine goals while hoping for seventy—a level nobody had reached in over thirty years.

In the first round of the playoffs, with Matthews fighting a mysterious illness, the Leafs fell to the Boston Bruins in seven games. David Pastrňák scored the deciding goal in overtime. When it mattered most, Pastrňák found a way to get the job done.

With a few long-term contracts offering the front office little room to move, Leafs fans worry that the lack of playoff success may extend into the next decade.

As of yet, Matthews has not proven himself to be a postseason leader. His playoff years, with one or two exceptions, have been clunkers. And Marner's playoff exploits have been rather ordinary. The pair must face their mirrors daily and ask themselves, "Why am I so unlike other Leafs who preceded me—men like Gilmour, Clark, Salming, Sittler, Kennedy, Bentley and Apps? I've had more than enough time to prove I belong with those Leaf icons at playoff time."

Neither wants to be remembered as among the highest-scoring, highest-paid players in the game, but also among the biggest postseason disappointments.

Obviously, the Leaf front office forgives Matthews his annual playoff plummets because in August 2023 he was handed a four-year, $53 million contract extension to remain with the team. The average annual value of Matthews's new deal is $13.25 million, which makes him the highest-paid player in the NHL.

If King Clancy, a Hall of Fame Leaf, were still living, he'd say, "Gee, I started in the NHL at $800." And the late Johnny Bower, another Hall of Famer, might add, "I came up from the American League in my thirties and made—I think—$10,000. And we won Stanley Cups."

A LAST LOOK BACK

WELL, IT seems I'm the only hockey broadcaster alive who has helped call a Leaf Stanley Cup-winning game.

It's been well over half a century and I can close my eyes and see it all unfold again. Leafs and Habs in '67. At Maple Leaf Gardens. Leafs leading 2–1 in the last minute of play. A faceoff to the left of Sawchuk. Imlach barking orders. Sending his old men out. "You guys hold the fort. I'm relying on you."

Defenceman Allan Stanley going stick-to-stick with Jean Béliveau. He would tell me later, "When I take faceoffs, I cheat."

And he cheated this time. Nudged Béliveau enough for a penalty. But there was no call. The puck went to Bob Pulford, who saw George Armstrong break out of the Leaf zone on the right wing. Pulford's slick pass right to Army's stick. A flick of the wrists, and the Chief slipped it into the empty net. Game over! The Cup won!

Come on, Leafs. More than half a century later, let's see another season unfold like that one.

You came close in '23, failing by one or two wrist flicks to get past the Florida Panthers, losing a crucial Game 5 in OT by 3–2, the closest of scores.

But there was no indication you wanted or demanded more. Not one player said, "We must be held accountable. We are responsible for our demise."

Remember what my friend Joe Bowen said on an earlier page in this tome. Joe growled, "I'm seventy-one and I've been calling Leafs games on radio for four decades. Will I ever—and I mean EVER—get to call a Stanley Cup game?"

Don't despair, Joe. This season. Or the next. Or the one after that. Hockey miracles do happen.

"Yeah," says Joe, "but neither one us may be around to see it, much less call it."

True enough, Joe. But we've survived long enough to see Stanley

Cup history made by others. Imagine a team only six years old, the Vegas Golden Knights, skating off triumphantly with Lord Stanley's venerable trophy—once the size of a bowling ball and now so huge and heavy it takes a well-muscled NHLer to lift it overhead. Future winners may feel shame when it slips from their arms and crashes to the ice.

Toronto's latest coach, Craig Berube, lifted it—once.

Berube became partly responsible for the most amazing turnarounds in NHL history. On New Year's Day, 2019, the Blues were dead last in the NHL, with thirty-four points. They would then post a record of 30–10–5, the best record of any team in the league over that stretch. In the postseason, the Blues beat the Winnipeg Jets in six games; the Dallas Stars in seven; and the San Jose Sharks in six to earn a berth in the Stanley Cup Final.

On June 12, 2019, they won hockey's ultimate prize, defeating the Boston Bruins 4–1 in Game 7. Never has a team in last place on New Year's Day risen to Stanley Cup ownership and a giddy amount of hockey glory.

Will Berube achieve another minor miracle and lead his Leafs deep into the 2025 playoffs? If he does, they'll be naming streets, schools and arenas after him. A thousand young parents will gleefully name their next baby—girl or boy—Craig.

A FINAL THOUGHT

I DEDICATE this book to one of the greatest of Leafs, a man who will always be in our hockey hearts, a man who will always be a Maple Leaf Forever—the late Börje Salming, who died on November 24, 2022.

Salming, a fixture on the Maple Leafs' blue line for sixteen years, was seventy-one years old.

Before his death, an odd thing happened one night. I felt the need to get up from bed and write a letter to Börje.

> *Hi Börje:*
>
> I had a dream about you tonight. Not surprising, because you have been on my mind for some time now,

ever since I heard about your battle with amyotrophic lateral sclerosis (ALS). You are a very remarkable, courageous man to deal with such a life-taking blow.

In my dream, I witnessed the emotional rush you created by appearing next to Leaf ambassador Darryl Sittler on TV the other night. Enough tears were shed to replenish the low water levels on the mighty Mississippi.

I got to know you from the start of your splendid career. You were the first great European player and you excelled as you rose from beginner to best. I always put you high on my list of the most skilful players I've seen, and now I can add the bravest of all.

I recall a playoff game at the Gardens against the infamous Broad Street Bullies—Stanley Cup champions then—and how they followed coach Fred Shero's orders to "take care of Salming. I don't care how." One of the Flyers, knowing you were not a fighter, punished you with a flurry of blows to the head—a dozen hard jolts, perhaps—but you shook them off, you did not buckle. And later you led a brilliant rush for a perfect shot that eluded Flyers goalie Bernie Parent. The standing ovation you received an instant later was like no other.

I woke from my dream and said to myself, *Börje was reaching out to you. Get up and write down all you recall of it. Dreams are so easily forgotten.*

So, Börje, that's what I'm doing.

In my dream, I was standing in freezing temperatures, waiting for you, outside Maple Leaf Gardens. I wanted to tell you how much you were admired—and, yes, loved—by fans everywhere. And when you saw me shivering in the cold, you came right over and gave me a bear hug. Your concern for me overwhelmed me. You said, "We've got to get you home. You're freezing. Where do you live?" I told you "Willowdale," even though I haven't lived in Willowdale in ten years. But it was where I lived when you were a Leaf.

You slapped a button on a wall, and in seconds a Swedish racing car, painted in blue and yellow stripes, came roaring down a ramp and the driver motioned me over. "Get in," he said. "Börje's worried about you."

He began to drive me home, but then Harold Ballard appeared and waved us down. I rolled down my window.

"Börje says you're a good guy," Ballard said, smiling. "I never liked you much, but Börje says I've misjudged you. You want to come back and work for me?"

I had always wanted to be part of the Leaf family, but I was older now, much older. I got out of your car to talk to Ballard when a man rushed over and took my elbow. I said, "Who are you?"

He laughed and said, "I worked in accounting for Ballard when he hired you years ago as head of public relations. We all laughed because you were the lowest-paid PR man in the NHL."

It was true. But I desperately needed a job back then. And it was a front-office job with the Leafs. I was sorry it didn't last.

I approached Ballard and said, "Harold, it's too late now. Too late for both of us. Börje Salming just showed me he really cares about me. You never cared."

I returned to the warmth of Börje's car, and the driver smiled and patted me on the back. He'd heard my remark. Then he raced off with me. To Willowdale, I think, even though I wasn't sure I still lived there anymore.

I had seen the images of you standing next to your old friend and teammate Darryl Sittler at the Scotiabank Arena. And you were both crying, with all of Canada watching. You had lost the ability to speak. Your face was contorted. Your arms were stiff. Sittler helped you raise one arm for a feeble wave and the crowd erupted, showering you with love and affection and the utmost respect.

But in my dream, your face was youthful, smooth-skinned and smiling. Your words came easily. They were comforting and sincere. You'd shown so much empathy and concern. And I began to cry, along with the millions of fans who adored you.

I cried because you'd been so kind to me, so determined to help. I knew you'd always been a good man, a player who showed no fear even when those roughneck Philadelphia Flyers tried to send you back to Sweden with shattered dreams, with nothing more than broken bones to show for your desire to play in the NHL.

How they failed. How ashamed some of them must feel now.

When I woke from my dream, I felt my pillow and it was damp.

So, Börje you were awesome. You flew over from Sweden to greet old friends. You were able to walk out to centre ice, Sittler and Tiger Williams by your side, knowing it would be your last time on hockey ice, stoically waving a final salute as an entire nation roared greetings that said, "Welcome home" and "We love you," accompanied by a massive outpouring of sobs and tears and grief and despair as they agonized over your gutsy, gallant battle with an incurable disease that was nearing its end. I can't think of a more emotional few moments in hockey's rich history than those.

But your friends had rushed off with you. You were in the arena, surrounded by former teammates—Sittler, Lanny McDonald, Tiger Williams. And Mats Sundin, another great Swedish Leaf on whom you were an influence. They loved you. You felt at home there. You were all bonding again. Having fun.

And it was so much fun to see.

Börje, you can't possibly know that the old man you comforted in a dream is also dealing with an incurable issue, a rare heart disease. But in his case, there's a treatment—a very expensive one—that prolongs life. That's a night-and-day difference between the two of us. In your case, ALS appears to have evil, sinister characteristics, cruelly singling out superstars of sport, like New York Yankee great Lou Gehrig and now you, the best of the Leafs—Börje Salming.

This old man is not overly concerned about his own final moments. They may come in ten minutes or ten years. He will never hear ovations like you have. Nor should he. You were a shining star, the King of Hockey. You have earned every "Bravo, Börje." This old guy has lived into his nineties, and that's unexpected—a gift. He accepts every day as a bonus. His life has been full, his accomplishments not numerous but satisfying, his many blunders forgotten. His life is almost complete.

A few days ago, he was thinking—if he could, if it would make a difference—he would offer his expensive, life-saving pills to Börje Salming, if it meant the great Swede he so admires might get to enjoy another few months on Mother Earth.

Ah, Börje, this news just came in. I'm so sad. Your demise came too fast. Everyone will be devastated, especially your Leaf teammates, your opponents, your fans worldwide.

Peace be with you.

Thank you for befriending me in my dream. It was a unique, awesome and inexplicable way of reaching out to me while I slept.

Brian McFarlane

ACKNOWLEDGMENTS

Special thanks to special people who helped make this book possible.

To Publisher Matt Joudrey, Managing Editor Alana Brooker, Copy and Proof Editor Courtney Bill, and Graphic Designer Lucas c Pauls at At Bay Press.

To those who helped in the photo search—Joe Rizzuto, Andy McCall, Paul Patskou, and Ernie Fitzsimmons.

And to associate Dave Batson.

And finally, to Substantive Editor Lloyd Davis.

And to my wife, Joan, who perused these pages looking for pucks that flew off the pages into the crowd carrying commas and periods and a few pertinent facts with them. We may not have retrieved them all but we did our best—as always.

BRIAN MCFARLANE is known as Canada's foremost hockey historian, a man who has been a player, a writer, and a broadcaster of the game for over fifty years. In 2020, he was named to the Order of Canada. For 27 years he served as a host and commentator on Hockey Night in Canada. In 1960, he became the first Canadian to work on U.S. hockey telecasts with CBS. In the seventies, he hosted the NBC hockey telecasts. He has written close to 100 books and his book sales are estimated at well over a million copies. In 1995 he was inducted into the media section of the Hockey Hall of Fame. He is also a member of five other Sports Halls of Fame. He has been married to his wife Joan for 68 years. They have three children, six grandchildren and five great grandchildren.

OUR AT BAY PRESS ARTISTIC COMMUNITY:

Publisher – **Matt Joudrey**
Managing Editor – **Alana Brooker**
Substantive Editor – **Lloyd Davis**
Copy Editor – **Courtney Bill**
Proof Editor – **Courtney Bill**
Graphic Designer – **Lucas c Pauls**
Layout – **Lucas c Pauls and Matt Joudrey**
Publicity and Marketing – **Savita Singh**

Thanks for purchasing this book
and for supporting authors and artists.
As a token of gratitude, please scan the
QR code for exclusive content from this title.